Time for a European Federation

Peter Lang

Bruxelles · Bern · Berlin · New York · Oxford · Wien

Yannis Karamitsios

Time for a European Federation

How Europe could remain relevant in the century of globalization, climate change and the fourth industrial revolution

Europe of Cultures / Dialogues
Vol. 24

© P.I.E. PETER LANG s.a.
 Éditions scientifiques internationales
 Brussels, 2022
 1 avenue Maurice, B-1050 Bruxelles, Belgium
 brussels@peterlang.com ; www.peterlang.com

ISBN 978-2-87574-428-9   ISSN 2031-3519
ePDF 978-2-87574-429-6   DOI 10.3726/b18952
ePub 978-2-87574-430-2   D/2021/5678/66

Bibliographic information published by "Die Deutsche Nationalbibliothek".

"Die Deutsche National Bibliothek" lists this publication in the "Deutsche Nationalbibliografie"; detailed bibliographic data is available on the Internet at <http://dnb.de>.

Table of Contents

Part III Major policy sectors of the new European Federation

Acknowledgements and disclaimer

The creation of this book was realised thanks to the contribution of several persons.

Brooks Tigner carried out the linguistic revision. He worked on literally every single word of this text, improving and enriching its English, identifying gaps and inconsistencies, and spotting the parts that needed further elaboration. I am very grateful for his support.

Christos Bezirtzoglou stood behind the initial concept. We spent long hours discussing together the project's basic notions, structure, and strategic objectives. He contributed sources and contacts who helped its development and to reach its maturity. I am also grateful to him.

Anita Seprenyi, Franzesco Guerzoni, Julia Stark, and Kiril Mitrov reviewed several parts of the script. Their valuable comments made it more accurate and thorough, and widened its perspectives.

The publishing house, Peter Lang, contributed its friendly, constructive, and professional co-operation. They embraced this bold political proposal with a very supportive attitude – not easy in a time lacking "euroenthusiasm" – while working diligently to improve its analysis in all respects. I am very grateful for this opportunity.

Most important, a word of special gratitude to my wife Katarzyna and daughter Dimitra for their patience during the long days of work that finally brought this text to fruition. Thanks to their understanding, my concentration on the task proved much easier.

Finally, I should note that I am employed by the European Commission and I am also member of several associations with political and social activity. I must thus clarify that all views expressed in this book are strictly personal and do not represent the positions of those organisations.

Preface

"The time for European sovereignty has come. It is time Europe took its destiny into its own hands. It is time Europe developed what I coined "*Weltpolitikfähigkeit*" – the capacity to play a role, as a Union, in shaping global affairs. Europe has to become a more sovereign actor in international relations. European sovereignty is born of Member States' national sovereignty and does not replace it. Sharing sovereignty – when and where needed – makes each of our nation states stronger."

This is an extract from the 'State of the Union' speech I delivered in 2018 to the European Parliament, as President of the European Commission, which was among the guiding principles of my term in office between 2014 and 2019. We launched European defence, an extraordinary step forward since this policy area was not part of the Commission's remit. We launched the 'Juncker Plan', generating €550 billion in investments all across the Union. We concluded important trade agreements with Japan and Canada, showing that the EU remains an important global economic player. We introduced significant social programmes. And we worked for a more political Commission to make sure the entire Union attains a stronger political image and dimension.

Several events have since occurred that confirm my insistence on the need for European sovereignty: the UK's withdrawal from the EU; the growing assertiveness of other big powers such as China; the climate crisis; the recent Indo-Pacific alliance of the USA, Australia, and UK that bypasses European partners; and of course the Covid-19 pandemic. They all remind us, as Europeans, of our common challenges and the need to take control of our destiny together.

Yannis Karamitsios's book proffers a bold proposal for the future of Europe, namely its unification under a sovereign federal state. He argues that this is the only way to move forward in this century of burgeoning globalisation, climate change, and the impact of the fourth industrial revolution. European states can compete, and cooperate, with the rest of the world – but only as an integrated entity. We must seek common answers to the major questions of our time: geopolitical competition, diplomacy and defence, new technologies, ecological threats, and energy security, just to name a few.

Of course, not everyone would agree that Europe should evolve into a federation: some would counter that such a goal is too premature, risky or unrealistic in our present era. I think they are right, for the time being. However, no matter whether one endorses the idea or not, we must acknowledge the huge leaps in European integration that have unfolded in recent decades. Twenty-six European countries share a common border space thanks to the Schengen area, for example. Thirty share a common economic space via the European Economic Area (EEA), and nineteen nations share a common currency, the euro. More recently, efforts are under way to create a Health Union, something unimaginable before the Covid-19 pandemic. All these are signs of progress towards stronger – not weaker – European sovereignty.

I am hopeful that this journey will continue successfully. The road is undoubtedly bumpy. There are still gaps in the mentality and culture of EU member states, an inevitable consequence of our union's now too-large membership. Back in the 1980s, when I attended my first Council meeting as Luxembourg's young Employment Minister, there were only 10 EU countries. Now there are 27 and growing, as are the challenges.

Immigration remains a divisive issue that puts European solidarity to the test. Illiberal governments have unfortunately become a reality within the EU. Schengen came under heavy pressure during the Syrian refugee crisis and continues to be challenged during the pandemic. Bitter disagreements have taken place between certain 'frugal' rich EU members and other, poorer states during negotiations over the pandemic recovery budget. And it will most probably continue like this.

On the other hand, our political resilience is remarkable. We have built up strong institutions and solidarity supported by hundreds of economic, social, and environmental programs. We negotiate international treaties as a single force. We have stood united in the face of Brexit and the ongoing pandemic.

Our next advancements need fresh ideas and political courage. This book offers not only a framework but also the substance for a federal European polity. It touches upon a very wide and complex set of issues, from education to defence, from social security to the economy, immigration, industry, and much more. We may not all agree about the content of its proposals, but we should definitely welcome its debate on how to shape and pull those policies together. It provides federalists one more tool for their future proposals. Yet it also offers to all other Europeans the means to consider the direction of their societies...today, as the European Union, and tomorrow – if they so wish – as a European Federation.

Jean-Claude Juncker

Former President of the European Commission

Prologue

The European federalist movement has its origins in the 1920s, 1930s and 1940s. The idea of a European and world federation surfaced in 1941 as the "Ventotene manifesto", co-authored by Italians Altiero Spinelli and Ernesto Rossi.[1] Federalist organisations, like the Union of European Federalists (UEF), have been continuously active since those years. Other various organisations, seminars, manifestos and texts have also appeared since then, stressing the need for a more united Europe and driving a constructive debate on how to reach that objective. With the arrival of COVID-19 in 2020, the rationale for federalism has intensified due to pandemic's extraordinary stresses and strains on societies and the sense that little will be achieved without enhanced European unity and solidarity.

This text promulgates our position in support of the federalist idea. We propose the creation of a new sovereign entity, the "European Federation" (EF), to succeed and replace the European Union (EU) and its member states, with the latter becoming constituent parts of that federation. The EF would, ideally, include all EU-27 member states of 2021 and the United Kingdom (UK), which, despite Brexit, should be welcomed back into the European family due to its size, economy, population, culture and global clout. The EF would also embrace other willing countries such as Norway, Iceland, Switzerland and the western Balkans nations. It would thus stretch from the Arctic Ocean to the Mediterranean, and from the Atlantic to the borders of Russia, Belarus, Ukraine, and Turkey.

Yet our analysis calls for more than just forging a new European entity. Simply creating a structure is not enough: strategic choices to meet the challenges of the 21st century need to be clearly defined. Therefore this treatise stands apart from its predecessors by focusing on a comprehensive set of proposals for a European federation's foundation. This comprises a constitutional framework, the EF's institutions and, most important, substantive policies for its economy, growth, social issues, defence and foreign affairs. Moreover, it explains how to achieve these within a budgetary framework and an annual expenditure of less than €8 trillion (in 2021 prices).

This forward-looking analysis focuses on a specific end-destination. We do not therefore linger on current EU affairs such as post-Brexit negotiations, the EU's budget for 2021–2027, or how to respond to the COVID-19 crisis. We however do use such topics as examples of factors that must be taken into account in the long-term.

Our analysis is structured in three main parts. The first Part deals with the conceptual framework for e federal European republic. The opening chapter introduces the historic imperative for creating a European federation. The second chapter elaborates its ideological framework. The second Part describes and analyses the four pillars needed to build such a European federation: political (Chapter 3), economic (Chapter 4), security (Chapter 5) and socio-cultural governance (Chapter 6). The third and final more policy-oriented Part deals with the major policies and instruments for developing a true European federation: immigration and demographic policy (Chapter 7), agriculture and food policy (Chapter 8), enterprises, industry and employment (Chapter 9) and climate policy, infrastructure networks and circular economy (Chapter 10).

Finally, it should be noted that this analysis is neither a specialist tome nor an academic thesis. It does not aim for an authoritative position on every topic, and should not be taken as such. It is a politically argued analysis with a forward looking perspective. It thus falls to experts to advise their politicians, policy makers, enterprises and civil society groups on how best to use it.

Part I

CONCEPTUAL FRAMEWORK FOR A EUROPEAN FEDERATION

This text introduces a quite radical political proposal to the Old World: the wholesale replacement of 27 advanced European nation-states, as well as their common international organisation (the EU), by a new and cohesive sovereign federal republic. It is thus essential to explain the historic necessity for such a move and, more important, the federal entity's basic character and ideological principles that would underpin its functioning – principles that justify the detailed proposals in the following chapters.

Chapter 1

The historic need for a European Federation

1.1. *Europe at the beginning of the 21st century: A brief state of play*

The 21st century is one of extreme globalisation. It is an era whose challenges demand large-scale approaches. The international game of power politics, prosperity and competition is bigger than ever. All the numbers – whether pertaining to people, resources, commerce, capital, investments, communication, transport, debts, or trade – count in the billions or trillions. In such an environment, the political and economic players have to be large or specialised enough to compete successfully and thus safeguard their interests and values, especially as the world is gradually cohering into evermore integrated regional blocks: from ASEAN in South East Asia and Mercosur in South America, to the African Union. Small political or economic entities will inevitably be shunted to the margins and irrelevance.

Are individual EU member states strong enough to face that challenge? According to one estimate, not a single EU nation will count among the top eight economies of the world by 2050.[2] It is also doubtful whether any will figure among the top military powers either. Even today's most populous EU country of Germany ranks only 19th in the global list of countries by population.[3]

Europe as a whole needs to evaluate its position on the global scene. It must reassess and define its identity. Where does it stand compared to other powers? How is it going to deal with current and future geopolitical, ecological and economic trends? What are its origins and what does that mean to its people? Let's first put some "big picture" facts on the table to illustrate the challenges.

As the 21st century has entered its third decade, a post-Brexit EU still retains a prominent global position. Its economy is the second biggest on the planet, smaller only than that of the United States.[4] It has the world's third largest population of approximately 447 million people, trailing only China and India. It has enjoyed seven decades of peace, an unprecedented achievement in Europe's long history. It has advanced human rights more than any other society in history and has achieved the highest quality of social welfare. And it is an international organisation with the highest degree of integration among its members.

The EU's impact on the world remains significant. It ranks first in both inbound and outbound international investments. It is the world's largest trader in manufactured goods and services, and the biggest trade partner of 80 countries (by comparison, the U.S. is the biggest partner of only 20).[5] It is the greatest international aid donor on the planet[6] and the global champion in food safety rules, health standards, renewable energy and organic farming. The majority of EU member states figure on the top-30 of the Human Development Reports of the United Nations.[7] All these achievements should be seen as important competitive advantages: they contribute to a stronger, more productive and more sustainable Europe. They help make the world as a whole a better place to live. They thus need to be safeguarded and further enhanced.

In many other areas, however, the EU's prospects look bleak in 2021. Brexit and the rise of national populist governments, political parties and movements in some EU countries have shaken the foundations of Europe's political structure. The regimes of Poland and Hungary, for example, bluntly defy European values, EU law and warnings from Brussels, yet remain highly popular (partly due to their insistence on preserving national sovereignty). Their popular support raises questions about the public's faith in a common European vision. The COVID-19 crisis has further increased the already high public debts. Moreover, the EU faces a set of broader existential threats which, if left unchallenged, will likely push Europe permanently to the margins of the international community and history.

1.2. Five existential challenges for Europe

The threats are a mix of global issues and ones specific to Europe, framed by the competition with other continents. The most relevant challenges to Europe's prosperity and freedom in the coming decades are: economic, financial, and productive decline; demographic stagnation; climate change; energy dependence; and exclusion from technological innovations.

1.2.1. Europe's economic, financial and productive decline compared to the rest of the world

The EU has experienced only small growth in its gross domestic product (GDP) since the economic crisis of 2008. Never spiking higher than 3 % of annual GDP, its average annual growth has averaged below 2 %,[8] while China, India and other important competitors have grown at rates exceeding 6 %. Meanwhile, the EU's overall public debt, at some 90 % of annual GDP in 2020, is significantly higher than that of most emerging economies of the world[9] and, moreover, is projected to rise much higher due to the economic impact of the COVID-19 pandemic. By contrast, in 2020 China had a debt-to-GDP ratio of 66 %, Mexico 45 %, Indonesia 38 %, and Kazakhstan 23 %.[10] While it is normal that debt-to-GDP rates for developing economies are lower, with bigger margins for growth, and those for other mature western economies are higher due to their smaller margins for growth, this trend nonetheless has worrying implications for Europe's global position.

Wealth and power are gradually shifting to the southern and eastern hemispheres, and the Pacific region. We only have to ponder that, in 1984, China's economy accounted for a mere 2.4 % of the global economy, while today its share is 18 % and growing.[11] Conversely, the EU's share of the global economy will have dipped from 30 % in 1995 to less than 20 % in 2030.[12] And for the first time in history, the volume of "south-to-south" trade is starting to compete with the volume of "south-to-north" trade.[13] Indeed, the globe's economic centre of gravity has moved eastwards and will continue to do so through the next decades. The EU's declining share of the global economy has slowed for a while thanks to its continuous enlargements since 1995. But future enlargements will be marginal and, post-Brexit, the EU has lost its second biggest economic engine. It is therefore likely that the EU's relative decline vis-à-vis the rest of the world will accelerate compared to the previous years.[14]

Manufacturing is led by Asia and North America, with the majority of world's goods produced in China, Japan, South Korea, India and the U.S. alone[15] Most commodities in energy, food and other sectors are produced outside Europe, where developing countries will increasingly use them for their own development rather than for export to our continent. By exploiting lower labour, environmental or safety standards, they compete with Europe via a more advantageous position that exerts great pressure on our society and economy.

In addition, and partly as a result, several European countries and regions suffer persistently high levels of debt and unemployment, and large trade- or current-account deficits. Globalisation entails opportunities but also high costs for Europe and the western world in general.

1.2.2. The demographic deficit: An ageing and stagnant population

By the year 2050, the combined EU-27 and the UK's current population of 508 million is projected to peak at 525 million, and then slightly decline. This is a meagre increase of less than 4 %. At the same time, global population is estimated to jump from 7.5 to more than 9 billion – an increase of more than 20 %.[16]

The median age of the EU-28's population is over 42 years. This is higher than that of the USA (38), China (37), Brazil (32), Mexico (28), India (27) and every African country.[17] The slowing pace of birth rate is alarming. In 2017, 5.08 million children were born in the EU-28, which roughly corresponds to a birth rate of 9.9 per 1000. It is part of the declining birth-rate trend in Europe: from 16.3 in 1970 to 12.8 in 1985 to 10.6 in 2000.[18] This slide is a major competitive disadvantage, and one projected to grow dramatically over the next generations. For example, between 1965 and 2015 Europe's share of the global population contracted from 13 % to 7 %.[19] By the end of this century, it is projected to shrink to only 4.1 %.[20]

These stark figures send a clear message: Europeans are growing older and falling in numbers compared to the rest of the planet.

This demographic decline is not just one among other problems. It is an existential threat and should be treated as such. Europe is likely to suffer a lack of talent, new ideas and vitality. Europe's age pyramid will invert, with its upper "old age" layers spreading wider than the lower ones. In 2006, there were four people of working age (15–64) for each person aged 65 or over; by 2050, that ratio is projected to fall to just two working people supporting the others.[21] This will have a devastating impact on our pensions funds, social security systems and the ability of our workforce to sustain its retired population, with obvious implications for Europe's overall productivity and creativity.

1.2.3. The menace of climate change: Food dependence and water scarcity

The EU's agriculture and food sector are still productive and of high quality. Its imports and exports of agricultural products with non-EU countries are generally balanced.[22] For decades this equilibrium has ensured that Europeans no longer worry about hunger, malnutrition or lack of food.

However, Europe is now threatened by climate change and a subsequent ecological crisis. Its continent is getting warmer and, in many parts, drier. The years 2020 and 2019 were respectively the second and third warmest on record for the world.[23] According to one estimate, temperatures were more than 1.2 degree Celsius above Europe's average for the 1981–2010 period.[24] Globally, the years between 2014 and 2019 were the hottest since records began in the 19th century, with average temperatures between 1.1C and 1.2C higher than pre-industrial times.[25]

Europe's glacial regions are in retreat. Glaciers in the Alps have lost nearly half of their volume since 1900. Under a moderate climate change scenario, the volume of all European glaciers will decline by at least 22 % – and possibly much more – by 2100.[26] This will lead to water shortages and serious ecological disruptions.

In southern Europe water is growing scarcer while soil degrades as desertification advances across the region. Spain's situation is characteristic of the coming threat. According to the UN's respective research, nearly three-quarters of the country's territory could grapple with desertification, with 18 % at high risk of turning irreversibly into desert landscape.[27] The southern regions of Portugal and Italy, southeastern Greece, Malta, Cyprus and the Black Sea border regions of Romania and Bulgaria also face serious rates of desertification.[28] In addition, due to the combination of higher temperatures and increased global trade, plant pests and diseases, previously found only in tropical or subtropical regions, are advancing to more northern latitudes. This could inflict heavy economic and environmental damage on many of crops and forests.

Without serious mitigation of greenhouse gas emissions, the annual climate-related damage across Europe may amount to 2 % of the EU-28's GDP. The geographical distribution of climate damage is asymmetric, however, with a clear bias against Europe's southern regions. The resulting welfare losses range from almost zero in northern Europe to

3 % of GDP for Europe's southern regions.[29] Most of the economic loss will probably stem from increased mortality, coastal damage and reduced agricultural production.

Such trends threaten our agriculture, forests, water basins and, ultimately, our food and water security. A climate-resilient, resource-efficient Europe must thus become a priority. An infertile, deteriorating natural environment will engender unacceptable risks if we are forced to import a majority of the foodstuffs we need to sustain our society.

Our problem with food security is further linked to the wider impact of climate change on global food security. According to the Food and Agriculture Organisation (FAO), demand for food is likely to grow by 70 % until 2050 due to demographic growth and changes in diet and income.[30]

The strategic global warming question for Europe is: how are we going to cope, as the rest of the world grow hungrier and less eager to share its food resources with us?

1.2.4. Energy dependence on other countries

In 2018 the EU imported 58 % of the total energy it consumed at a cost of more than €1 billion a day. Specifically, it imported 90 % of its crude oil, 69 % of its natural gas, 42 % of its coal and other solid fuels and 40 % of its uranium and other nuclear fuels[31]

The main imported energy product was petroleum products, with crude oil being the main component and accounting for almost two-thirds of the EU's energy imports. This was trailed by imports of gas (24 %) and solid fossil fuels (8 %). The number of supplier countries is very limited, which hangs a question over the EU's future energy security. Two-thirds of its crude oil imports came from just six countries: Russia (30 %), Iraq (9 %), and Saudi Arabia, Norway, Kazakhstan, and Nigeria (7 % each). Nearly three-quarters of the EU's imports of natural gas came from only three: Russia (40 %), Norway (18 %) and Algeria (11 %). Within Europe, energy dependence varies wildly according to the country, from levels below 40 % in Estonia, Denmark, Bulgaria, Romania, and Sweden to more than 70 % in Italy, Belgium, Lithuania, Cyprus, Malta and Luxembourg.[32]

Europe's general level of dependence is unacceptable for its future prosperity and security. Despite their decline over time, fossil fuels (oil, coal and natural gas) will remain important factors in the world's energy mix for several more decades, since they are still abundant and cheaper than most renewable sources. Especially natural gas is going to be used as a 'transition fuel' before our economy becomes carbon neutral. So, during that time Europe risks becoming hostage to geopolitical developments that compromise its energy supply.

That dependence also poses an existential threat to Europe linked, once again, to the demographics. The expected rise in global population over the next three decades will generate a surge in energy demand from other parts of the world, which may push Europe to the margins as other secure their energy supplies. If Europe does not reverse its energy dependence, it will have to grapple with the consequences such as trade deficits, geopolitical volatility, and overall political and military insecurity due to gaps in its respective supplies. The sharp rise of energy prices in autumn 2021 sent a clear warning to all European countries.

Therefore, urgent action must be taken to increase our domestic energy production and self-sufficiency, through development of a carbon-free and circular economy.

1.2.5. Exclusion from the leading edge of fourth industrial revolution

Artificial intelligence, autonomous vehicles, robotics, gene technology, the internet of things, 3D printing and biometrics are only a few of the emerging technologies starting to influence our lives and how our economies operate. All these have been grouped under the term "fourth industrial revolution", which stands apart from its predecessors: the first revolution arising from steam power, the second involving electricity, and the third digital revolution that begun in the 1980s and continues today. As the World Economic Forum notes, the fourth revolution opens a new chapter in human development, enabled by the extraordinary technology advances of the three preceding ones.[33] As a result, the "fourth-wave" advances are merging the physical, digital and biological worlds in ways unique to their intensity, innovation and unpredictability.

While questions remain about the fourth industrial revolution's impact on the global labour force and how people will co-exist and communicate with one another, its technological trends are clear: nothing will go untouched. All human activities will be modified or disrupted, while entirely new economies and ways of human interaction will emerge. The prospects are not encouraging, however, that Europe will have a leading position in this new era.

In 2020 there was no EU entity in the world's top 10 internet or semiconductor companies,[34] while only one figured among the top-10 information technology companies. Looking ahead, few observers expect Europe to produce any player of the scale and impact of Amazon, Google, Huawei, Facebook, Microsoft, Xiaomi, Apple, Samsung, or IBM. Why is this, and what does it mean for Europe's future?

US and Asian firms are indisputable leaders in these fields. Most of the remarkable advances in artificial intelligence, virtual reality, synthetic biology or life prolongation take place in other regions' laboratories, not Europe's. Not surprisingly, the locus of innovation and knowledge production is moving from West to East. China and East Asia are rapidly increasing their global share of university students, researchers, and patents, with China predicted to have as many researchers as the combined total of the EU and US by 2030. India is also emerging as an international scientific force.[35]

Europe dominated history during the 19th and early 20th centuries thanks to its industrial revolution and control of the most advanced technologies of the time. That is no longer the case in our century. Our innovative spirit does not seem to be as sharp as it once was. We consume rather than produce science and technology. Gone are the days of our cutting-edge inventions such as the airplane, internal combustion engine or cinema.

One could argue, of course, that technological knowledge is no longer localised as it was in the past. Most technological advances spread rapidly around the world, moving easily to the realm of common ownership. However, the major beneficiaries of new knowledge and innovations are their creators rather than the users: they control the trends and adapt them to their strategic objectives.

The fourth industrial revolution is re-defining the basic notions of life, nature, war, security and well-being. If Europe loses the race to artificial intelligence, digital innovations or life sciences, it will lose a technological century. It will miss the opportunity to fundamentally determine the shape of our public and private domains. Such a gap in knowledge and technological prowess would severely handicap our continent. Europe must bolster and speed up its ability to lead, rather than follow, technological innovation. This is critical to remain relevant in terms of power and progress in the 21st century.

1.3. Scenarios for the way ahead – Why a European Federation?

The above described situation requires a new vision for the European region to deal with the 21st century's unfolding developments. Europe's current structures seem not to be well equipped for managing these changes. Therefore further integration is more than needed.

While the mid-1980s unleashed parallel dynamics – i.e., increasing integration via treaty amendments (1986, 1992, 1997, 2000 and 2009) alongside membership enlargement in various waves (1986, 1995, 2004, 2007 and 2013) – these processes slowed or even began reversing after 2010. This gives reason for serious concern.

Several scenarios about the way ahead surface periodically by governments, think tanks, political parties, pressure groups and various scholars. Among the most prominent has been, since March 2021, the launch of the "Conference on the Future of Europe", a one-year effort steered by the Commission, European Parliament and Council to give Europeans "a greater say" over what the EU does and how it works on their behalf.[36] Its purpose has been to "pave the way to launching a series of debates and discussions to empower people from every corner of Europe to share their ideas to help shape Europe's future".

Thus Europe's citizens, civil society groups, other stakeholders, and public authorities – European, national, regional, and local – have been given the opportunity to organise events and contribute ideas within that process. Responsibility for the Conference has fallen to the European Commission, European Parliament and the European Council, whose presidents have held its Joint Presidency. The latter has been supported by an Executive Board (co-chaired by the three institutions), which regularly reports to the Presidency. The Executive Board has been responsible for overseeing the Conference's progression, and preparing each meetings of the Conference Plenary, including citizens' input and its follow up. The Executive Board also has had the task of transparently drawing up the final report in full collaboration with the Conference Plenary. The report has been agreed to be published digitally on a multilingual platform, with the conference's three institutions obliged to swiftly examine how to act on the documents's recommendations within their respective area of responsibility, as laid down in the Treaties.[37]

It remains to be seen whether this overarching institutional effort will, in the long-term, lead to any new constitutional benchmark for European unification.

The possible outcome of such initiatives, present or past, can be summarised under one of the following four basic scenarios: "Medieval Kingdoms", "Four-Freedoms", "Europe à la carte" or the "European Federation" scenario.

– *The "Medieval Kingdoms" scenario*

Under this scenario, the EU dissolves entirely or declines to irrelevance, with Brexit as a starting point. Every European state would constitute its own entity, possibly with links to a regional union with its neighbours. During our century's second decade, several EU member states – like Poland, Italy, Hungary – began resisting the application of various EU rules, policies or principles to their territory, positing that national sovereignty was primary. Notions of "Polexit", "Frexit", "Grexit" and others surfaced, though they never materialised. Nonetheless, journalists and scholars at the fringes of the left and right seized the moment to argue that nations were revolting against globalisation and their people against international elites. Steve Bannon, chief strategist of Donald Trump's presidential campaign of 2016 and highly skilled in selling "populism versus elitism", embodied that narrative. He campaigned vigorously in the EU for an alliance of national populist parties during the EP's May 2019 elections. Although the results fell short of his efforts, they confirm to some extent the centrifugal tendencies that have emerged within Europe during the past ten years.

The "Medieval" scenario is dismissed as simply outdated and dangerously out of step with history. It would yank Europeans back to the dark ages of multi-directional friction among small, isolated states, leading to local economic and cultural wars that would disastrously fragment Europe's business community. The citizens of our small continent would be divided by poverty, isolation and irrelevance. Fortunately, the vast majority of political Europe considers this option neither desirable nor realistic. Almost all Eurobarometers, the regular public opinion surveys carried out by the European Commission, confirm the support of the majority of EU people to the union. It is also encouraging that national populist, euro-sceptic and sovereigntist parties won fewer than 180 of 790 seats in the 2019 EP elections.

– The "four-freedoms Union" scenario

Here the EU reverts back to its European Economic Community profile (the historic EEC), based on a huge free trade zone, customs union and enhanced integration in selected areas, but little beyond that. There would be a strong focus on the single market's "four freedoms" for the movement of goods, services, people, and capital, with the participating nations retaining their sovereignty over many other competences. This is the option traditionally favoured by the UK, which pushed for expansion of the EU territory and markets while resisting integration of its social policy and judicial sectors.

This option, too, should be considered an anachronism. As the experience of 1970s and 1980s showed, a free trade zone and customs union alone were not adequate to fully serve the interests of the participating states and their publics. Regionalised state-to-state relations are complex and cannot survive by economic ties alone. They require co-ordination of their social, political, judicial, security and environmental affairs. Thus, the 12 EEC countries in 1992 shifted their constitutional basis to form the EU. Beyond a certain point, a higher level of political, economic and institutional integration is necessary to supplement the achievements of free trade, to produce a more functional "union of nations".

– The "Europe à la carte" scenario

Here the EU continues, more or less in its current form, as a joining of sovereign states with different sub-groupings of integration (Eurozone, Schengenland, closer defence or fiscal integration, etc.). The EU would likely achieve a certain degree of supranational unification – more than today but alongside national control over taxation, defence and foreign policy. Depending on their level of participation in EU policies, the member states would position themselves within concentric circles of increasing co-operation, either close to the centre, and thus greater integration, or further away in the outer orbits. Such circles already exist regarding the eurozone whose hard core is monetary union, orbited by EU, then the European Economic Area (comprising the EU and three more European countries) and, finally, broader regional co-operation.

This model was proposed by French President Emmanuel Macron in his Sorbonne address of September 2017.[38] Although we welcome the spirt of that speech, along with any initiative for more European integration, we believe this option is not ambitious enough. It carries the risk of perpetuating counterproductive national competition between EU member states, as well as incoherent policies, excessive red tape and unnecessary economic and political delay as the EU tries to catch up with the rest of the world. Indeed, this is the EU's current state of affairs, troubled by endless internal inconsistencies in the application of its policies. Its members are still divided between south and north, east and west, liberal and authoritarian, big and small, rich and poor. With such differences, the EU's current structure cannot produce a common European direction.

– *The "European Federation" scenario*

Under this scenario, the EU shifts to a federal sovereign state, entitled the "European Federation" (EF). All EU member states and the UK, as well as like-minded countries from Scandinavia, the Balkans and central Europe, would voluntarily surrender their sovereignty and become constituent states of the new federal entity. The EF would take over their seats within the United Nations and all other international organisations and fora. A radical reform of institutions and systems would have to occur. Strongly rooted national habits and cultures would have to adapt gradually to the new reality. Joint frameworks, from harmonised criminal legislation to a common military force, would have to be established. This would also demand serious investments and certain short-term national sacrifices for the sake of Europe's long-term prosperity.

This last scenario is the preferred proposal to the people of Europe, even if it is the most difficult one, particularly in an era of growing euro-scepticism and resistance to globalisation. Yet it is the only way for Europe to stay at centre-stage in world affairs and avoid marginalisation. Only this formula offers Europe the chance to be a leader and provider of progress, wealth and ideas rather than their passive follower and recipient. A federal European state is the only way to face the future's global challenges – as a single force and a reaffirmation of the mission of an "even-closer union among the peoples of Europe" (Article 1, Treaty of European Union). Linking together is the best way for us to become stronger and more effective in defending and projecting our interests and values.

However, addressing Europe's existential challenges is not the only reason to move in that direction. A federal Europe would become a major, self-sufficient geopolitical power, as strong as or stronger than the USA, Russia or China. It would be a model for other regional federations around the planet. Ultimately, it could inspire a global federation of nations based on the principles of peaceful co-existence, human rights, social justice and sustainable development.

Our idea of a European Federation is not an original one. It has been surfaced in various guises before, sometimes as the "United States of Europe". However the difference between those proposals and our analysis is that we elaborate with precision the policy choices needed to implement the concept in order to achieve full institutional integration.

In a nutshell, we support the case for a new European federal state with a more open, dynamic, global and competitive orientation. We argue for an entity that rests on the principles of federalism, liberalism and ecological development, principles that Europe has generated and developed over the centuries. We stand in favour of a state with a common fiscal, monetary and economic space – and a common people with equal rights and freedoms of movement, residence and work conditions. That state would, for the first time in Europe's history, obtain a common defence force and a common long-term strategy regarding its neighbourhood and the wider world. Our policy proposals place innovation, entrepreneurship and sustainability at the heart of a competitive production model. Social cohesion would be achieved by offering more opportunities and access to all versus simply granting subsidies to specific groups. Moreover, a robust economic strategy would be required to shape common European policies in energy, agriculture, food, manufacturing, advanced technologies, health, education and social welfare.

In short, the above elements are the essence to what a European Federation should comprise. Critics may label that vision utopic, but muddling along as Europe is doing today will only lead to its decline. Radical change requires radical thinking. The ideological principles of such a European Federation are laid down in the following chapter, while detailed proposals for its institutions and policies are laid out in the next ones.

Chapter 2

The ideological framework of the European Federation

Every political programme must first be defined by clear ideological principles. Those must inspire a common vision and purpose for its citizenry to gain its trust.

The envisioned federal republic would be based on four ideological principles. They should be explicitly cited in the EF's constitution as the building blocks of a sovereign state. These are federalism, liberalism, ecological development and common European humanistic values. Those principles and values have historically proven to be most successful in building free and prosperous societies. They were first established in Europe and closely linked to our way of life. They should therefore be safeguarded as our political heritage and developed further.

2.1. Federalism

Federalism is the notion that a political organisation may consist of different nations and territories that share a common government and distributed powers at regional, national and supranational levels.

Federalism has been used in Europe as a framework for many polities: monarchies, republics and communist states. It is the current form of governance in Germany, Austria, Belgium, Switzerland and Bosnia and Herzegovina. Lesser types of federalism are also practised in other countries: Italy, although not a federal state, has granted significant powers to its regions. In Spain, UK, Denmark and Greece, one or more regions have high degree of autonomy (Catalonia and the Basque country in Spain; Scotland and Northern Ireland in the UK; Mount Athos in Greece; Greenland and the Faeroe Islands in Denmark).

In all those countries the federal choice has been the result of various factors: co-existence of different linguistic, religious or ethnic groups, or co-existence of different regions geographically separated by natural borders. In the EF's case, federalism would be the product of all those factors – and more. It would be the natural choice for responding to the challenges of globalisation in a more effective, coherent manner. Indeed, globalisation, arguably, is the first reason to establish a federal structure in Europe.

Federalism is the most realistic option for linking millions of different people together under a common political structure. Historic examples of federalism such as those of the USA, India, Brazil or Canada are indicative: they stand in contrast to centralised unitary states which are deemed as more distant and less democratic for their citizens. Federalism can be symmetric, where all constituent entities have the same status (Switzerland, Austria) or asymmetric (Spain, UK) where certain regions have a higher degree of autonomy in an otherwise centralised state. Federalism can express itself nationally (Germany) or at the supranational level, the EU being the example par excellence of such integration with federal elements, though it is not yet a true federation.

The proposed EF would be a symmetric federation with constituent states of equal standing: this is the simplest option to ensure a smooth transition from the current EU structure, with its equal member states, to a European Federation. One could also argue for a federation of regions, versus states, since this would be closer to the citizenry and local governance. While we would support a high degree of autonomy for regions within a federal Europe, our preference is for a federation of constituent states as the more realistic option due to each people's strong historical association with their nation state. With some notable exceptions, most Europeans are more attached to the nation than their region. Thus a Polish feels more "Polish" than, say, Silesian, a Greek favours Greece over just Thessaly and so on. People would not like to see their countries disappear from the political map.

To reassure its citizens, a federalist Europe would need to convey twin messages. First, it would have to convince Europe's peoples that they are no longer citizens of relatively small countries but rather belong to a larger, secure and prosperous global power whose goal is to defend their interests in a fiercely competitive global environment. In other words: citizen confidence in the benefits of the federal project. Such confidence has been lost in Europe in recent decades due to the rise of increasingly bigger players on the world state.

Second, federalism should ensure, via decentralisation and the principle of subsidiarity, that Europe's peoples and cultures enjoy an appropriate degree of autonomy. Federal governance should respect local traditions, identities and perceptions. A citizen in Seville should feel European, but would also need to preserve his or her Spanish and Andalusian identity. More detailed proposals are presented in Chapter 6 dealing with socio-cultural governance.

Finally, it is debatable whether federalism should be seen as a neutral institutional framework capable of accommodating all possible ideologies (democracies, dictatorships, communism, liberalism, socialism, nationalism, etc.) or whether it should function as a unitary ideology unto itself. In the EF's case, we would see it both ways. Federalism would offer a neutral institutional framework for the functioning of a new state that could evolve in different directions, depending on the results of each election: conservatism, liberalism, social democracy etc. But it would also carry some inherent ideological elements. Since the EF would be a free union of different states and people, its federalism would embody the notions of anti-nationalism, along with pacifism and solidarity. It would serve as the main tool against national, local, ethnic or racial chauvinism. It would be the ideal political tool to eliminate discrimination between people and administrative regions within a wide area. These are all features that contain a clear ideological character and have no place in a nationalist or authoritarian regime.

2.2. Liberalism

Liberalism constitutes the main political pillar of societies across the EU and should remain the cornerstone of EF policies, objectives and vision. Historically, liberalism has emerged in three main forms. These readily co-exist and complement each other: classic, economic and social liberalism.

- Classic liberalism revolves around the idea of individual emancipation. It consists of classic civil and political rights, democratic representation, free political organisation, secularism, rule of law, equality before the law, non-discrimination and freedom of conscience, speech, press and religion. A product of England's revolution and the Enlightenment, it formed the ideological foundations of the American and French revolutions whose intellectual godfathers were persons like Adam Smith, John Locke, Jean-Baptiste Say, Thomas Malthus or David Ricardo. It emerged as a response to the prevailing oligarchy and feudalism of the 17th and 18th centuries and, in the following century, as a reaction to the excesses of the industrial revolution and urbanisation in Europe and the United States. At liberalism's core are civil liberties derived from the rule of law and, above all, freedom of the individual by limiting the power of government.

- Economic liberalism rests on the idea that the economy must function according to the individual and the free choices of society thus its principles of market economy, laissez-faire economic policy, protection of private property and free competition among economic actors. Classical liberal economists called for the abolition of feudal and mercantilist restrictions on countries' manufacturing and internal commerce, and for an end to the restrictions that governments imposed on foreign imports to protect domestic producers. They firmly believed in the superiority of a self-regulating market.[39]

This form of liberalism has driven the astonishing increase in global wealth for the past two centuries. We are convinced that freedom of trade and entrepreneurship must lie at the heart of all our policies because these have shown that they create wealth and overall progress for all segments of society. State intervention in the economy should aim only at creating a favourable framework for this progress and preventing economic abuse of people's rights, safety risks or environmental damage.

- Finally, social liberalism aims to guarantee the fulfilment of individual freedoms through social justice. Its objective is the creation of appropriate conditions under which all members of the society obtain equal opportunities to progress according to their abilities. It demands social infrastructure (education, public health, labour rights, etc.) to ensure that individuals are equipped to meet their needs, regardless of their initial wealth or social status.

Building on earlier liberal thought, social liberalism spread during the second half of the 1800s and into the 1900s when its adherents declared that rewards generated by the market were too crude a measure of a person's contribution to society. Moreover, they considered that the market ignored the needs of those lacking in opportunity or economically exploited. The market alone could not address basic human needs such as education, housing, health, public hygiene and other societal needs. They thus pushed for labour rights (e.g. through trade unions) and government-funded social services.[40]

History reveals that a combination of these three forms of liberalism offers the best guarantees for individual and collective progress. That was, for instance, the gist of New Deal policies in the USA (1930s–1940s), and has been the basis of Europe's progress since the 1950s. In our times of financial crises, however, liberalism has come under fire from those who argue, falsely, that it only represents the interests of the "neoliberal establishment".

Such accusations should be ignored. Liberal ideals have been successfully tested and developed for more than 200 years and they are increasingly embraced by a majority of the planet, even by communist states (China, Vietnam) that have steadily switched to the former "heresy" of free market economies. Thanks to the opening of global trade and the adoption of liberal policies, more than one billion people worldwide, especially in India and China, escaped from absolute poverty in the intervening years since 1990.[41]

Europe should remain faithful to what it created, as an example to the world: individual freedoms, open societies, free markets, social welfare and social cohesion. No other ideological framework has better served the basic needs of human nature in terms of self-fulfilment, self-determination, freedom, ambition, and the quest for progress.

2.3. Ecological development

Climate change, environmental degradation, depletion of resources, poverty, inequality, and lately public health and protection from epidemics, are humanity's prime concerns for the 21st century. They often exacerbate each other and represent major ethical and existential challenges for our future.

It is argued that Europe's ecological policies should reach beyond mere environmental protection and sustainable development. A new governing *principle of ecological development* should be defined. This implies a development that respects, to the most reasonable extent possible, all forms of human, animal and other life – one that treats the natural environment in a co-operative and complementary manner, versus one that is dominant and exploitative.

Basically, this version of ecological development would rest on the classic concept of sustainable development, namely progress that fulfils today's needs without compromising opportunities for future generations to fulfil their own.[42] However, given our century's looming challenges, we need a concept of ecological development that reaches for distant horizons, beyond the mere management of resources.

This notion of ecological development should foster an all-embracing moral stance towards life and the dignity of humankind and the animal kingdom. It should promulgate an ethical view whereby humans pursue mutual co-operation and avoid the domination of one by the other.

Ecological development should thus take into account the principles of social ecology as developed by the American social theorist, Murray Bookchin, who argued for a world that "re-harmonises" human communities with the natural world, while celebrating diversity, creativity and freedom. This ideology considers all lifeforms are interrelated and of equal importance, contrary to mankind's preference for hierarchical structures. Humans are not masters of the natural environment and our global ecosystem, but simple parts of it. Social ecology draws its perspective from the idea that ecological problems are inevitably the results of social dysfunctions in human society, and especially in authoritarianism and hierarchical relations. Humans treat one other as superior or inferior, masters or servants, and similar to the way they treat nature. In Bookchin's view, social factors such as racism, sexism or colonialism are closely linked with environmental problems such as the destruction of natural habitats and the ravening exploitation of resources. Social dysfunctions should not be injected into relations with nature.[43]

Ecological development should further encompass the principles of political ecology that reach for a more equal distribution of the costs and benefits of environmental change or exploitation. The unequal distribution of those costs and benefits alters power relationships between social groups at the expense of their weaker elements. It inevitably reinforces social and economic inequalities since any change in environmental conditions affects the political and economic state of societies. Therefore, those affected the most by nature's exploitation should be compensated and allowed to help define the policies that impact their environment.[44] Political ecology can thus be a tool to improve environmental governance, facilitate the decisions that communities make concerning their natural environment and reveal how unequal relations within and between societies affect it.

In the same vein, ecological development should bring fundamental non-economic values to the core of our political choices. Though frequently neglected, these deserve the highest priority: the values of a common cultural heritage, landscapes, traditions, communal services, leisure activities, self-organisation and volunteerism. Our lives are not only about money, consumption or infrastructure. They are grounded in human relations, beliefs and aesthetics. All these elements must be reintroduced, in a clear way, into our public discourse and actions.

How to apply the principle of ecological development in practice? The EU already has an advanced environmental policy, probably the world's most progressive. Its pillars are precaution, prevention, and – via the 'polluter pays' principle – rectifying pollution at source. As stated by Article 11 of the Treaty on the Functioning of the European Union (TFEU): *"Environmental protection requirements must be integrated into the definition and implementation of the Union's policies and activities, in particular with a view to promoting sustainable development."*

Stretching back to 1973, the EU's multiannual environmental action programmes have set the framework for future action in all areas of ecological policy. As a result, the EU has promulgated an impressive set of sectoral environmental legislation for air and water quality, soil protection, noise pollution and waste management.[45] This is complemented by a solid array of programmes and rules regarding cultural heritage and preservation, and urban and rural landscapes. More recently, the "European Green Deal", launched by the Commission in December 2019, aims for zero net carbon emissions by 2050. This new cross-cutting strategy will support the 'greening' of all sectors of the economy, industry, consumption, large-scale infrastructure, transport, food and agriculture, construction, taxation, and social benefits.[46] We will expand on this very ambitious project in the following chapters.

The EF would have to build on that *acquis*, while introducing its own approach to ecological development for the core aspects of daily life. This would set more ambitious targets in critical environmental areas such as recycling, carbon-free energy, forest protection, water use and the reduction of pesticides. Chapter 10 offers specific ideas on climate policy and the circular economy.

A federal Europe would promote the principles of political ecology by introducing more inclusive practices for public consultation and participation in projects with serious environmental effects (we lay down in the next chapter our ideas about democratic governance). It would ensure that those affected the most by environmental damages would be substantially supported and compensated.

The EF would promote social ecology by developing programmes focusing on communal solidarity for those in need, volunteerism for social and environmental action, environmentally friendly and co-operative enterprises and, finally, fair trade schemes to support developing countries.

A renewed ethical approach would be introduced for the treatment of animals, including new policies to reduce meat production and consumption in order to reduce animal suffering and protect our nature (for more detailed proposals on these issues, see Chapter 8 on agriculture).

2.4. European humanistic values

Common European humanistic values underpin our principles of federalism, liberalism and ecological development, all overlapping to a great extent and girded by history. But they also reach further. These are "deep values", first developed in classic Greco-Roman times, then complemented by the Christian tradition, revamped by the Renaissance and finally codified during the Age of Enlightenment, the French Revolution and subsequent struggles for social justice with the birth of the industrial revolution.

These values consist, first and above all, in the idea of humanism: the inherent value of human beings, anchored in their ability to improve their own lives through the use of reason, compassion and ingenuity as opposed to exploitative cruelty, irrationality, and brutality.[47] The roots of the term trace back to the notion of 'humanitas', as developed by Cicero in ancient Rome as an educational and political ideal. At later stages, the term acquired the qualities of benevolence, compassion and mercy, and then more advanced characteristics such as judgement, eloquence and prudence.[48] Indeed, Europe has traditionally placed humans beings and their dignity at the centre of its philosophy. That approach has exerted a cross-cutting influence over its politics, literature, arts and daily life for several centuries.

A significant characteristic of humanism is the idea of solidarity, whose roots largely stem from the traditions and philosophies of the three Aramaic religions: Christianity, Islam and Judaism. The term first

appeared in the Napoleonic Civil Code of 1804 as a legal concept, refer-
ring to a common responsibility for debts incurred by one member of a
group. But it soon developed into a sociological and political concept.
French philosophers, Charles Fourier among the first, began to deploy
'solidarity' as a principle characterised by reciprocal sympathy among
persons bound together in a community. Fourier was the first to associ-
ate solidarity and social policy, arguing that it should include the sharing of resources with people in need, a guaranteed minimum income
and public support for families.[49] Another contemporary philosopher,
Auguste Comte, posited that the primary task of government is to sustain and bolster society's sense of solidarity as the only way to avoid
excessive specialization and isolation of its groups.

Many scholars since then, from liberals to marxists, have debated the
value and role of solidarity in creating a successful society.[50] What is not
disputed, however, is that it is a guiding principle for Europe's labour
movements, Catholicism's social instruction and the political theory of
the continent's Social Democratic and Christian Democratic parties.
It is the cornerstone of a long concatenation of social programmes and
movements.

Another culminating achievement of European political thinking is the doctrine of the social contract according to which individuals surrender some of their freedoms to state authority in exchange for
the protection of the remaining rights.[51] Here the state is considered as
institutional expression of society, with its mission to serve, not rule, its
constituents via implicit "contractual" terms. The first contracting party
(citizens) offer their taxes, obedience to legislation and even their lives
during war. The other contractual party (the state) offers in return security, public utilities, infrastructure and whatever else citizens need to live
and prosper within an organized, civilised framework. One aspect of this
contract has been the emergence of the social state that ensures safety
nets for the weak: the state moderates the excesses of extreme liberalism
on one hand and of communitarianism on the other one.

A final European value of our interest, is the idea of progress. Faith
in scientific, technological and intellectual advancement is central to the
improvement of human life, and must remain our constant objective.[52]
Philosophical proponents of Progress maintain that the human condition has improved over the course of history and will continue to do so.
Its earliest theorists needed first to define human well-being to prove that
it increases over time. As indicators, they pointed to freedom, happiness

and the realisation of human capabilities. Other theorists interpreted human well-being as a single value or as a set of incommensurable values empirically connected.[53] Theories of progress depend heavily on their historic context, variously highlighting the predominance of science or the more concrete means of production.

Doctrines of progress first appeared in 18th century Europe, epitomizing that time and place's optimism, reaching its peak in the following century. However, after the horrendous world wars of the 20th century and their industrial scales of destruction, that idea's glow has suffered from scepticism. In any event, over the four last centuries Europe has experienced the longest and most consistent scientific, technological, artistic and intellectual period of progress in history. It is an impressive journey that has liberated humanity from illiteracy, superstition, slavery, and blind submission to authority. It is the triumph of reason over irrationality, and optimism over the dark pessimism of the middle ages. We can still tap into the rich inspirations behind the Idea of Progress, the fundaments of which lie within the Enlightenment, Encyclopedism[54] and Modernism of the 18th, 19th and 20th centuries.

2.5. Practical tools for our common political lives

Such ideological principles should not hibernate in books, however. As practical tools for the EF's politics and decisions, they should be explicitly mentioned as preamble justifications in all the EF's laws and in its explanations of policy and programmes. Humanism and solidarity should be laid down, for instance, as the guideposts for any law regulating welfare policy, whether for immigrants, unemployed or the disabled. The notion of the social contract should explicitly justify any measures that restrict freedoms or rights (e.g., confinement or travel restrictions due to the COVID-19 pandemic) for the purpose of securing other, more important freedoms and rights (e.g., life and health). The idea of progress would be the cornerstone of any programme promoting scientific research.

These principles can, of course, be interpreted as contradictory. Free economic activity usually harms nature in one way or the other, thus it contravenes the principle of ecological development. Economic liberalism can also function in opposition to social liberalism since the interests of enterprises can conflict with the interests of their employees.

Efforts should be made to apply these principles in a balanced way by moderating excesses. That means focusing not only on the points of conflict surrounding an excess but their reconciliation. A robust enterprise can also support employees' rights. An expanding carbon-free economy can boost profits while respecting nature.

In sum, theories should be treated as a set of living tools to shed light on, and help implement, daily policies. They should be codified in the EF's constitution as European values, and taught as subjects in all European schools, occupying a central place in education, social policy, civil activity, and political discourse. Ultimately, they will constitute the intellectual raw material for creating new European identities, politics and a way of life.

2.6. The European federalist movement

In the final section of this second chapter it would be useful to briefly examine the history of the European federalist movement to understand how it has elicited the above-mentioned ideological principles over the last decades.

The notion of a "United States of Europe" was initially circulated by Victor Hugo in his speech to the International Peace Congress of 1849 in Paris. However, the first organised movement around the concept appeared only after the First World War. The idea of a unified European state was introduced in Richard von Coudehove-Kalergi's manifesto of 1923, the *Paneuropa*, which favoured social democracy as an improvement on "the feudal aristocracy of the sword". This prompted creation of the International Paneuropean Union, which still exists as the oldest movement campaigning for European unity.[55] In 1925, Coudenhove-Kalergi began publication of his three-volume work, "The fight for Paneuropa, 1925–1928". In 1926 the organisation's first Congress was held in Vienna where its 2,000 delegates elected him as president of its Central Council, a position he held until his death in 1972.

Similar ideas were later evinced by Aristide Briand when he addressed the League of Nations in September 1929, advocating a European Federal Union. The next year, in fact, he submitted to the French government a "Memorandum on the Organisation of a Regime of European Federal Union".

The subsequent World War swiftly put an end to any dreams of a federated Europe, united in peace. However, that war also sowed the seeds for the birth of a new version that was articulated by Altiero Spinelli, an anti-fascist Italian activist. While serving a long-term sentence – imposed by Mussolini – on the small island of Ventotene, he and Ernesto Rossi in 1941 drafted their "Manifesto for a Free, United Europe", more widely known as the "Ventotene Manifesto". Here the authors attributed the events leading to World War II to the existence of nation states. Their text argued strongly against both the form and nationalism of the modern nation state: "[...] *the nation is no longer viewed as the historical product of co-existence between men who, as the result of a lengthy historical process, have acquired greater unity in their customs and aspirations and who see their State as being the most effective means of organising collective life within the context of all human society. Rather the nation has become a divine entity, an organism which must only consider its own existence, its own development, without the least regard for the damage that others may suffer from this.*"

They therefore concluded that a European federation needed to be put in place. In 1943, Spinelli founded the "Movimento federalista europeo" (European Federalist Movement) in Milan. During the next 40 years he was a dominant figure in what became the post-war European federalist movement.

After the war, nearly 80 federalist groups from 16 European countries gathered in in September 1946 in Hertenstein, Switzerland, to declare their support for federalism and adopt a political programme. The delegates were convinced that only a European Federation, united in its diversity, could prevent a repetition of the disastrous global wars sparked by their region. In December of that year they officially established the Union of European Federalists (UEF) with its mission to co-ordinate and organise the various movements into a federal structure.

The UEF started off campaigning for a "European Federal Pact" by organising a petition, signed by thousands of citizens and eminent personalities, that requested the transformation of the Advisory Assembly of the Council of Europe into a Constituent Assembly of the European Federation. It also lobbied for creation of the European Defence Community (EDF) and its political equivalent. However, those campaigns bore no fruit. Subsequently, the UEF developed two political camps. One insisted on a constitutional path, whose supporters included Altiero Spinelli, leading directly to a European federal state. The other side advocated a more step-by-step approach via a gradual but increasing level of integration, with a common market as the first step. Dissonance between the two finally led, in 1956, to the UEF's split into two separate organisations, the "Movement Federaliste Europeen" (M.F.E.) – favouring the constitutional "big bang" approach – and the more gradualist "Action Europeenne Federaliste (A.E.F.)".

In 1973, however, the two organisations rejoined forces by re-establishing the UEF. The reason? Their joint aspiration to push for a closer political, economic and monetary union, and to campaign for direct elections regarding the European Parliament (EP). That proved more successful for the mid- and long-term: the EP's first direct elections took place in 1979; the long-standing "European Economic Community" transformed into the European Union in 1993 accompanied by the birth of its internal market; and the EU achieved monetary union with the eurozone's creation in 2002. The UEF doggedly pushed for all those objectives during its campaigns via petitions, lobbying, press articles, demonstrations. The latter, in particular, occasionally produced spectacular results. For example, during a European Council meeting in Milan, on 28 June 1985, approximately 100,000 people gathered in the biggest federalist rally ever seen, demanding a review of the Community treaties.

The UEF was not alone it its drive for federalism. Another parallel effort also unfolded after WWII, at a higher level, by the "European Movement". During 7–10 May 1948, around 800 delegates from around Europe gathered in The Hague for their Congress of Europe. Organised by the International Committee of Movements for European Unity and presided over by Winston Churchill, the event brought together its enthusiasts to debate how to develop a European Union. Aside from Churchill, its participants included important political figures such as Konrad Adenauer, Harold Macmillan, Paul-Henry Spaak, Albert Coppé, and Altiero Spinelli. This landmark conference led to the European Movement, created on 25 October 1948. Duncan Sandys was chosen as the Movement's President, with Léon Blum, Winston Churchill, Alcide De Gasperi, and Paul-Henri Spaak elected as Honorary Presidents.

The Movement's first major achievement was to create the Council of Europe in May 1949, the European organisation that upholds human rights, democracy, and the rule of law. It also founded the "Collège d'Europe" in Bruges[56] and the European Centre of Culture in Geneva. Since 1948 the European Movement has actively fought for the most important goals of European integration: direct elections of the European Parliament by all European citizens, the European Union Treaty, and above all a European Constitution.[57]

The year 2005 marked the peak for the federalist movement with its initiative for a Treaty establishing a Constitution for Europe, but also a major setback. The goal was to create a consolidated constitution for the EU, replacing its existing treaties with a single text and giving legal force to the Charter of Fundamental Rights. Critically, too, it would have expanded qualified majority voting within the Council of Ministers into policy areas historically decided by unanimity among the EU's member states, thus enhancing the union's supranational dimension. The Treaty was signed on 29 October 2004 by representatives of the 25 EU member states at the time, and subsequently ratified by 18 of them. However, it was rejected by French and Dutch voters in May and June 2005, which brought the ratification process to an halt. A substantial opportunity to create a more federal structure for Europe had been missed.

Yet federalist movements have continued unabated since then. In 2010 the 'Spinelli Group' was created, a network of federalist-minded members of the European Parliament (MEPs). Founded by Guy Verhofstadt, Belgian MEP and former prime minister, and MEPs Daniel Cohn-Bendit (Germany) Sylvie Goulard (France) and Isabelle Durant (Belgium), the group aims to "find a federal majority among members of the European Parliament on important subjects". Echoing the Ventotene Manifesto's sentiment, their declaration calls on all MEPs and European citizens to fight against nationalism and intergovernmentalism by accelerating European integration among countries in support of a federal Europe.[58]

The period subsequent to 2010 has seen the emergence of new federalist forces as a reaction to Euro-sceptic populist movements and events such as Brexit. For example, Volt Europe, the first pan-European political movement, was created in 2017. Only four years later in 2021, it managed to get almost 60 representatives elected to posts across various European, national, regional or local parliaments. Volt argues that Europe's national parties have reached their viable limits, while populist promises are putting Europe's very peace at risk. Thus, the rationale behind its creation: to conduct politics for and within a federal Europe, across the borders of its constituent countries.[59] That said, the party's electoral successes between 2019 and 2021 have been limited to just a few countries, most notably Germany and the Netherlands. Its appeal to southern and eastern European states has, so far, been negligible.

In addition to Volt Europe, other movements have sprung up in the wake of Brexit such as "Stand Up for Europe" and "Alliance 4 Europe", both aspiring to co-ordinate, support, and motivate pro-EU organisations and citizens. They were particularly active regarding the European Parliament's elections of 2019 when the risk of a euro-sceptic majority was looming on the horizon. Fortunately that was averted. However, as of 2021, those organisations are still known to only a small circle of euro-enthusiasts and have yet to become well known household names.

In sum, such movements and parties have been based, to various degrees, on the ideological principles elucidated above. Apart from the federalist idea in general, they all stress the need for peaceful co-existence, respect for human dignity, democracy and the rule of law, and solidarity between countries, regions and individuals. Indeed, each movement has derived inspiration from the notion of a common European cultural heritage, adapting its ideals to the narratives of their time.

Part II

THE FOUR PILLARS OF THE EUROPEAN FEDERATION

In Part Two of our analysis the major characteristics of the proposed European Federation are elaborated. Four pillars are identified which the EU currently lacks and needs, if it is to advance to the level of a fully sovereign, federal and functional European Republic. These are:

(1) common political and democratic governance, with joint institutions, rule of law framework and human rights protection (Chapter 3),
(2) common economic governance via a full economic, fiscal, monetary and banking union (Chapter 4),
(3) common foreign, defence and security governance (Chapter 5), and
(4) common socio-cultural governance and the development of a common European identity (Chapter 6)

The pillars are equally essential for a truly sovereign state. If one or more is missing or functions badly, the state will fail or seriously weaken.

Chapter 3

Political governance, democratic institutions and human rights

Every sovereign state needs solid institutions to be governed effectively and to ensure the security and trust of its citizens. While the EU is an international organisation with a high level of integration among its member states, it is not a sovereign state or even a confederation of states. It lacks a constitution, a central government, an all-encompassing supreme court, a central bank or a parliament elected from lists of European-level candidates. Creating the EF would unavoidably require the establishment of new political institutions and forms of democratic governance.

This chapter elucidates our proposals for the EF's political governance, institutions, constitution and its membership. Democratic governance would be the vector for direct democracy, citizens' participation in decision-making, effective public administration, prevention of corruption and, finally, widespread support for civic education. It would further need a robust framework to advocate human rights, the abolition of all forms of discrimination, respect for minorities and a judicial system designed to protect those rights, while supporting the economy and other needs of society.

3.1. Political governance

3.1.1. The basic framework

The EF would be governed as a federal republic consisting of constituent states. It would replace and succeed the current EU member states, plus any other European state that wished to join and respect its rules.

EF governance would be based on classic democratic principles as developed since the 18th century: division of powers (executive, legislative and judicial), parliamentary representation based on popular vote and a comprehensive system of governmental checks and balances.

To ensure a functioning polity, the EF would have to be led by a parliament as the legislative branch, and a government as the executive branch. Both would serve simultaneous four-year terms following a general election. A federal court of justice would carry out classic checks on the legislative and the executive branches.

As a union of constituent states and hundreds of millions of people, we posit that an additional layer of checks would be needed to control the functioning of the EF's institutions. This could be an EF "Council of Governance" consisting of representatives from the constituent states, regions, professional associations and civil society.

All these central institutions would be seated in Brussels – and Brussels alone – as the EF's capital city (meaning no more "travelling circus" to other cities such as Luxembourg or Strasbourg). Siting everything in the Belgian capital would, at a stroke, reduce costs, red tape and wasted hours of travel that afflict EU institutions today. It would also send an important message to the public about efficiency and respect for taxpayer resources.

3.1.2. Federalism and the principle of subsidiarity

The principle of subsidiarity, and its scope of application, is a central topic at the heart of any federation, but also of the European project since its inception in the 1950s. It was established as an EU governance doctrine by the Treaty of Maastricht of 1992 and remains a basic principle of European and national policies. According to Article 5(3) of today's Treaty on European Union, *"under the principle of subsidiarity, in areas which do not fall within its exclusive competence, the Union shall act only if and in so far as the objectives of the proposed action cannot be sufficiently achieved by the Member States, either at central level or at regional and local level, but can rather, by reason of the scale or effects of the proposed action, be better achieved at Union level."*[60]

Due to the EF's large and heterogeneous nature, its federalism should rest on four hierarchical layers: the EF federal government and other federal institutions; the constituent states (replacing the EU's current member states); regions; and municipalities.

The powers at each level would be explicitly defined in the EF constitution which would clarify that, in cases where powers are not explicitly granted to the EF's constituent states, regions or municipalities, they would devolve to the highest level, i.e., the federal government. This would be important to ensure legal clarity and enhance the EF's sovereignty. This approach would be justified by the fact that, due to the large scale of global competition or challenges, the objectives of the federation can only be achieved at the highest level, as we will have to find common answers on international trade, investments, scientific advancements, ethical issues, ecological policies and of course defense and security.

Constituent states and regions would retain clearly defined competences and thus enjoy a sense of ownership over the EF's political integration. This would be the most realistic approach, as the central EF government would lack the resources to deal directly with all topics concerning the lives of more than half a billion people. Subsidiarity would thus be the principle for preventing centrifugal tendencies while fostering a sense of unity across its member states' populations.

The responsibilities of the EF's states and regions would include policy best handled at local level. This would include topics such as health, education and environmental policy, basic infrastructure management, public order, cultural policy, sports and religious affairs.

3.1.3. The constitution

The EF would be established and governed by its own constitution, inspired by the traditions of its constituent states. This founding document would set up the new federation as a sovereign state, subject to international law, and a member in all international organisations and treaties.

It would define the governing principles of democracy, federalism, rule of law, free market economy, human rights, ecological development and European humanistic values. It would lay down the separation of powers and the checks and balances among the executive, legislative and judicial branches. It would list, describe, and regulate EF institutions and create a system of judicial and other protection against abuses perpetrated by any of the three branches. It would also establish common European military forces, given the high importance of defence. A bill of rights, included as a legally binding annex, would transpose the respective international treaties on civil and social rights.

Contrary to the tradition of the European states, the Constitution would be a short document, only consisting of 70–80 articles, thus avoiding the minute details of EU treaties and state constitutions. Together, these articles –especially if written in a simple way that would reasonate with the ordinary public – would create the governing framework and principles for the new state to function. They would further empower the government and the parliament to adopt more specific legislation on all other matters of federal competence.

3.1.4. The parliament

The EF Parliament would be elected directly through general multiparty elections. Its composition would be subject to minimum quotas of representation per constituent state and region. It could be either unicameral or bicameral.

A bicameral parliament is well suited for a large federal structure such as the EF, with an upper chamber representing the constituent states and a lower chamber directly representing the people. This would ensure mutual control between the two parts of the legislature. This is the choice of federal states such as the U.S. (House of Representatives and Senate) or Germany (Bundestag and Bundesrat). It is also the case in Italy where, though not a federal state, its citizenry opted for strong but mutually controlled institutions (Chamber of Deputies and Senate) to avoid a repetition of Mussolini's fascist regime. The advantage of a bicameral parliament thus lies with its increased level of checks and balances, the solid representation of its constituent entities and its stronger spirit of federalism.

However, one could also argue in favour of a unicameral parliament as a simpler, more efficient legislative process. This would prevent deadlocks on issues while increasing the visibility and accountability of its elected representatives vis-à-vis their constituencies. A unicameral parliament would directly represent the people, thus enhancing the federation's political identity and unity. It would perhaps offer a more efficient solution for creating a truly European 'demos'.

Our preference would be a unicameral parliament for the purpose of simplicity, legislative efficiency and its more direct connection between citizens and representatives. It would avert lengthy procedures for adopting legislation, which can take years in the U.S. Congress or at EU level, whose two legislative bodies (the European Parliament and the Council) often find it hard to reach agreements. We acknowledge, however, the merits that a bicameral structure would offer for a large federation, espe-cially one whose constituent states would insist on having their say on federal affairs. Therefore, we do not exclude that option. In any event, the EF's states and other parts of European society would be institution-ally represented via its Council of Governance (explained below).

The members of the EF parliament would not exceed 800. This would be important, in order to function effectively, and this is also close to today's number of the members of the European Parliament.

The electoral system would be proportional representation, with a low threshold for a political party to enter the parliament (e.g. 2 %). Such a system is necessary to democratically reflect the great diversity of European people and their political choices. It would be crucial to ensure that the biggest possible number of votes is represented. It must be acknowledged, however, that such a system would lead to the forma-tion of coalition governments in almost all cases. That was the case, for instance, of the European Parliament that emerged after its May 2019 elections. Had this been the EF parliament, at least three parties would have been necessary to form a majority coalition to support an EF gov-ernment. We would exclude the "first-past-the-post system" where the first party in a constituency assumes its representation, even if it won with less than a majority of the votes. This system distorts the election results and usually leaves unrepresented the majority of votes cast. That is what the UK does, with its winning parties that are hugely over-repre-sented in its parliament.

A certain number of members of the EF parliament, say 100, would be elected from a common European list. For instance, a political party that gained 30 % of the votes at European level would appoint 30 of those 100 members, and so on. The remaining 700 members would rep-resent regional constituencies based on proportional representation, i.e., the size of their population. Electoral law would determine the precise size of those constituencies. Out of the respect for the constituent states, we would try to avoid cross-border constituencies (such as Italy's south Tyrol and Austria's north Tyrol) in preference for those that remain wholly within the states' national borders.

Only Europe-wide political parties would participate in EF parlia-mentary elections. Each party would have to maintain branches in a substantial number of constituent states (e.g. a minimum of 60 % of the constituent states) to ensure its European and supra-national credentials.

The parties would be obliged to include in their ranks and candidate lists a minimum representation of all nationalities, and a minimum representation for women. Their funding from the federal budget would be minimal and provided under strict conditions. Any private funding higher than a certain amount (e.g. 3,000 euros) would have to be publicized in a register accessible to all. The same would apply to the campaign funding of individuals at all elected levels.

The EF parliament would exercise the classic powers of modern national legislatures by investing its confidence in, and control over, the EF's government. That would be carried out by an absolute majority vote within parliament, with the power to withdraw its confidence by the same mechanism.

In cases where the government did not complete its four-year mandate (e.g. due to a resignation or withdrawal of confidence), the parliament would appoint a new government to complete its mandate without need for a general election. A general election that interrupted the Parliament's mandate would only be possible under extraordinary circumstances specified by the EF's constitution and endorsed by a qualified majority vote of its members (e.g. 70 %). This would be key to ensure the normality of election cycles and guarantee political stability and continuity. Such a rule, known as the Fixed-Term Parliaments Act, was introduced in 2011 in the UK, for instance.

The parliament would vote on the republic's annual budget and other important measures as determined by the constitution via a specific qualified majority (e.g. 60 % of members). Qualified majorities would ensure a broad consensus on the most critical matters, such as the ratification of international treaties or the privatisation or nationalisation of strategic sectors. A simple majority would be required for all other acts.

3.1.5. The government

The EF government would be the Republic's executive branch.

It would be headed by a president and two vice-presidents. It would also comprise ministries covering all the major policy areas: foreign affairs, defence, economy, trade, justice and human rights, industry, agriculture, energy, environment, immigration, and so on. It would be administratively supported by an EF "Administrative Commission" that would succeed and replace, to a substantial extent, today's European Commission as the EF's central civil service and ministries.

The government would be empowered by the constitution and the parliament to issue executive decrees on technical issues of lesser political importance, where no parliamentary vote would be required. It would negotiate treaties, oversee the EF's security and defence forces and execute the federation's diplomacy and foreign affairs. It would execute the budget and submit to parliament the legislative bills falling under the federation's competence.

The president of the EF government would also be its head of state. He or she would shoulder ultimate political responsibility for the federation's affairs, with their office serving as the "face of Europe" to the rest of the world. In this way, the head of state would also have full executive powers but would be subject to the democratic control of parliament. This would be a hybrid of the presidential and prime-ministerial system. Conversely, its disadvantage would lie in the office's possible instability: while presidents are independently elected for a fixed term and rarely removed, a president who was also head of a parliamentary government could fall at any moment if losing parliament's confidence.

Alternatively, the head of the government could be the prime minister, while the head of state was president with ceremonial tasks only and elected by the EF parliament. This is the model followed today in many European republics such as Germany, Greece, Italy and Hungary. This model's advantage is that the president, though without substantial executive competences, would be the ultimate guarantor of the functioning of the state. His or her post would provide for a dual system of checks and balances within the executive branch of power. If something went very wrong in the execution of the tasks of the government, the president would offer a guarantee of normality by steering proceedings in his/her capacity as an independent senior personage. On the other hand, one could argue that it would not be appropriate for a major power, such as the EF, to be led constitutionally by a figurehead not treated as an equal by the other powerful presidents of China, Russia or the United States. Therefore the first option is preferable, namely a head of state who would also be head of the government with executive powers.

The EF government's two vice-presidents would hold distinct positions above all the ministers. One would function as first vice-president who, if needed, would succeed or temporarily replace the president.

Together, the two vice-presidents would co-ordinate the government's agenda and ensure the coherence of its policies by linking the ministers' work to government's broader programmes on important matters, such as social cohesion, sustainable development, security or defence.

3.1.6. The Council of Governance

Routine functions of the EF parliament and government would be controlled by the Council of Governance, comprised of representatives from all the central governments, parliaments and regions of the constituent states, as well as professional associations and civil society.

The Council's mandate would cover the following:

- to be consulted before adoption of any act of the government or parliament. Although it would not vote on those acts, its feedback would be officially taken into account and examined by the two other branches before adopting them;
- to exercise a veto by qualified majority of 70 % of its members against any act of the government or parliament considered as contrary to the interests of EF society;
- to exercise a veto by qualified majority of 70 % of its members against any act of government or parliament considered as breaching the EF's constitution and, in particular, its principle of subsidiarity.

The Council's purpose would thus be to act as an important check on the two other institutions. It would not be a co-legislator but a last resort in cases where it was determined that the other branches were acting against the EF constitution or the will of its people. The government, parliament and Council of Governance would have the right to challenge each other's positions before the European Supreme Court, to deter abuses of power.

The composition of the Council of Governance and the election of its members would be guided by specific constitutional provisions. Several seats would have to be reserved for the constituent states' governments, parliaments and regions, while others would be reserved for representatives of professional associations and civil society groups. Their appointment could be partly based on practices of the EU's current Committee of Regions and European Social and Economic Committee.

It would serve a four-years term parallel to the term of parliament. It would also be accountable to the public by submitting annual reports of its activities to the EF and national parliaments, and answering citizens' petitions. It would act, partly, as society's official "lobbyist" vis-à-vis the other EF institutions, with a strong role of intervention and control.

3.1.7. The judiciary

There would be three divisions of the judiciary – civil, administrative and criminal – plus prosecutors' offices to adjudicate on all matters of EF competence. There would be three courts of instance: first, second (appeal courts) and the European Supreme Court. The latter would also serve as the highest constitutional court to decide on matters of federal responsibility and other constitutional affairs.

The courts would have branches in all EF constituent states. Each judge and prosecutor would be appointed, promoted or dismissed by independent judicial and prosecutorial assessment boards composed of senior judges, legal academics, and government experts. For reasons of democratic accountability, all members and the president of the European Supreme Court would be nominated by the EF government and appointed by the parliament. They would each serve a single long-term of nine years, thus ensuring their democratic credentials and independence because they would not care to be re-elected. The courts' functioning would be supported by federal judicial and prosecutorial schools and career-long training cycles.

The judiciary would be administered by the EF's Ministry of Justice and Human Rights, which would have responsibility for drafting civil, administrative and criminal legislation, regulating and supporting the court's administration, and providing its infrastructure and resources. More detailed proposals on rule of law and the judiciary are presented in the next sectors of this chapter.

3.1.8. The Central Bank

The EF monetary policy would be designed and administered by its Central Bank. This would subsume the EU's current European Central Bank and its primary responsibility for monetary policy, supervising Europe's private banks and issuing the euro.

The bank would be independent but democratically accountable, governed by a board of directors, perhaps 15-strong, who would serve seven-year, non-renewable terms. This would safeguard their independence, while removing concerns about re-election. One third of the board would be appointed by the government, another by the parliament and the final third by a body representing commercial and investment banks in the EF. Its directors would be qualified professionals with strong financial backgrounds who would elect the central bank's president as its top official.

The Central Bank president would attend regular hearings of the EF parliament's Committee on Economic and Monetary Affairs, where he/she would present the bank's policy decisions. Other members of the board, or senior executives within the bank's administration, could also attend ad-hoc hearings of the parliamentary committee to explain the bank's position on specific topics.

The central bank would be obliged to issue annual reports on its activities, the state of the euro and the state of Europe's banking sector. Its reports would be submitted to the EF's government, parliament and Council of Governance, and it would answer to written or oral questions from parliament. All such measures would aim to make the bank an independent but also democratically accountable institution.

More detailed proposals on the EF's monetary and banking policy are presented in the next chapter.

3.1.9. Other institutions and advisory bodies

Several other independent EF institutions would be created by the federation's constitution to succeed their EU counterparts today. Their leaders would all be elected by the EF Parliament to ensure their democratic legitimacy, and enjoy a long, but single term to ensure their independence. These institutions include:

(a) a Court of Auditors as the independent authority to verify if the EF's budget has been implemented correctly and whether its funds have been spent legally and with sound management. Its mission would be to improve the EF's financial management and promote accountability and transparency. It would act as the state's financial 'watchdog', warning policy makers about any possible derailing of financial policy.

(b) an Ombudsman's office as the independent authority investigating complaints against EF institutions regarding maladministration. It would help citizens, business and civil society to solve their issues with EF authorities. It would also proactively address broader systemic issues and signal EF authorities about any structural problems within their administration.

(c) a Data Protection Supervisor as an independent authority to monitor the processing of personal data in EF institutions and provide advice to EF institutions on such matters. It would focus in particular on the application of new technologies regarding personal data.

All such bodies would also be seated in Brussels. Their competences would exceed those of today's EU institutions, as requisite for a large sovereign federal state.

Following current EU practice, the EF would turn for support in its policy making to independent EF agencies for scientific, technical and policy advice to the government and parliament. These agencies would be expanded or modified as needed.[61] In the spirit of decentralisation, we would favour a spreading of these independent federal agencies across European cities to promote the EF's visibility and contacts with Europe's population. This would mimic the siting of EU agencies in various locales, such as the European Food Safety Authority (EFSA) in Parma, European Border and Coast Guard Agency (Frontex) in Warsaw, European Environment Agency (EEA) in Copenhagen or the European Fisheries Control Agency (EFCA) in Vigo, Spain.

3.1.10. Accession to, and exit from, the EF

Federalism is based on the voluntary union of political entities. In the case of the EF, it would include the right to voluntarily exit from it, if a constituent state's population so wished.

All EU states and the UK would have the automatic right to join the EF. The same would apply to other European states, and especially members of EFTA (European Free Trade Association, namely Iceland, Norway, Switzerland, Lichtenstein) as well as others fulfilling the so-called "Copenhagen criteria",[62] agreed during the EU's 1993 summit in the Danish capital. These comprise:

- political criteria: the stability of institutions guaranteeing democracy, rule of law, human rights, and respect for and protection of minorities;
- economic criteria: a functioning market economy and the capacity to cope with competition and market forces;
- the administrative and institutional capacity to effectively implement legislation and the ability to take on the obligations of membership.

Consequently, we would support the accession of all European states west of Turkey and the post-Soviet republics since those states are, as of 2021, closest to fulfilling those criteria. A subsequent enlargement of the EF to include Turkey, Ukraine or other post-Soviet republics could be reviewed later, but only after their societies have achieved a true reform of their political governance and economy.

The accession of any state to the EF would have to enjoy a wide consensus of its public in view of the very substantial transfer of sovereign power that membership would entail. For this reason, the decision would have to be subjected to a popular referendum. The accession vote would require an approval threshold of 55 % of casted votes, and a participation threshold of 50 % of all registered voters. Alternatively, and instead of a referendum, it would require a qualified majority of the national parliament of the acceding state, namely three-fifth of the plenary's national parliament's members.

Equally, every constituent state would have the right to exit the EF via a referendum based on an approval threshold of 60 % and a participation threshold of 55 % of the exiting nation's registered voters. Exits from the EF should be more difficult than entries; otherwise any EF constituent state could be tempted to organise referenda on a whim or each time it was dissatisfied with federal policy. Referenda to withdraw should thus be subject to tougher requirements than those to join the federation.

3.1.11. Road map towards the establishment of the EF

As explained in Prologue, no current or forthcoming developments regarding 2021 or 2022 are discussed. One of these is the "Conference on the Future of Europe", during which EU institutions and civil society will have examined possible constitutional changes. It is however highly unlikely that the conference's conclusions will embrace a true federalist vision.

Therefore a road map is suggested with practical steps to shift from the current state of affairs to the proposed European federation.

A first set of preparatory steps would need to be taken by the EU member states at inter-governmental level, without need to change the EU Treaties. These steps could be completed within four years and would create the political and economic framework for ensuring a smooth transition to the EF. They would require that all EU member states:

(1) agree at inter-governmental level to join their defence forces under a joint command, military doctrine and budget;

(2) join the eurozone, with no opt-outs;

(3) approve at inter-governmental level a joint fiscal policy that unifies their financial assets and liabilities. This would include limits on public deficits, debt, borrowing and spending policies – all supervised and co-ordinated by a member of the European Commission who would be designated as a kind of eurozone's Minister of Finance.

These three steps would be crucial to forge a joint economic, monetary and defence space preceding the new federal sovereign state's creation.

At the same time, another set of steps would be taken in parallel as a road map specifically aiming at the creation of the EF. These include in chronological order:

(1) Creation of a European constituent assembly to draft the constitution and agree on the EF's establishment, with a view to succeeding the EU and its member states. The assembly would consist of members of the European Parliament (MEPs), members of national parliaments of the EU's member states, officials from EU governments, and representatives of professional organisations and civil society. Following its creation, the Assembly would have to produce the draft constitution within two years.

(2) Referenda would take place in all EU member states and other willing European states to establish the EF. As explained above, this would require a 55 % "yes" vote and a turn-out higher than 50 % of a nation's registered voters. As an alternative, and instead of a referendum, accession could be decided by a national parliament's qualified majority at at least three-fifths (3/5) of its members.

(3) The EF's creation would take place with the accession of at least 20 states. For the union to have a realistic chance of survival, France, Germany and Italy would have to belong to its core, as founding members of the EEC and because they represent the three biggest economies and populations of the EU. Poland and Spain would also be important due to their size. Other EU member states that voted against joining the federation would remain independent sovereign countries. They could create, together with the EF, a new economic partnership based on a customs union, internal market and integrated co-operation in important sectors as is the case today with the European Economic Area (EEA).

(4) Immediately after the formal establishment of the EF, the first elections would take place for the EF parliament, which in turn would elect the EF's first government and president.

(5) All important institutions would be established within two years. Following the EF's creation, a transitional period of five years would see the transfer of the former EU member states' institutions, defence forces, assets and liabilities to the EF, and the settlement of other technical details.

This schedule could prove feasible. Admittedly, it could take several years to complete this roadmap. But in extraordinary times, when confronted by events such as war, financial crisis or natural catastrophes, these would be catalysts for accelerated political advancements. In that case, the roadmap would be likely realised in a much shorter period.

3.2. Democratic governance

The EU and its member states have often been accused of abiding the so-called "democratic deficit" where decisions are allegedly taken in closed rooms by bureaucrats, lobbyists and politicians with little regard for society's concerns. In many member states, people do not trust the political system because it is perceived to be controlled by self-serving elites. People express these grievances against public administrations because they perceive them as inefficient or corrupt, or both. Such views are stronger in southern and eastern Europe, while trust in public governance is higher in northern Europe (see later reference to Transparency International's surveys).

Mistrust in a political system is dangerous. Lack of public confidence in governance usually leads to the growth of undemocratic and reactionary forces. We must bear in mind that the Internet's explosive growth and that of social media have introduced a serious variable: everyone now has a say in public affairs. This is definitely a sign of progress, but it also means all are exposed to the influence of the enemies of democracy and basic freedoms – far more so than a few decades ago.

Following four measures are critical to the EF's democratic foundation by cementing the public's confidence in its political system: (1) greater use of referenda at all levels of governance; (2) wider public participation in decision-making; (3) more efficient and transparent public administration; and (4) a strong framework against corruption. In addition, a strong programme of civic education would have to unfold across the federation to create informed, responsible, and rationally-minded citizens. All those factors, if well combined, would likely boost trust in public institutions and the federation we propose.

3.2.1. Referenda at all levels

Referenda are the ultimate tools of direct democracy and the empowerment of people. They are an important part of the institutional blueprint we propose for a democratic and federal EF. However, referenda involve certain risks. They can distort democracy if their questions are not clearly defined, if voters are not well informed about the subjects in question or if the process or the timing of a referendum is manipulated by authorities to misdirect the public's will. Referenda can also be divisive if they touch on cultural or deep ideological issues (e.g. the legalisation of drugs). They should be handled with care.

There is a rich and diverse history of referenda in Europe. Their procedures vary according to the constitution of each European state and the subject matter, with some referenda binding and others not. More than 40 EU-related referenda have been held across the EU nations, candidate member states and their territories since 1972, most commonly on the subject of whether to join the EU, adopt the euro, make EU treaty amendments or participate in EU-related policies. National referenda have also been held on very specific questions: Portugal asked its citizens in 1998 to approve a new system of regionalisation. Luxembourg held a referendum in 2015 to change its election rules. Ireland used the mechanism in 2018 to overturn the country's constitutional ban on abortion. Moreover, the constitution of many countries makes room for referenda at local and regional levels as well. But the 'world champion' is

Switzerland where such voting is a cornerstone of its political life and a main instrument of governance: Swiss voters can demand, regardless the government's position, a binding referendum at either federal, cantonal or municipal level.

In the EF, referenda would be a routine procedure for local and regional governance. In order to respect the representative character of local democracies, however, they would be non-binding and consultative in nature only. Elected municipal and regional councils would always have the final say in deciding the matter in question, with the proviso that, if those authorities ignored or moved against the results of a referendum, they would be obliged to present a reasoned opinion justifying their decision.

Municipalities and regions would be urged to fix one or two dates per year (e.g. mid-May and mid-November) when local citizens could vote on one or more questions of local or regional importance. These would introduce a simple "Yes" or "No" pair of responses or multiple choice options, depending on the complexity of the subject. Some examples could be:

(a) "Do you support making your city centre permanently car-free? (Yes / No)"

(b) "Which of the following projects do you prefer to renovate a central part of your community? (Options: A, B, C, D)"

(c) "Would you support the expansion of our region's port? (Yes / No)"

(d) "A sum amount of [x euros] has been earmarked for cultural projects in our region. Please choose three priority projects from the following list (Options: A, B, C, D, E, F)".

All referenda would have to be well prepared by giving voters at least two months to learn and debate the topic(s) prior to a vote. Local authorities would offer a summary of the pros and cons to help citizens sort through the complexity of each topic. Where necessary, they would present a simplified version of expert analyses or impact assessments on, for instance, the social and economic effects of converting an urban area into a car-free zone. This would be important to avoid polarisation and over-simplified positions. Direct democracy requires that rational citizens make well-educated decisions.

Crucially, referenda would be organised at either EF level or that of its constituent states on critical political and policy issues, such as the accession of other countries to the federation. Given the enormity of the scale of such endeavours (400 million or more eligible voters), clear rules would have to be set concerning their initiation, organization and prior public debate. The launch of each EF-level referendum would be subject to prior endorsement by the EF's government, parliament and Council of Governance. Referenda at EF level could be initiated by a certain number or percentage of its citizens (e.g. 3 million) via an electronic platform modelled after the current online system of the European Citizens' Initiative.[63] These exercises in democracy could be merely consultative or function as a binding mandate for the authorities to act, under an action narrowly linked to the referendum's target objective.

3.2.2. Democratisation of public decision-making

Democracy not only concerns the right to elect representatives or directly vote on specific subject matters, but also daily opportunities to influence decision-making on the multitude of topics that define our lives. No every executive decision can be decided by referendum, of course, so people should have at least the opportunity to be consulted in the early preparatory phases of rules, which should be carried out in an organised and substantial manner.

In the EF, every municipal, regional, state or federal regulatory act would be subject to a sufficiently lengthy public consultation (e.g. two months) prior to its adoption. Citizens would have the opportunity to transparently submit their feedback on a draft act's content. Their respective public administrations would help with these submissions by guiding debate on specific topics. It would, obviously, be necessary for citizens to understand the essence of substantial policy issues before expressing a view on them.

For instance, in the case of a new draft law on the reduction of the use of plastic, the public would have the opportunity to comment on the draft's specific provisions regarding the targeted types of plastic for withdrawal, the modes of recycling or financing schemes, or penalties in cases of non-compliance with the new rules. Most important, they would also have a say in the costs and benefits of such a scheme.

All public consultations would be online. However, complementary to this, we would favour live meetings with citizens, especially on issues of local interest. Thus, for instance, if a municipality aimed to change its school programme or method of garbage collection, these could be discussed in open public sessions with citizens in a municipal town hall. Both forms of consultation would boost citizen trust in their public administrations, not to mention the accountability of public officials.

Public authorities would summarise and make public the results of each consultation. Any final adopted act would be accompanied by a concise report indicating what has been changed as a result of the public consultation, and why certain kinds of citizen feedback were accepted or rejected.

Further to this, the EF would regularly set up more general debates on horizontal and long-term issues, such as industrial, bio-ethics or energy policy. Particular inspiration is drawn from the French tradition of "grenelles", a term born by the first conference of social stakeholders in May 1968 in Paris's Rue de Grenelle. In 2007 France launched its "Grenelle de l'environnement" to include representatives of national and local government, industry, labour, professional associations and non-governmental organisations. All participated on an equal footing, with the goal of reaching a common position on climate change, energy, bio-diversity and natural resources, health and environment, employment and competitiveness. This led in 2008 to the French National Assembly's adoption of the "First Grenelle Act", which orients the country's general policy for the coming decades. Specific laws have since flowed from this.

Similar approaches are followed by other governments or EU institutions as they define their broad, long-term thematic policies. The EF would build on that tradition by holding its own "grenelles" in the most inclusive way possible. The objective of each would be to adopt legally binding programmes and acts, and to gain the trust of the partners who helped shape the legislative frameworks. The perception of ownership would be key to winning hearts and minds in the public arena.

3.2.3. Public administration: Efficient, responsible, transparent and accountable

The EF's public administration would imperatively have to be more efficient than that of many EU member states. In 2018, for example, the EU-28 member states' collective public sector employed some 75 million people – or one public servant for every seven citizens. As Europe's single biggest "industry" responsible for nearly 50 % of GDP, it employed

25 % of its total workforce, of which 16 % laboured for national governments alone. Efficiency of government varies widely among them. According to a 2015 World Bank report, Bulgaria, Greece, Romania, Croatia, Italy and Hungary had low levels of government effectiveness, while Germany, the UK and the Scandinavian countries had the highest. Government effectiveness correlated strongly with competitiveness of an economy.[64]

The EF's public administration would first focus on increasing its transparency and efficiency through digitalisation by following the example of Estonia, whose administration is almost entirely virtual. All documents in Estonia are online and everything is backed by the cloud. If needed, Estonians could decamp to a new continent, boot up, and reconstitute their government exactly as they were before.[65] The public administration of Greece also made a big step forward in 2020 by offering to issue many official certificates (e.g. family composition) online. It also assigned to each citizen a single electronic identity for all their dealings with the public administration. Similar digital leaps have occurred in many administrations in Europe and the rest of the world due to the social distancing measures of the COVID-19 pandemic.

The vast majority of administrative transactions with EF public authorities would be carried out exclusively online. Tax declarations, personal certificates, applications for social benefits, business registration, land registry submissions or construction permits, as well as other functions, would only take place electronically, supported by the necessary secure algorithms. This would include all types of payments between citizens and the state such as the payment of fees or tax refunds. The overall goal would be the automisation of all routine public authority transactions that do not require discretionary decisions. Every citizen would possess a unique digital code and bank account to facilitate their transactions with the state.

The transfer of so many public services to the online domain would of course require time and large investments. But it is already happening at an accelerating pace in the early 2020s. There would be some initial disadvantages: older people not acquainted with information technology, for example, could have difficulties adapting to the new approach. Systems could suffer technical teething problems with consequences for service for the citizen. A heavy reliance on digitisation would render society more vulnerable to organised cyber-attacks, hackers or large scale glitches. However, such problems would not be insurmountable. At points-of-service older citizens could be assisted by technical personnel or by computers configured especially for their use. At any rate, each EF authority would have to consider how to set up help lines and back-up personnel for the public at large and to guard against technical glitches and cyber-attacks.

The large scale of digitation would drastically reduce the size of public administration workforces currently required to physically handle traditional paperwork. Conversely, with that reduction, other public services would see an increase in their personnel. This would be the case for medical doctors and nurses or judges and prosecutors, where the human dimension is irreplaceable and, moreover, acutely needed during emergencies as the COVID-19 pandemic has shown. Civil servants would be employed mainly in areas where their mental skills, judgement and compassion brought added value to the work of machines.

Many public services could be merged to achieve economies of scale (e.g. Europe's patchwork of national health and social security systems would be consolidated into a single large European one). As a priority, the EF administration would do an inventory of all existing national public services and employees to reduce unneeded or overlapping functions and cost.

The payroll of civil services would be drastically reduced in such areas as taxation, which would be simplified by EF legislation, as proposed in the next chapter. Similar reductions in personnel would occur in Europe's social policy sectors, thanks to the simpler procedures we propose in our chapter on social protection. The EF would have a budget to cover a total payroll of 30 million central government employees – approximately 6 % of the total population, or less than one civil servant per 16 citizens. Most central government employees would be hired on a permanent basis to bolster their careers with a sense of security and independence. All would be hired via an examination tailored to each government policy sector, with appointments decided by panels of at least three independent experts. The performance of career public servants would be regularly assessed by independent panels.

An independent European Public Recruitment Agency would be in charge of selecting personnel for the EF civil service. It would design the process according to the requirements of each sector (e.g. economists, medical doctors, sanitary inspectors, etc.). The agency would be modelled on the EU's existing European Personnel Selection Office (EPSO).

The civil service in its entirety would be non-political to maintain its professionalism and the state's continuity between changes of governments. Every government would have the right to appoint their choice of people to certain political posts, but this would be limited to very low percentage of the total central government posts, and only for specific positions defined by law.

3.2.4. A strong framework against corruption

Corruption remains one of the biggest challenges for any society. Corruption lowers investment levels, distorts competition and suppresses the amount and efficient use of public money. It is estimated that the economic costs incurred by corruption in the EU approach €120 billion per year,[66] equivalent to 1 % of its GDP and almost equalling the union's annual operating budget itself.

Corruption has many faces. It may take the form of political bribes or activities committed by and with organised criminal groups, petty private-to-private corruption or the abuse of power by a public official for private gain . Four out of five EU citizens consider corruption as a major problem in their country.[67] 37 % of all EU businesses say it creates problems for their sector, with 60 % avowing that bribery and the use of personal contacts is often the easiest way to obtain certain public services.[68]

At the same time, many of the former EU's member states rank among the least corrupt in the world on the list of Transparency International, the organisation that tracks global corruption. This is particularly true for Scandinavian countries and Germany.[69]

In the EF, a robust and independent European anti-corruption authority would be created to monitor the performance of its public services and ensure the enforcement of anti-corruption legislation. The EF would allocate a substantial amount, at the scale of €10 billion per year, to the authority. This would cover the latter's staffing, training, equipment, housing, technical needs, digitation and security. A tailored regulatory framework would ensure the wide-ranging executive and prosecutorial powers necessary for its flexibility and independence. The authority would annually report to the EF's parliament and Ministry of Justice. There would be sufficient funding for special anti-corruption police units and prosecutors to take on organised criminal groups. However, corruption cannot be tackled by administrative judicial procedures alone.

All pressure groups (professional organisations, trade unions, NGOs, professional lobbyists, etc.) would be registered in EF public registers. Their contacts with public officials at all levels, from EF President down to municipal councillors, would be officially recorded and made public. Any non-recorded or non-publicised meeting would be considered a serious criminal and administrative offence for all involved in the meeting. Further, all companies established or operating in the EF would be forced to publicly register their beneficial owners, up to and including the ultimate physical beneficiary.

All files, information and official correspondence of public administrations, including internal official correspondence, would be accessible to the public. This would be carried out either through publication of the information on official websites, or by disclosing it upon specific request by any individual, with some safeguards to secure confidential evidence, protect private data of officials, and prevent abusive or pointlessly recurrent requests. A special legal framework would empower citizens to actively engage in the monitoring of public service, and support community monitoring initiatives aimed at detecting corruption, verifying the dispersal of public funds and improving the quality of public services.

The EF would actively pursue the closure of international financial loopholes. Corrupt public officials or members of criminal organisations need access to the international financial system to launder and hide their ill-gotten funds, so it is essential to block their access. Financial centres operating in the EF, such as banks or investments funds, would have to apply specific procedures to identity and stop the processing of proceeds from suspected money laundering activities or dubious offshore locations.

The Federation's European Anticorruption Authority and other public or financial institutions would be specially equipped with the technology to uncover money-laundering, fraud or tax evasion such as artificial intelligence to help the EF's financial centres and authorities trace patterns of illegal activity.[70] Transparency International UK and World Bank are both moving in this direction. The latter is developing a programme in co-operation with Microsoft's research group, for example, to enable the bank to see links between patterns of winning and losing bidders on banks' contracts to beneficial-ownership information around the globe. The programme's users can thus map networks of relations, locations, and bidders' use of shell companies and off-shore jurisdictions to minimise risks before a contract is issued.[71] There are many more examples of how similar programmes, based on the new technologies of machine learning and big data crunching, could be used to identify corruption, from international to local levels.

Overall, we believe that many of the measures described in this and other chapters would help reduce corruption linked to public authorities. The digitalisation of public services combined with decent salaries for civil servants, a higher number of judges and prosecutors, simpler and lower taxes, simplification of social protection, registered lobby groups and a more transparent process of decision-making would without doubt reduce the instances and sources of corruption. Simply put: a well-paid civil servant would be less motivated to receive bribes. A well-served citizenry would not feel the need to proffer the bribes. Moreover, simplification of regulations would reduce the margins for abuse of power.

3.2.5. Civic education – a tool of emancipation

Another important element for a successful political governance of any state is the civic education of its citizens. It rests on the idea that citizens should understand the critical political choices of their society and actively shape them in a rational manner. The many objectives of EF authorities would only be paper achievements if its people do not share them in practice. Is the European public ready to support the principles and policies that we are proposing through this text? We would say: possibly yes, if the right preparatory work is carried out at European level and especially in education.

However, we should acknowledge that a sizeable segment of European society – impossible to quantify with precision – is still indifferent, suspicious or hostile to such ideas. Many remain prone to xenophobia, irrationality, superstition, prejudice or negative stereotypes against certain groups of people. They oppose secularism. They are indifferent to the separation of executive, legislative and judicial powers. They are receptive to fake news, irrational explanations of events and conspiracy theories, the most recent concerning the source and spread of the COVID-19 pandemic (i.e. the virus is a hoax, is has been released by big firms or caused by G5 networks). They vote for populist or nationalistic political parties. They are only sensitive to human rights abuses if these are committed against an affiliated group (e.g. against nation X), while remaining indifferent or even supportive of abuses when committed against presumably hostile groups (e.g. against religion Y or minority Z). They reject the difficult policy choices necessary for society's long-term benefit (e.g. moderation in public spending) and instead accuse Europe's "elites" or "oligarchy" of defining those choices. Their decisions and emotions are dominated by irrationality, self-interest and prejudice versus reason and values.

Such people are not necessarily poorly educated. Many are highly educated, wealthy and privileged. Any individual can think that way, without even realising it. Such attitudes can also be traced to education and the values received from families, schools, media and social circles. Those instincts must be harnessed for good and not evil. We thus believe a prime EF task would be the civic education of all members of its society with the aim of fostering consensual decisions, rational thinking, mutual respect among individuals and a healthy democracy.

Civic education is education in self-government. It must promote a reasoned commitment to the values and principles of democracy. According to Margaret Stimmann Branson: *"A message of importance [...] is that politics need not be [...] a zero-sum game. The idea that 'winner takes all' has no place in a democracy, because if losers lose all they will opt out of the democratic game. Sharing is essential in a democratic society - the sharing of power, of resources and of responsibilities. In a democratic society the possibility of effecting social change is ever present, if citizens have the knowledge, the skills and the will to bring it about. That knowledge, those skills and the will or necessary traits of private and public character are the products of a good civic education."*[72]

We subscribe to that view. Civic education should embrace shared values, rights and responsibilities. This is the raw material of a progressive and vibrant society. The basic subjects that form the pillars of civic education, ones with which all European citizens should be well acquainted, comprise:

- the institutions of the state, its mode of governance and the separation of the executive, legislative and judicial power;
- basic elements of human rights, tolerance, non-discrimination, and anti-racism;
- the possibilities to participate in local, regional, and national governance;
- the principles of secularism;
- the rational reception of news against prejudice, hate speech, and conspiracy theories;

- the basic principles of sustainable development, with a focus on everyday matters such as recycling, energy efficiency, reduction of fossil fuel consumption, and air pollution;
- the basic principles of solidarity: how to respect the rights and freedoms of other citizens and how to offer support to the weak and dispossessed;
- the values of volunteerism, civil initiatives, and self-organisation;
- the rationale of fiscal and economic policies: why are taxes imposed on citizens and how they are spent.

Civic education is not a one-time process or period. It envelopes people's lives and needs, evolving with society. In the EF's case, we would split it in two tracks: civic education as part of basic school education, and civic education as a life-long process.

The first and most important step would be the inclusion of civic education in the curricula of schools across the federation. Its elements would be taught in simple terms to children of all ages, with the idea of engaging them in acts of civil participation and teaching the value of volunteerism, participation in public life and a rational filtering of what they hear, see or read. During each year of school, children would learn how and why we have moved from the EEC to the EU and finally to the EF. They would learn about the core values of the EF's constitution and what it means for our daily lives. As a separate subject for instruction, civic education would be taught by specially trained teachers.

Civic education for adults would be more challenging as they are exposed to many more diverse sources of information and opinions, including the media, not to mention professional, social and civil groups and their activities. Thus, the EF would need a synergic programme involving government, public administration, civil society and media.

EF governmental institutions would communicate their policies in a transparent and simple manner. Hard choices would need to be explained with honesty so that people understood and accepted them. If an austerity measure is adopted, public authorities would have to clarify in a simple manner why is it needed and what policy areas it would serve The public will support these measures if they understand the sacrifices asked from them.

The EF's ministries would explain in clear and simple words their mission and the basics of their policies. Some examples: the website of the Ministry of Justice would inform citizens about the basic legal procedures: civil, criminal and administrative. Why are they separated and what purpose does each serve? What is the role of the public prosecutor or the investigating judge? What are the basic principles of family law or civil law?

The EF Parliament would inform citizens about its mission, its committees and tasks, and how these work. How can a citizen contact a member of the EF Parliament? How can citizens submit petitions? How does the Parliament control the EF's other branches?

The EF Central Bank would educate the public about the basics of financial and monetary policy. What is inflation? What is the central interest rate, and when does it go up or down? What is quantitative easing? Why do the banks need capital buffers, which may sometimes restrict their lending potential?

The EF Ministry of Environment would offer the most rational and documented information about climate change, our responsibility to tackle it, the value of recycling, how best to do it, how to save energy, how to protect the forests, how to contribute to cleaner urban air, and so on.

Media bear a huge responsibility in educating the public, not only about current events but also the "why" and its context. Media should also lead by example in its elimination of fake news, hate speech, racism, and the mistreatment of minorities. We know, of course, that this is easy to state but difficult to implement: freedom of speech and information inevitably include some rotten apples, and always will. The EF would, if needed, impose rules or sanctions on social media platforms and conventional media that tolerate or promote disinformation. A code of conduct would be adopted by all EF media and social media platforms on how to engage in citizens' education about their most important rights and obligations, and the functioning of democracy. A good start has been made through the Code Practice on disinformation, a worldwide self-regulatory set of standards promulgated in October 2018 to fight disinformation. Its signatories include social and conventional media platforms, leading social networks and the advertising industry. Each of them is committed to fighting suspicious or fake accounts and websites and bots, while improving the visibility of authoritative content and making political advertising more transparent.[73]

NGOs, trade unions and all forms of citizen associations would bear their share of responsibility. They could, for instance, inform their members and the wider public about the possibilities to participate in charities, protect the environment, support workers' or pension rights, lead a healthier life, the benefits of vaccination, and so on to name just a few examples.

Indeed, life-long civic education is a complex exercise. It would require the engagement of many different actors who themselves might have a different understanding of its content and purpose. Admittedly, it could be a futile exercise: despite whatever funding or manpower invested in the campaign, many might still end up mired in ignorance, tribalism and prejudice simply because they would find it easier and more comforting. That is human nature, but the overall effort to alter or overcome it would still be worth it.

3.2.6. Different human rights standards in the EU – a problem to be fixed

The EU can be proud of having the highest degree of human rights protection in the world. This achievement is one of the guiding principles and objectives of EU policy, according to Article 2 of its treaty. All EU Member States have qualified as 'free' in Freedom House's 2018 report, with each being either 'full' or 'flawed' democracies, according to *The Economist Intelligence Unit Democracy Index* of 2020. Nine EU member states scored among the 15 highest countries for press freedom in 2020, according to the World Press Freedom Index. Despite ups and downs in those rankings from one year to the next, the survey's big picture leads us safely to the conclusion that we live in a union of free and democratic societies whose respect for human dignity and rights exceeds that of anywhere else in the world.[74] It is an achievement to safeguard.

The progressive development of human rights can be divided into three generations, according to the historic period in which they emerged. First and foremost are the classic civil and political rights and freedoms such as the right to life, dignity, a fair judicial process and the freedom of expression, consciousness, and religion, as they were first shaped in the 18th and 19th century. The second state, usually referred to as comprising social and economic rights as developed in the 19th and 20th century, includes the right to education, health, work and social security. The third, sometimes referred to as 'collective rights', includes the right to peace, a healthy environment, data protection, and a transparent public administration.

The adoption in 2009 of the EU's Charter of Fundamental Rights, under the Lisbon Treaty, as a legally binding set of rules, was a major step forward. Enjoying the same legal status as the EU's treaties, it strengthens the protection of those rights by making them more visible to EU citizens and binding on EU authorities.

However, this should only be seen as a start. A true integration of fundamental rights into the political life of Europe can only be ensured through Europe's political unification. We believe that human rights should not be subject to the principle of subsidiarity, namely to approaches at state or regional level. They are universal and must guarantee the same protection and opportunities for all human beings. Unfortunately, this is not yet the case in the EU due to varying standards applied across its member states. It is one of the main signs that we have yet to become a union of equal citizens. There are still many differences in interpretations and applications of human rights. We would like to present some examples:

– The EU is split between regions that respect and guarantee gay rights, for example, and those that do not. In 2020, most EU member states recognised same-sex marriage or a form of civil union. On the other hand, Bulgaria, Croatia, Hungary, Latvia, Lithuania, Poland and Slovakia recognise no form of same-sex unions, with marriage defined as a union only between a man and a woman.

– The EU is also split between those regions that permit citizens to use certain drugs and others that punish the consumption of exactly the same substances. Portugal, for instance, has abolished all criminal penalties for personal drug possession since 2001, while the Netherlands has a policy of non-enforcement of fines for cannabis possession. But in a large majority of EU member states, the possession of drugs is a criminal act.

– Elsewhere, the EU is split into regions of varying gender equality. According to a 2020 report from the European Institute for Gender Equality, Sweden achieved the best index score at 83.8 (based on a scale of 100), followed by Denmark at 77.4. Conversely, Greece and Hungary sat at the bottom with 52.2 and 53 respectively.[75] It seems that women in southern and eastern Europe – countries that score lower than the EU average of 67.9 –still have a long way to go to reach the level of the western and northern Europe.

– There are other sharp disparities among the member states, too. For example, many restrictions exist across the EU about where citizens can live, work or own property. It is absolutely natural for France to allow a Parisian to move and settle in Marseille without hindrances. By the same token, Latvian, Irish or any other EU citizens should have the same indisputable right to move, work, invest or conduct their lives, whether in Italy, Romania or elsewhere in the union without restriction. This is not, however, reality: major discrepancies surround, for instance, the status of posted workers – employees who carry out a service in another EU member state on a temporary basis but do not enjoy the full labour rights of the host state. That, unfortunately, is the EU's situation today, despite its major progress in creating the internal market and its four freedoms.

Only within the EF would it be possible for Europe's citizens to move, work, settle, marry, establish associations, vote, run for office, seek justice or be sentenced in the same way and without discrimination, regardless of where they lived in the federation. Only within such a framework, too, would the rights for women rise to the same level of protection across the European continent.

The EF would thus be a space for the free exercise of individual choices and rights, with no variations from one region to the next – meaning it would be fully in the spirit of the liberal principles elaborated in the previous chapter. Some fundamental changes would thus be introduced to terminate the existing discriminatory situation in the EU.

3.2.7. A common non-discriminatory legal framework for all EF citizens

The EF would adopt its own civil and criminal codes applicable across all its territory. It would have its own administrative, family, inheritance and penitentiary laws. This joint legal framework would combine the best elements of all the legal traditions of Europe's continental and common law. It would be the first step towards a union of universal rights and obligations for all, without variance within individual constituent states or regions.

All EF citizens would have the absolute freedom to move, settle, work, or study in any region within the federation, without restriction or discrimination. There would be no extra administrative procedures apart from the obligation to notify local authorities of a citizen's new residence and occupation, preferably by electronic means. The EU's current administrative problems with posted workers would no longer exist, as all EF citizens would be governed by the same social security rules, as we describe in the succeeding chapters. Such a unified space of freedom would create the ideal platform for millions of people to freely move about and develop their potential according to the same opportunities.

The EF would strictly apply the principle of equal pay for equal work to eliminate gender discrimination in the workplace. It would further introduce strict rules for the prevention of sexual harassment in the workplace (which regularly targets women) and support social programmes to ease the 'family or career dilemma' (see Chapter 6 on social policy and Chapter 7 on demographic policy). It would also elaborate policy to encourage and facilitate the promotion of women to managerial positions and jobs with higher salaries and career prospects. We are not fully convinced that gender quotas in high managerial positions are always the best approach: sometimes women are accorded a board position simply to comply with the respective rules, without them being necessarily more qualified or motivated than their male colleagues who may have been excluded due to quotas. On the other hand, it is an undeniable fact that men are over-represented in posts with higher salaries and responsibilities: in 2019, 64 % of managers, 73 % of board members and 83 % of senior executives in the EU were men – and not just because of their higher merit.[76] For such reasons, a mixture of measures would be introduced to help both women and companies gain the most benefit from each other: a certain degree of quotas for female representation, financial incentives for companies that demonstrate a better gender balance in higher posts, strict non-discriminatory frameworks for promotion regardless of gender, as well as special counselling and training programmes for women in business or public sectors where they are still far less present than men.

All EF citizens would have the same choices concerning their private lives and families, regardless of sexual orientation. Same-sex couples would have full rights to marriage, with all its entitlements, and full rights to adopt children to enjoy their right to family life.

The possession and marketing of certain soft drugs would be legalised under strict conditions. Although the legalisation of those drugs would likely lead to some proliferation of their use, their consumption would be safer, better controlled and help reduce many forms of criminality linked to illegal drug trafficking. This would also, to a large extent, alleviate the workload of police and judicial authorities, while reducing Europe's prison population and the miseries linked to imprisonment for relatively minor crimes.

All women would have control over their own bodies, and the choice of abortion at the early stages of pregnancy. Abortion is not our preferred option, meaning EF authorities would pursue an active campaign of sexual education to prevent unwanted pregnancies, especially at a young age. But it is in the interest of society that this option remains legal and safe.

The same rules would apply to euthanasia. The EF would allow individuals the right to choose any form of euthanasia in case of prolonged or unbearable suffering, and would set clear protocols for each form of it.

Church and state across the EF would be strictly separated. Religion is a personal spiritual affair with no relationship to citizenship. Marriage, divorce and death fall within the realm of the state, regardless of religious custom or procedure. Therefore citizens would be obliged to respect and obey the civil ceremonies and procedures governing those three life events, with the freedom to add parallel religious ceremonies as an option. Any existing laws on blasphemy would be abolished: no one could be punished for insulting a religion any more strictly than for insulting any other subject of dignity. Any and all religious symbols would be removed from the working environment of public buildings.

Minority groups would be treated with respect for their identities and needs. Minority linguistic groups would have the right to use and learn their own language, even if it was not one of the official languages of the EF or its constituent states. Minority religious groups would have the possibility to use their own temples, schools, cemeteries and other sites, and to celebrate their own holy days. Minority ethnic groups would have access to special education courses about their culture and history. There would be no positive discrimination for minorities regarding employment or social benefits since all citizens must be treated in the same way. We would, however, support the introduction of incentives and programmes to support their development and integration with the societies where they live in, such as those for Europe's Roma people.

Finally, we should anticipate how rights and freedoms will need to be protected in the future. The risks are great that future privacy will be undermined by the massive digitalisation of our lives such as facial recognition technology and the use of big data by companies and public authorities. The EF would set very strict rules for the protection of personal data, prohibiting its disclosure by public or private actors and requiring that it is processed in the most transparent ways possible. Major fines and other penalties would be imposed on all who violated those rules.

The EF would also reject the practice of "social scoring", which has already taken off in China and could spread elsewhere. It assigns a score of trustworthiness to individuals based on their behaviour or background, ranging from evidence of past criminal activity, for example, to the patently absurd such as incorrectly sorting house waste or failing to show up for a restaurant reservation. As a result, in China people have been blacklisted or denied for defined periods basic public goods or access to air or railway tickets. As social activities become inter-connected via technology, the temptation of general state surveillance over every aspect of our lives will grow. Indeed, the first tentative signs of that trend emerged during the COVID-19 pandemic. EF authorities would constitutionally limit that kind of surveillance, e.g. by only allowing practices necessary for public safety, such as cameras on the streets or public transport.

3.2.8. High judicial and prosecutorial standards

In keeping with Europe post-WWII political tradition, the EF would be governed by law and not by arbitrary force. Thus, an exemplary judicial system would be imperative to control executive power, protect citizens' rights and ensure their confidence in state institutions. Moreover, a strong judiciary is a necessary pre-condition for economic development and investor trust.

The EF would aim for the highest standards for the performance of its judges, prosecutors and court administration. The EF's Ministry of Justice would ensure an appropriate functioning of the federation's judicial, prosecutorial and prison systems, supervise the functioning of its judicial administration and foster a robust legal framework with access to justice for all.

Given the prevailing differences in legal standards across EU member states, this would be a tall order. The judicial sector in several EU member states is notorious for delay, whose courts deliver their first instance rulings only after two or three years, with subsequent rulings stretching well beyond that. This fails to deliver justice fairly or to uphold the rights of citizens.[77] According to recent figures, a first instance case takes, on average, more than 400 days to be completed in Italy, 500 days in Greece and 1,000 days in Poland and Cyprus.[78] The average length of judicial review of competition cases is more than three years in Belgium, Bulgaria, Cyprus, Czech Republic, Denmark, Malta and Poland.[79]

Understaffed judicial sectors and poor working conditions for judges, prosecutors and judicial administrators account for the delays and gaps, which directly affect the economy. According to a study by the European Commission's Joint Research Centre (JRC), there is a strong statistical correlation between the length of proceedings (a proxy for efficiency of the judiciary) and the economic performance of a member state's enterprises.[80]

In countries, like Poland, the government has directly interfered with the independence of the judiciary and came in straight conflict with the EU institutions in this respect. Meanwhile, corruption or fear of organised crime can intimidate or deter judges from performing their tasks in several member states. The EF would thus need to introduce some structural changes to reverse this situation.

The appointment, evaluation, promotion or dismissal of any judge or prosecutor would be decided exclusively by independent EF judicial and prosecutorial councils comprised of high-ranking judges, prosecutors and independent legal experts such as law professors. The federation would make a serious political commitment to building up a highly efficient judicial sector, funded with the necessary resources for its realisation. Its judicial policy would encompass a set of decisive measures.

First of all, it would include generous salaries for judges and prosecutors to reduce the temptations of corruption. They would occupy the top notch of civil service in recognition of their role in protecting human rights, the EF's economy and society. They would be guaranteed a steady career, with judges and prosecutors involved in sensitive criminal cases having special security protection and benefits.

It would be combined with the employment of a higher number of judges, prosecutors and administrative personnel to reduce backlogs. This would be an essential element for the timely delivery of justice. The number of permanent judges was 21 per 100,000 inhabitants in the EU in 2016.[81] In the EF, this number would increase to 30 or more, namely a total of more than 150,000 judges and prosecutors altogether. This large number of professionals would be perhaps the most crucial factor for the much needed acceleration of court cases, and true delivery of justice and business confidence in the rule of law.

Criminal legislation would be simplified and alternative penalties would be introduced, such as social work for petty or non-violent crimes. Violent crimes would be punished more stringently than others, while imprisonment would be mainly reserved for violent criminals.

Old court buildings would be refurbished and new court buildings would be created to ensure an efficient and safe environment for judicial work. It is difficult to underestimate the value of adequate premises and infrastructure for the appropriate functioning of a judicial system. There would be quotas for administrative personnel per constituent state and region, as well as quotas for working space per personnel. Great importance would be given to properly equipped premises with the necessary IT systems and data bases.

Artificial intelligence and big data technologies would be used to help reduce judicial workloads by processing and producing electronic court files, assessing evidence, classifying the most important information needed for decisions and using reliable statistical approaches as required. Computers would not replace judges in reaching a decision, but simply assist them. Some routine cases, where no intellectual discretion is needed as a first step, however, could be automated. Typical cases of 'computerised' court rulings might entail administrative fines for standard offenses, validation of certain categories of contracts or mutually agreed divorces. At any rate, these automated rulings would be subject to human supervision.

Finally, the EF would create its own schools for judges and prosecutors for regular, life-long training. There would be at least one school in each EF constituent state, designed to keep judges and prosecutors up to date on the latest technologies to help them carry out their tasks more efficiently. Completion of the schools' two-years programme, based on intensive practical court training and an extensive series of mock trials, would be an entry requirement for hiring.

3.3. Concluding summary

The EF would be a federation with its own constitution and political institutions: the parliament, the government, the Council of Governance, the judiciary, the Central Bank and other bodies. It would have specific procedures for the accession and exit of states. In order to move from the current EU status to the federal state of the EF, a particular roadmap should be followed starting from a European constituent assembly.

Democratic governance would however need more than political institutions: it would be based on referenda promoting direct democracy, participation of citizens in public decision-making, an accountable public administration, a framework against corruption and permanent civic education to create well informed and rational citizens. Democracy also requires a robust framework for the uniform protection of human rights and a robust judiciary system to serve citizen's rights and the economy. Of course important budgetary consequences are linked to the creation of such a EF and need to be carefully taken into account.

Chapter 4

Economic governance through an economic, fiscal, monetary and banking union

4.1. The need for an economic, fiscal, monetary and banking union

The EU has an advanced economic union with an internal market for most products and services, accompanied however by only a restricted monetary union (the eurozone, with a limited constituency of member states), plus a partial eurozone banking union supervised by the European Central Bank (ECB). The EU lacks a fiscal union because its member states continue to control their own national budgets, taxes, debts, surpluses and deficits. But as experience has shown with the eurozone crisis of the early 2010s or the Covid-19 pandemic, a monetary union with no corresponding fiscal union is wide open to instability due to the heterogeneity of national public debt and deficits, combined with the member states' divergent fiscal priorities. Lack of a common fiscal and monetary union carries direct consequences for an economic union where varying currency, inflation and tax rates undermine both the competition of enterprises and the functioning of the internal market.

For instance, as the third biggest economy in the eurozone, Italy faced the abyss of public debt default due to the COVID-19 pandemic in 2020. This is just one example of one weak link that could place at mortal risk the eurozone' entire financial chain. And why? Because no strong institutions exist to align the zone's fiscal policies. Italy, along with Spain and other important economies, simply could not manage alone without the active support of the other zone countries. Moreover, the richer members and their banks would have seen their own solvency threatened if their weaker partners went bankrupt. The key-word at that time was 'solidarity': support from the north to the south, and from those countries least affected by the crisis to those most affected by it. However we cannot continue eternally on this basis of voluntary solidarity and goodwill. We will need solid institutions and a true union to avoid such scenarios in the future. The decision of the European Council of July 2020 to commonly borrow up to €750 billion as a part of a recovery fund to address the effects of COVID-19 pandemic, has been an unprecedented step and a good start to move to a certain level of fiscal federalism.

For the EU to evolve into a sovereign EF, there will have to be a joint fiscal policy, single currency, a fully integrated banking system and a completely integrated economy and market. Without these, no real union is possible and no equitable economic or social policies can be developed in a coherent manner. Without them, Europe will remain a splintered economic space characterised by unsustainable debts and deficits in some regions alongside big surpluses in others, and all the uneven economic growth and disparities in employment and social development that will drag along behind it.

An economic union of different countries is based on the principles of common customs and markets. This is currently the case for the EU thanks to the achievements of its former iteration, the European Economic Community (EEC). The EU's economic dimension was enhanced by creation of its internal market in the early 1990s, but that is still incomplete. As of 2021, policy areas involving digital services or intellectual property rights remain fragmented across the EU member states. According to one estimate, removing the remaining barriers to a digital single market alone could add as much as €415 billion to Europe's GDP.[82] In contrast to the EU's economy, the EF's would be a fully integrated one for faster growth, fairer competition and a more coherent society.

The EF's fiscal union would be based on the principle of fiscal federalism whereby the collection of revenues and the allocation of expenditures would be clearly defined for each level of the federal administration (federal, constituent state, regional and municipal). Taxes and spending at the federal level would enjoy the greatest share compared to lower government levels, thus ensuring the primacy of federal policies. The federal government of the republic would be the main revenue collector, spender and debtor – and not its constituent states or local authorities. Otherwise, the substance of EF policies and powers would risk draining away for lack of cohesion and adequate sources of financing.

The EF's monetary union would see the adoption of the euro as the only currency for all EF states and with no possibility for opt-out.

A single currency is a state's financial flag and symbol of its sovereignty. Those European countries not belonging to the EF, however, would have the possibility to join its currency union, provided certain conditions are fulfilled and that their inclusion would be mutually beneficial.

The EF's banking union would see the transfer of responsibility for banking policy from state to federal level. This would fall under supervision of a single Central Bank that would absorb and replace the national central banks of the constituent states. All public and private banks would come under common rules for their establishment, supervision, borrowing, lending, capital requirements, resolution and anything else essential to their functioning and mission.

In sum, the EF's economic, fiscal, monetary, and banking union would be governed by a single Ministry of Finance and Economy and a single Central Bank. Such an integrated structure is fundamental for carrying out coherent financial and economic policies

Finally, the importance of having a strong economy and financial stability for the EF is crucial. This is the cornerstone for building common trust in a new state, its mission and institutions. It is also the foundation for all the other pillars we present in the following chapters, from a credible common defence to social policies. As the deep financial crises of the 1930s and 2008 showed, a weak economy leads to general frustration with a system and its institutions. Populism, racism, xenophobia, protectionism, and pessimism can quickly replace rationality, tolerance, openness and optimism. Avoiding these symptoms should be our top priority, and the best way to achieve what would be a truly European and inclusive economy, with clear strategic directions.

A more detailed analysis of the proposed EF's economic, fiscal, monetary, and banking policy is outlined in the following sections.

4.2. Economic policy: The ten commandments

The EF economy would function on the basis of certain principles that we present in the form of "ten commandments". They introduce a general framework friendly to business and investments. In our view, this is the optimal framework for remaining competitive with other regions of the world, while best serving the needs of the European society. They are:

4.2.1. Entrepreneurship first

A society's wealth is created more by private enterprises than any other source. Enterprises create the vast majority of goods, services, jobs, and tax revenues that we need to function as an organised and civilised community of people. A country with few or weak enterprises is a poor one. We therefore place the 'entrepreneurship first' idea at the top of EF economic policies. European people should live with the perception that it is a great choice to operate enterprises in Europe, no matter their size, and also to work for them or with them.

The EF would define the basic framework for entrepreneurial success: a reduction of red tape, more investment opportunities, easier access to capital, simpler employment rules, simpler bankruptcy procedures. The philosophy of our entire policy here revolves around the idea that Europe's citizens should benefit from as much support as possible in order to launch or operate a productive and innovative business of any type or scale: from the smallest local company to the largest international firm.

4.2.2. Simple and low taxation

Taxation must shrink in size and complexity. In our view, wealth should remain in the hands of the people who produce or earn it, and they should use it as they wish. This is what we perceive as fair policy and in line with our vision for a liberal Europe. Only the smallest necessary fraction of people's income should be transferred to the state, and only insofar as it contributes to social progress. The EF should set the example of a modern state where taxes are returned to the citizen in the form of high-value services. People will more easily accept the imposition of taxes if these are seen as investments for the public's benefit.

We also see a need for a simple tax code consisting of a just a few pages. In this spirit, we propose the imposition of only three taxes: (a) VAT (value added tax) as a general transaction tax; (b) income tax; and (c) a corporate earnings tax. A more detailed presentation of our taxation proposals is outlined in the next section on fiscal policy.

4.2.3. Attraction of foreign direct investments

In our vision, Europe should become the magnet for the world's money and trust for doing business. Creating a favourable environment for foreign direct investments (FDI) must be a central EF economic goal. There are two kinds of foreign direct investments: the creation of new productive assets by foreigner owners (e.g. through the construction of a new hotel or shopping mall on European territory) or the purchase of existing assets by foreign investors (e.g. through acquisitions or mergers with existing European enterprises).

The EF would send a clear welcoming signal to the world. Both types of FDI would enjoy tax breaks or reduced taxation for an initial period. Investment procedures would be simplified, and mergers and acquisitions of companies would be facilitated via fresh sources of foreign capital. Special bilateral chambers (e.g. Euro-Chinese, Euro-American, Euro-Russian, Euro-Indian, and so on) would be set up with prominent business leaders to facilitate trade partnerships. European economic diplomacy (see next chapter) would also play an active part in advertising and promoting European companies by informing the international community about the business-friendly nature of European policies.

On the other hand, foreign investment in strategic infrastructure would be subject to security scrutiny and conditions. We have in mind the most recent example of Chinese companies such as Huawei and ZTE. Their rising dominance in the area of 5G deployment has stirred great controversy and confusion in western countries when considering them as telecommunication suppliers or investors due to security concerns. The EF would impose a vetting process to block or restrict foreign investments if they posed a serious risk, whatever the nature, to the EF's security.

4.2.4. Export-driven economy

Aside from attracting international capital into Europe via foreign direct investment, our economic policy would also aim to generate wealth through exports. Europe must once again become a leading manufacturing power that exports high-value goods to the rest of the planet. This is a realistic prospect. Many parts of the globe are gaining in wealth and keen to consume high quality goods and services of the calibre produced in Europe. Our region's public authorities must play their role in guiding European business toward the most promising international markets. Exports could further be promoted through specialised export help-desks (more details in chapter 9).

4.2.5. Focus on ecological development and circular economy

The European economy must meet the increasing expectations of its citizens to live in a sustainable environment where the protection of nature and life would be a top priority. Economic development should resonate with ecological development. It should evolve toward a circular economy that recycles, recovers and reuses resources instead of one-way consumption and disposal. The EU's precautionary "polluter pays" principles would continue to apply across all EF policies.

Public investment and business incentives would focus on clean energy and transport, while policies would be on the optimal use of garbage as a potential source of economic wealth or productive re-use. The highest tax rates would apply to production and consumption that exact the highest environmental and health costs. The EF would not only tally the environmental cost of each kind of economic activity, but would focus on the economic benefits of nature's protection.

The EF would base its economic development on the objectives and principles of the European Green Deal, launched by the EU in December 2019. As the European Commission noted when unveiling the initiative, it encapsulates a new strategy for a resource-efficient and competitive economy that produces no net emissions of greenhouse gases by 2050 and which decouples economic growth from resource use.[83] More detailed proposals on the EF's climate and circular economy policy are developed in Chapter 10.

4.2.6. Knowledge-based economy

A knowledge-based economy relies more on skills, intellect and innovation rather than material production and consumption. It is the overarching component to the economy where intellectual capabilities are far more important than natural resources. In our 'post-industrial' revolution, countries and companies increasingly compete for information and know-how rather than material goods. Data, patents, trade secrets, and business intelligence constitute the new currency, sometimes more valuable than money itself.

The EF would support a legal and administrative framework to generate incentives for the dissemination and use of scientific and other types of knowledge to stimulate and create growth. It would invest in a highly skilled labour force, because, no matter how sophisticated a country's infrastructure, it serves little purpose without the qualified employees and employers to make use of it effectively. The EF would also put its money into a dynamic information network to facilitate the flow and processing of information by as many members of society as possible. Academic and research institutes in the EF would be closely linked to daily business and production. Their activities would focus on practical business applications. Chambers of commerce and business associations would actively inform and train their members about the latest opportunities emerging from scientific breakthroughs such as big data processing, blockchain or new energy efficiency techniques. Business rules would be drafted in close co-operation with the scientific community. Universities, financial institutions and the EF's telecommunication, energy and information sectors would steer this horizontal mission.

More details on the links between EF's business policy, new technologies and high education are set out in Chapters 6 and 9.

4.2.7. Business clustering and hubs of excellence

Economic sectors benefit more if their enterprises are clustered and developed in the same area. Clustering enhances both the competition and co-operation between enterprises. One thinks immediately of the examples of Silicon Valley and information technology (IT), Hollywood and film-making or Detroit for cars. According to one study, productivity in clusters is much higher than average non-clustered productivity, and it increases with the cluster's strength, ranging from 10 %-15 % above average for basic-performing and medium-performing clusters to twice as high (+140 %) for high-performing clusters.[84]

By operating in close proximity to one other, business entities interact in a more dynamic fashion and evolve into something bigger than the sum of its parts. Their employers may change job within the sector without having to physically move away from their region, while at the same time the clustering effect makes it is easier to attract highly qualified employees from other areas.

This is already underway in a number of regions across Europe but would be enhanced by a more tailored framework under the EF's aegis. One can point to many current examples in Italian fashion, German engineering, Baltic IT start-ups, Anglo-Irish financial services,

Scandinavia's wood and paper industry and others. Many of these sectors and geographic regions could host world-class hubs of excellence, subject to favourable production and investment conditions. The EF would designate special "cluster zones" for certain sectors that offered a more favourable business and investment environment. It would mobilise the EF's resources and co-ordinate with its banks to support the clusters with the necessary infrastructure.

4.2.8. Public spending: No higher than 50 % of annual GDP, with a focus on strategic investments

Government (or "public") spending is usually defined as the expenditure of central, state and local governments, including social security outlays. In 2019, the EU-28's public spending amounted to 45.8 % of the EU's annual GDP.[85] That proportion is moreover expected to significantly rise in the short- and mid-term, however, due to the COVID-19 crisis which has contracted national GDPs and led to fiscal stimuli to ameliorate the social and economic damage.

For the EF, annual public spending would be held to below 50 % of GDP, both in normal times and, preferably, during periods of crisis too. A 50 % rate translates to something less than €8 trillion per year in current 2021 values, if we calculate on the basis of EU-27 plus UK GDP in 2019[86] (the last 'normal' year before the pandemic, when the combined GDP of the EU-27 and the UK reached approximately €16 trillion). We believe it would be crucial to stay below this ceiling to make room for Europe's private economy to flourish. Of course, from an ideological point of view, we would prefer a lower rate, and perhaps this could be achieved from 2030 onward. However, such an objective does not seem likely in the 2020s because of the COVID-19 pandemic's impact.

To boost the efficient use of public money, government spending would need to favour strategic investment over short-term subsidies, shored up by responsible governance that reflects the needs of present and future generations. We see opportunities for such strategic investments in the areas of advanced technological research, basic infrastructure, carbon-free energy and demographic policies. Appendix I summarises the annual amounts we envisage per sector for the EF's annual budget, with the goal of keeping public expenses below the 50 % target.

4.2.9. Public – private partnerships and investment banks

European business will need access to financing and capital, under the guidance of specialised institutions. We would support the creation of several "sister" European banks to boost growth and jobs, each with a sectorial focus:

- a European Bank on Primary Industries for agriculture, fisheries, forestry and the mining of minerals and metals;
- a European Bank on Secondary Industries for large industrial players producing finished goods;
- a European Bank on Advanced Technologies and Tertiary Industries for advanced technology and research; and
- a European Bank on Entrepreneurial Development ("EBED"), with a focus on micro-finance, small start-ups and small and medium enterprises.

These banks would be public-owned but independent institutions whose operations and lending would be co-ordinated with the federation's Ministry of Economy. They would function through public-private partnerships and thus serve to leverage private sector projects. They could replace or complement the EU's existing European Investment Bank (EIB). It could be argued of course that such an approach would generate a lot of mega-banks and bureaucracies. However, this would be a realistic choice due to the need to financially support all those big programmes that we propose in this text through a central and better co-ordinated banking group, without of course excluding the role of the other private banks and financial institutions.

One should note here that public-private partnerships (PPPs) would have to become more efficient under the EF than they are in the EU today. While PPPs enable public authorities to support business and the society with large-scale infrastructure projects (such as motorways or telecommunication), they also tend to hamper competition and weaken the negotiating position of private contractors. PPPs take longer to set up due to public sector procedures, which create more delays in their execution than for purely private projects. Finally, PPPs frequently suffer from inadequate planning or misplaced expectations, with overly optimistic forecasts compared to their actual end results.[87]

For these reasons, the EF's rules for PPPs would factor in more room for profit for their private partners and more emphasis on a swift conclusion of agreements and projects. Red tape linked to PPP's would be reduced. Any delays would be borne by the public partner of the contractual side. The selection of each PPP would be based on sound comparative analyses within a framework of pre-determined strategic priorities. The four above-mentioned banks would have to select partners with careful diligence and allocate loans prudently. This would be important for their reputation and ability to borrow cheaply on international markets.

4.2.10. Internal market

The EU's internal market remains incomplete regarding network industries, digital services, insurance companies, intellectual property rights, and certain other sectors.

In a survey of October 2018, almost 70 % of businesses responded negatively when asked if the single market was sufficiently integrated in their sector.[88] Moreover, the European Parliament's 2020 "Cost of non-Europe" study estimated that the benefits of removing the internal market's remaining barriers to create a truly single marketplace for goods and services could amount to €713 billion by 2030.[89]

Several factors account for the incomplete internal market. According to the Commission's policy paper of March 2020, the market is riddled by too many practical barriers for business. Companies complain about burdensome and overly complex administrative procedures when operating in another member state, uneven access to public procurement, national standards imposed on top of common EU rules, problems arising from cross-border purchases, too-high entry requirements for professionals from one member state that want to start their business in another, varying national taxation systems and so on.[90]

This disruptive state of affairs would cease with the EF's establishment. Uniform marketing rules for all sectors would apply directly across its territory without differentiation. The administrative procedures for setting up or running business would be the same everywhere within the EF's borders, meaning no more cross-border barriers or discriminatory practices. There would be no supplementary or hidden national or regional standards – critical to ensuring fair competition, legal certainty and confidence for all enterprises.

4.3. Fiscal policy

The EF would be a single fiscal entity with its own tax policy applicable across its entire territory. The EF central government would borrow, lend and guarantee credit towards all directions as a single legal entity, something not possible for the EU today. Its parliament would adopt the annual budget for all federal expenses, thus determining the EF's deficits and surpluses, debts, taxes, current-account balances and public expenses.

In line with our vision for a more efficient public sector, we have identified four strategic priorities for the EF's fiscal and public financial policies: (1) sustainability of public debt and the elimination of budget deficits; (2) simple and low taxation; (3) the profitable use of public assets; and (4) a rationalisation of public expenditures.

4.3.1. Sustainability of public debt and elimination of budget deficit

The first objective of the EF fiscal policy would be to maintain a sustainable public debt, at a rate below 85 % of the republic's annual GDP, and a balanced budget with zero deficit. Missing that target, with the resulting debts and deficits, could undermine the EF's financial independence and weaken its global status, thus putting its financial and political objectives at risk. That scenario would entail painful compromises to avoid bankruptcy, placing Europe at the mercy of its creditors: China, Japan and other Asian countries, Russia, the USA, large banks, sovereign wealth funds, hedge funds, and bond market speculators. It would impose strict austerity and slashes to social budgets. Is that what we need in the long-term?

Admittedly, our target figure of 85 % looks other-worldly at a time when EU member states and other western countries are heading in exactly the opposite direction to combat the economic fall-out of the COVID-19 pandemic: i.e., aggressive fiscal stimuli, heavy public borrowing and an abolition of limits on budget deficits. We agree, of course, with those choices as an obvious emergency response to an unprecedented global crisis with its potentially enormous impact. We are encouraged to see that, even in the early stages of the COVID crisis in March 2020, several EU leaders proposed the idea of "euro-bonds", or common borrowing by all eurozone members as a mutually supportive solution, and this proposal was adopted to a great extent by the conclusions of the European Council of 21 July 2020. It started being implemented in 2021 and hopefully over the next years too.[91] On the other hand, one must acknowledge that in the long run, once normal circumstances resume, European countries cannot continue as before with inflated debt and low-growth rates. This is not viable and it would block the EF from achieving its many other policy objectives.

Once the effects of the COVID-19 crisis are over, the EF would gradually adhere to specific deficit and debt ceilings. These would be strictly enforced via the supervision of an independent EF budget authority, which would annually report to the EF parliament, government and Council of Governance.

The EF constitution would allow for a maximum annual public deficit rate of 2 % of GDP, to be exceeded only in exceptional cases (e.g., war or a global financial crisis similar to those of 1929, 2008 or 2020–2021). These exceptions would require the approval of a three-quarters majority of the EF parliament. The figure of 2 % is an achievable target, as shown by EU member states' balance sheets in 2019 when – in the year before the outbreak of the COVID-19 pandemic – the eurozone countries reached an average deficit of 0.6 % and the EU countries 0.5 % of their annual GDP.[92] However, a deficit of 2 % would be the maximum, legally allowed limit – a safeguard, though not the preferred option. Our policy objective would be clear: no deficit at all. Even if this sounds crazy in 2021, when a sinking economy of 7 % or more has forced all Europe's countries to relax their economic policies, we must keep it as the golden rule for our future long-term fiscal policy.

The other strategic objective, linked to the zero deficit, would be the restriction of public debt to 85 % of the EF's GDP. This is less ambitious than the 60 % convergence criterion for joining the eurozone as agreed in Maastricht in 1991,[93] but it would be more realistic and appropriate for a post 2020-crisis Europe.

The EF would assume the national debts of all current EU member states. That collective debt amounted to 80.5 % of the EU's GDP in 2019[94], but in 2020 rose to 89.8 % and 97.3 % of the EU and the eurozone GDP respectively[95] and is now projected to grow much bigger in the coming years to meet the pandemic's financial exigencies. Merging all current national debts might seem unfair to the publics of fiscally responsible EU member states such as Germany, the Netherlands, Slovakia or the Baltic states. Indeed, it would mean that all the EF's citizens and tax payers would assume the debts of the EU's perennial over-spenders of Belgium, Cyprus, Greece, France, Italy, Portugal and Spain – countries whose debts in 2019 approached or exceeded 100 % of their GDP. However, this would have to be seen as a short-term sacrifice and expression of solidarity, one still affordable but necessary to shift to a true union. On a more positive note for the "donor" countries, it would benefit their business and industry, which would gain easier access to the markets of Europe's poorer regions. Creating a new sovereign republic would thus entail gains and losses for all: unifying our economies cannot be done without unifying our assets and liabilities.

Keeping debt relatively low would reduce annual debt servicing costs and its refinancing. The death-spiral of high interest leading to higher debt and then much higher rates would be avoided. The EF would aim to spend approximately no more than €500 billion per year (in 2021 prices) to service its debts. This amount may vary per the circumstances of each year, depending on the interest rates, maturity time of bonds and amounts borrowed.

Reducing our debt and borrowing would of course inflict short-term economic difficulties since it could also reduce Europe's access to easy or cheap borrowings of the present time. It would imply austerity measures with the risk of slower growth in the short-term. Yet any short-term losses would be more than compensated in the mid- and long-term by higher revenues flowing from bold policies friendly to business and production.

Moreover, the EF would take the lead on global initiatives to reduce public debt across the world, which in certain cases is ballooning out of control. There is the staggering $28 trillion in US debt in mid-2021, for example, or China's expanding public and private debt which, combined, now reaches 300 % of the country's GDP.[96] If such trends continue, we risk a global financial cataclysm that would take us all down.[97] Faced with such a gloomy prospect, a global agreement is needed to forgive portions of public debt. This is not an easy or fairly assigned solution, because it would hurt the finances of thousands of creditors: banks, other financial institutions, pension funds, sovereign state funds, creditor state budgets, and so on. It would not be wise to enter into the details of such a proposal: assessing the exact debt numbers, plus the costs and benefits of all aspects of a debt-relief equation would be a chaotic exercise. But, as a principle, we see no solution for the salvation of public finances other than slashing a reasonable amount of governments' debts – especially in low-growth regions such as Europe, all the more so in view of the pandemic's approaching aftermath.

4.3.2. Simple and low taxation

The EF's tax code would consist only of a few pages, one of the simplest in the world. It would rest on just three kinds of taxes: a general transactions tax (Value Added Tax), an income tax and a corporate tax. In particular, we would propose:

- a standard set of VAT rates for all services and transactions of goods, at three levels:
  • a reduced rate of 8 % for basic goods and services
  • a standard rate of1 8 % for other goods and services
  • a dissuasive rate of 40 % or more for socially or environmentally harmful products such as tobacco or fossil fuels.

The VAT would replace taxes for all existing transactions, including those on inheritance, sales and donations. The standard VAT level would be lower than the current VAT rates across the EU member states today.[98] For comparison, the lowest standard rate in 2019 was in Malta (18 %), with the highest rising to 27 % in Hungary.[99] The EF's low VAT rates would help boost demand, consumption and investment spending. They could thus strengthen business development, production, trade and the circulation of money. They would also support low-income consumers by increasing their purchasing power, thus increasing tax revenues for the EF budget.

- an income tax for physical persons

This would be a direct tax on all forms of income earned by individuals each year, whether professional salaries, dividends, rental or investment income. And it would be progressive, rising from 5 % for very low-incomes to 30 % for the highest income brackets.

It would mean that rich or ultra-rich persons would not be taxed excessively. We should not punish people for getting wealthy, and we should not deter people from aiming to get richer and to prosper. An ambitious society needs ambitious individuals to drive it forward. Such an approach would stand in sharp contrast to today's tax rates on private income in EU member states where the average income tax in 2020 was 38 %, and 41.5 % for the eurozone.[100]

– a corporate tax

This would be a direct tax on the profits of enterprises and any kind of business. It would be imposed on all corporations residing, or doing business, in the EF. It, too, would be progressive but never higher than 25 %. We support this ceiling, arguing that low corporate taxation would encourage entrepreneurship and attract foreign investments. It is time to end the big disparities than exist today across the EU: from 10 % in Bulgaria to almost 40 % in France.[101] This heterogeneity creates tax heavens within the Union and very unfair conditions for competition.

No annual property taxes would be levied for the mere possession of houses, cars, vessels or other assets. People must be free to enjoy the goods they obtain, being taxed only once for the goods at the moment of their purchase, inheritance or donation via the ordinary VAT rate of 17 %. Property taxes would only be imposed in exceptional cases of fiscal urgencies and following the approval by the qualified majority of the EF Parliament.

All transactions worth more than a specific value (e.g. 50 euros) would have to be executed electronically and taxed online once they are transacted. This is only logical in that all transactions are destined to become electronic within 10 or 20 years, with the use and circulation of coins and banknotes gradually withering away. A world dominated by electronic transactions would be an effective first step in combating tax evasion and increasing the transparency of company accounting. However, the EF would legislate strict provisions on data protection to defend the privacy of all engaged in such payments.

There would also be regional and municipal taxes subject to specific caps and limitations. As explained above, the EF federal government would be the main collector of taxes to better address the broader needs of its public and society.

Given the low levels of taxes proposed, fiscal exceptions in the EF would be rare to avoid a tax code stuffed with loopholes, derogations and footnotes that obviate the rules. For instance, no tax breaks would be granted to corporations or individuals for charitable donations: charities should be linked to social responsibility, not tax avoidance. Tax exceptions would be carefully targeted to boost only those activities of high social value or which attract foreign investments. It is worth repeating: the EF tax code would consist of just a few pages, easily understood by all citizens, business people and investors.

Yes, it is predictable that dozens of lobbies and professional associations would press for a more sophisticated tax system to defend their interests. Reality is complex and so is most tax legislation. On the other hand, there is another line of reasoning: that simple tax legislation can be, in and of itself, the best tax incentive. It encourages investment, growth, entrepreneurship, a healthy business environment, transparency and trust in public governance. Further, it would deter the flight of billions of euros from Europe to tax havens in the Caribbean and elsewhere, retaining the EF's money in Europe and encouraging its citizens to spend and invest more at home than abroad.

4.3.3. Public revenues stemming from common EF assets

Aside from taxation, an important source of public income would be generated by the rational use of public assets. A new database – the "EF Assets Inventory" – would be swiftly established to register all public assets within the EF's territory such as buildings, public lands or utility networks. Some of those assets would grant more benefits to the state and society if sold or leased rather than sitting empty or underused. The EF Assets Inventory could catalyse the use of state-owned enterprises, hotels, land holdings, islands, resorts, pipelines, roads, licencing rights and so on to generate billions of euros in revenue for public coffers.

That inventory would be managed by the EF Budget Authority, with its assets allocated according to sound procedures in public procurement and environmental protection guidelines. However, public utilities of strategic importance to all society would remain largely under public ownership or control. We draw inspiration from initiatives such as the "National Asset Register" compiled by the UK in 2007, an 1100-page book intended to help the government achieve "greater exploitation of under-utilised assets and the disposal of assets no longer required for service delivery". It aimed to "build on the significant progress, of £12.2bn since 2004–05, already made towards the target of £30bn of asset disposals by 2010–11".[102]

Part of the EF assets' revenues would be saved in a special 'rainy day' portfolio, meaning reserves of cash, golds, equities, bonds, cryptocurrencies and other assets that would be used as buffer in the case of difficult financial periods. That portfolio could take the form of a sovereign fund, that would be reinforced by €200 billion per year. It could follow the example of the very successful Government Pension Fund of Norway ("Oil fund"), the world's largest sovereign wealth fund, that was established in 1990 to invest the surplus revenues of the Norwegian petroleum sector.

4.3.4. Rationalisation of public expenditures

The first objective, as mentioned above – to keep a balanced budget and public debt at a sustainable level – would require certain fiscal sacrifices. We are against fiscal austerity because it slows growth, increases income inequality, deters social progress and fuels reactionary and undemocratic political movements. Therefore to avoid severe mid- or long-term austerity caused by high deficits and debts, the EF would need to proceed quickly with smart, bold or just common-sense cuts to our public spending.

As information technology and automation evolve, employment in the public sector could be gradually reduced. Retired civil servants would be replaced by more efficient technology instead of other civil servants. For instance, many tax officers would be replaced by computers thanks to increasing electronic taxation. Many desk-office jobs would be removed as public services shift to online representation. In general, we should aim for a rate of one civil servant per 30 citizens, as explained in the previous chapter.

Public spending for activities with little or negative social value should be eliminated or replaced by support for more productive ones. A general clean-up would be required for today's subsidies, tax benefits or allowances, which range from the unnecessary to the outrageous. Examples of public expenditure in the form of national or EU subsidies that would be slashed include: unwarranted sponsored holidays for certain groups of people; luxurious equipment for public offices; projects with frivolous or little intrinsic value such as requiring children to draw pictures of each other to develop "active European citizenship"; or the countless number of seminars each year where people gather from all corners of the continent at tax payers' expenses with no evidence of the events' added value for the participants themselves or society at large.

Billions of euros could be saved by rationalising public subsidies and projects. The EF administration's economy of scale would significantly contribute to this: for instance, there would be only one tax service, one civil aviation authority, one army or one statistical agency instead of today's 27 national ones.

4.4. Monetary policy

Monetary policy involves setting or influencing interest and exchange rates to support price stability and thus the economy. This is achieved through the supply of money, controlled by a central bank.

The EF would have its own monetary union and policy where the euro would be the single currency of the entire federation, without opt-outs for any region. This would stand in sharp contrast to the situation in 2021 where eight of the EU member states[103] were still outside the eurozone, using their national currencies instead.

The EF's strategic objective for its monetary policy would be two-fold: retaining the euro as a hard global reserve currency and keeping inflation below, if close to, 2 %.

4.4.1. The euro as single currency for the entire EF

The advantages of a single currency for a large economic space are many and serious. A single currency contributes to greater financial security and price stability. It creates a more credible framework for investment, savings, loans, businesses and long-term planning for industry and households. It supports fair competition and the integration of financial markets. It abolishes the inequalities and insecurities caused by currency fluctuations and the costs of currency exchanges. Companies and individuals need not worry about the conversion of their national currencies into francs, marks, pesetas, crowns or anything else as the vector for their transactions, commerce, shopping, travelling, studying or banking across Europe. A single currency also increases transparency by allowing price comparisons between goods and services across its economic space.

At the global level, the euro has already made Europe a heavy-weight currency champion. It is attractive to foreign governments as a reserve currency due to its strength and the confidence it inspires.

In 2019, the euro was the second most widely used currency in terms of its share of global payments, amounting to around 32 %. The US dollar, by comparison, accounted for 88 % of total payments (the total sum is 200 % because each currency trade always involves a currency pair; one currency is sold (e.g. US$) and another bought (€)).[104] Moreover, approximately 20 % of global foreign exchange holdings were held in euros,[105] making it the second reserve currency in the world, trailing only the US dollar. This is a significant advantage. Markets for world reserve currencies are vast, ensuring that bonds issued in them are in high demand. That is a major reason why borrowing in euros has been consistently cheap.

Furthermore, the euro offers to the European economy a shield against global financial threats. The large scale of the euro area makes it more resilient to international economic shocks such as foreign debt crises, currency market turbulence or sharp rises in the price of oil or other commodities. That stability is among the reasons why the euro area is an attractive destination for foreign investments and businesses, and why they prefer to use the euro for their transactions with European firms. Both sides gain from this, since it further reduces cost for European firms and the risk of losses caused by global currency fluctuations.[106] Not surprisingly, several countries lying outside the eurozone have linked their currencies to the euro for the higher stability it offers their own economies.

Finally, the euro represents the European economy's "flag", image and identity: the rest of the world identifies our continent with it. International financial institutions, such as the International Monetary Fund (IMF) and World Bank, closely follow the EU's euro-related policies and treat the currency almost as synonymous with the European economy.

4.4.2. Two strategic objectives of EF monetary policy: A strong euro and a low level of inflation

In principle, monetary policy is one of reaction to circumstances involving, for example, inflationary pressures, the global financial environment, trade balances, foreign currency fluctuations, geopolitical events, natural disasters or the outbreak of war. While it is impossible to forecast the specific monetary measures for all circumstances, we believe two strategic objectives should prevail as the basic framework for the EF's policy: retaining the euro as a hard currency and ensuring a low level of inflation.

There are solid reasons for the euro's retention as a "hard" global reserve currency. A 'hard currency' is widely accepted around the world as a form of payment for goods and services, and is expected to remain relatively stable albeit expensive.

As explained before, a hard currency offers many advantages. But some disadvantages too: expensive exports, the risk of very low inflation, addiction to cheap borrowing or competition from cheaper and more flexible currencies. However, when weighing the advantages against the disadvantages, we favour the "hard" currency option: its disadvantages could be offset by the economic growth, innovation and targeted investment flowing from a strong and stable euro.

To retain the euro as a hard currency, we must keep inflation rates below, but close to, 2 % over the medium term. This has been the target of the EU European Central Bank (ECB) for some years.[107] That 2 % target-value has a double objective. First, to deter high inflation that leads to a weak currency and low purchasing power (which chips away at income and leads to the impoverishment of a significant part of the population). And second: to avoid extremely low or negative inflation that slows economic growth, drains liquidity and invokes overall stagnation.

4.4.3. Ensuring a flexible approach in case of crisis

In periods of extraordinary difficulty, the EF Central Bank should be willing to explore all available tools to create liquidity for corporations and households, boost economic growth, achieve the desired inflation rates, and ensure a strong euro. Our analysis, of course, comes in the aftermath of the 2008 and 2020 financial crises and their subsequent national and regional financial impacts. Unfortunately, a global financial crisis of even greater scale may follow sooner or later. We are strongly convinced of the need to implement quick and flexible responses to extinguish small financial fires at their early stage, before they spread to catastrophic scales. It is worth mentioning that in 2012 a simple statement by Mario Draghi, then-president of the EU Central European Bank, that the bank would do 'whatever it takes' to save the euro, brought practically an end to the eurozone crisis at the time. We would favour the exploration of all possible means, however unorthodox, to make the EF's economic machine work as required by circumstances. With that in mind, the EF Central Bank would always be ready to consider one or more of the following actions:

(1) Quantitative easing

Here a central bank buys financial assets (e.g. bonds, mortgages, securities, etc.) from commercial banks and other financial institutions, consequently raising the price of those assets. This increases the supply of money for the commercial banks, which in turn are expected to supply it to business and households. By increasing the money supply and its circulation, quantitative easing is considered an unconventional growth mechanism in times of ultra-low inflation, growth and liquidity. The ECB launched a programme of quantitative easing in March 2015, which continued through 2016 and 2017. It produced satisfactory results by end-2017, since it led to increased growth and employment.[108] But the most spectacular action came in 2020 as a response to the COVID-19 crisis, when the ECB launched a "pandemic emergency purchase programme" worth a breath-taking 1.85 trillion euros, namely a temporary asset purchase programme of private and public sector securities.[109]

(2) Credit easing

Credit easing arises when a central bank purchases private sector assets such as corporate bonds and residential mortgage-backed securities. This normally increases the price of those assets and subsequently the value of the respective business and mortgaged properties, while supplying the market with more money. In response to the Great Recession of 2008–2009, the US Federal Reserve launched credit easing by purchasing large amounts of treasury bills and mortgage-backed-securities. As liquidity to the banking sector increased, interest rates fell, making money cheaper for institutions. That move prevented the overall collapse of US and many other banks.

(3) Monetary financing

This is the classic manoeuver whereby a central bank creates ("prints") money to directly finance government deficits or pay off public debt.

This is also known as debt monetisation. Monetary financing always has an inflationary effect, and is prohibited in a number of countries. Article 123 of the Treaty on the Functioning of the European Union (TFEU) explicitly prohibits the European Central Bank from financing public institutions. We would, however, retain it as one of the available options for the EF Central Bank, in case of very difficult situations.

(4) "Helicopter money"

This is perhaps the most extreme option, which has not yet been tested but could be worth considering should all other measures fail to deliver acceptable results. Here, the central bank makes payments directly to households or private business without the intervention of public authorities. It has been proposed by several economists as an alternative to quantitative easing, in cases where interest rates are close to zero and an economy remains weak or enters recession.[110] The idea was debated in the U.S. during the COVID-19 pandemic, where the government made three direct payments in 2020–2021 of $600, $1200 and $1400 checks to millions of eligible citizens. However it was not designed as money created by the central bank, but as a government subsidy based on government debt – so not a textbook case of helicopter money.[111]

It should be reiterated that we do not propose the above options as mainstream monetary policies. We simply introduce them as potential tools for consideration in cases where extraordinary circumstances demanded extraordinary action. We also note that all those options could entail setbacks and risks: hyperinflation, deficits in a central bank's balance sheet or very low-interest rates – things that hurt all creditors. But trade-offs are inevitable: each financial policy choice leads to winners and losers. The overall justification of a monetary measure should, however, be the specific circumstances and societal needs of the time.

Finally, the EF should keep its options open concerning the issuance or use of cryptocurrencies ('cryptos'), either as means of payments or assets for investments. Cryptocurrencies are digital assets designed to work as a medium of exchange of coins stored in a form of a computerized database, using strong cryptography to secure transaction records. They are typically not issued by a central authority, at least at the beginning of 2020s. However the future developments are anybody's guess. In April 2021, it was already a booming market. The combined value of cryptos stood at over €1.8 trillion, outstripping for instance US tech giant Apple at that time.[112] Of course nobody knows whether they are going to become major payment or investment assets in the future, or whether they will just turn out to be one more bubble to burst. The EF banking and public financial authorities must therefore follow a cautious but also open-minded approach to that new monetary and financial sector.

4.5. Banking policy

A healthy banking system is the foundation of any robust economy. Banks are important for providing the necessary capital for business and individuals. When a banking system fails, the entire economy comes to a halt with negative social impact on a massive scale.

Several years after the 2008 crisis and just before the COVID-19 pandemic of early 2020, the European banking sector was already in decline. According to Josef Ackermann, former chief executive of Deutsche Bank, American banks continued to dominate global markets and were more profitable and healthy than their European counterparts. After the 2008 crisis, the US government created the time and space for its commercial banks to clean-up their act, enabling the American economy to quickly start growing again. On the other side of the Atlantic, the eurozone moved from a financial crisis to a sovereign debt crisis, something that kept its banks in crisis mode for many more years. Americans consolidated their banks into bigger and more competitive entities, while the structure of Europe's more numerous and smaller banks remained more or less the same. American banks have fewer capital requirements and rely more on investment banking fees, while European banks rely more on interest lending and thus are more vulnerable to the ups and downs of economic cycles.[113]

Moreover, the global crisis of 2008 and Europe's subsequent sovereign debt crisis have tainted the big picture of its banks. Several became the "sick men" of the European economy whose balance sheets are burdened with non-performing loans, debts and toxic assets. In 2019, the total value of non-performing loans (NLP) of banks in the eurozone was estimated at approximately €630 billion, with the biggest problems afflicting Italian banks.[114] That was an improvement compared to previous years when such loans totalled close to €1 trillion. At the end of 2019, the NPL ratio reached a low point, after a continuous downward trend since 2016, amounting to 2.6 % of all loans.[115] Yet more deterioration is predicted for the years following the COVID-19 pandemic, though the exact numbers will be anyone's guess.

On a more positive note, the banks' capital buffers have improved compared to the previous years, as the European Central Bank's stress tests showed in 2018.[116] This suggests that Europe's banks have become more resilient to international economic shocks, as seen during the COVID-19 pandemic's aftershocks.

But European banks remain shaky for other reasons too. Many are exposed to derivatives valued in the billions of dollars, having extensively bet on their performance. Derivatives are financial contracts that "derive" their value from the performance of their underlying units, be they indexes, commodities, shares, mortgages, currencies or interest rates. Over-exposure to mortgage-backed derivatives for speculative purposes was behind the collapse of the US investment bank of Lehman Brothers in 2008, which nearly dragged down the entire US financial system as the value of the derivatives' underlying housing properties collapsed. Of course, many of those derivatives are used as insurance against other ones held by the same bank as follows: if one set of derivatives fails by moving in the wrong direction and produces losses, this would be compensated by other derivatives moving in the opposite direction. This is reassuring to a certain extent, but if several derivatives generate net losses by tens of billions of euros, we face the risk of a catastrophic domino effect between banks, and between funds, and then major fall-out for the actual, concrete economy. The total exposure of Deutsche Bank to notional derivatives at the end of 2018, for instance, stood at a terrifying €43.5 trillion.[117] Most of those underlying assets may be of good quality, of course, but who really knows how many bad apples among them could deliver a lethal blow to the bank and the whole banking system if another crisis hits the global economy?

4.5.1. The Liikainen report

In 2012, a group of experts led by Erkki Liikainen (then governor of the Bank of Finland and a member of the ECB) issued the so-called Liikainen Report,[118] which recommended the following actions:

– mandatory separation of proprietary trading and other high-risk trading from core banking activities;

- amendments to the use of bail-in instruments as a resolution tool;
- tighter capital requirements for trading assets and mortgages;
- stronger bank governance and control of banks, including measures to rein in executive bonuses.

Several years have since passed but we still consider most of the report's recommendations as a solid foundation for establishing a healthy banking system in Europe. Given the dense inter-connection of big banks around the world, it is important to make Europe's banks more resistant to global economic shocks. It is also imperative to prevent European banks from causing the next crises. Our banks must remain vigorous suppliers of cheap capital needed by European business to compete with the rest of the world.

4.5.2. Five strategic objectives for the banking sector

Based on Liikainen report, we have identified the following strategic objectives for the EF's banking system: (i) reduction of non-performing loans; (ii) separation of core banking activities from high-risk trading; (iii) reduction of exposure to derivatives and other high risk assets; (iv) stricter stress tests and capital requirements; (v) consolidation of small banks into larger ones.

- Reduction of non-performing loans

The EF should take bold action to relieve its banks, and subsequently its overall economy, of the current €630 billion portfolio -or whatever it would be in the future- of non-performing loans in the eurozone (only). A new "bad loans bank" should be created to take over the bad loans at discounted prices and focus on their management and potential recovery. The financing of that bank should be shared between the public budget, and the shareholders and bond holders of the banks holding the bad loans. The EF could participate with €300 billion, while the shareholders and bond holders would split the rest of the cost. The EF could allocate its starter capital in five instalments of €50 billion per year to mitigate the impact on its own budget.

This would definitely be a hard political choice since the state budget would be used to partly cover the losses of reckless bankers and borrowers. It would raise immediate issues of moral hazard that could encourage similar behaviour in the future by leaving it unpunished. On the other hand, we could see advantages for society too.

The bad-loans bank would purchase toxic loans at a discount, of which some could be subsequently re-sold to the original banks or other funds at higher prices when conditions – and their value – improve. The impact on the economy would be beneficial: a clean-up of toxic loans from the books of Europe's banks would give a new boost to their performance, while increasing trust in the banking system and lifting all sectors of the economy.

– Separation of core banking activities from high-risk trading

The Liikainen report proposes legal separation within a banking group of its high-risk financial activities from its deposit-taking operations. The former include proprietary trading in securities and derivatives and other actions closely linked to securities and derivatives markets. Banking groups would thus consist of separate deposit-taking and trading/investment activities.

We would support this approach. Separation would ensure that a bank's main tasks, namely deposit-taking and the provision of financial services to households and "main street" business, became safer. These core banking activities carry the highest social importance and levels of sensitivity: they should not be compromised by the potential failure of a bank's trading activities.

Such fire-walling would be complemented by already existing deposit guarantee schemes[119] that reimburse a certain portion of deposits to their owners when a bank fails (e.g. up to €100,000). In case of crises, it supports financial stability since it deters depositors from panic withdrawals.

– Reduction of exposure to derivatives and other high-risk assets

Limits should be set for the exposure of European banks to high-risk assets. While we strongly favour free markets and business choices, it would not be prudent to allow systemically important institutions to put Europe's entire economy on the line due to unshackled speculative practices. We are inspired by the famous U.S. "Dodd-Frank Act" which reduces systemic risk and increases the transparency of the marketing of derivatives. It led to the introduction of stricter requirements for bilateral derivative transactions, pre- and post-trade reporting, central clearing and the electronic execution of all standardised derivatives. The EU has adopted similar acts such as the European Market Infrastructure Regulation and the Market in Financial Instruments Directives.[120]

In the EF, leveraging, or the use of borrowed funds to buy assets, should be limited to a fixed maximum proportion, such as 25 leveraged euros per 1 euro of own capital. So-called "naked" exposure to derivatives, where a derivative position is backed by no countervailing hedged protection, would be prohibited or limited according to the size of a bank.

The EF's overall policy here should aim for a wider effort for such a reduction of leveraged risk in world markets, in co-ordination with other states and international organisations.

– Stricter stress tests and capital requirements

Stress tests would become tighter, with scenarios to include financial implosion at international scale. Given the financial crises of 2008 and COVID-19, it is obvious that risks are now more globalised and will likely occur more frequently too. Credit crunches in the U.S. or China could put the survival of many European banks in question. Regional conflicts, natural disasters, health crises, terrorist attacks and other such events are more likely than ever to cause domino effects on a global scale.

Stress tests must include tougher accounting for non-performing loans. They would be based on more adverse scenarios to plan for severe market turbulence, plus fines for misconduct. This would imply tighter capital requirements and higher depository buffers to absorb future shocks. The downside of this approach is a reduction of amounts available for lending to households and business. However, as past events have shown, it is better to be safe than sorry.

– Consolidation of small banks into larger ones

Europe is "overbanked". There are too many banks, several of them financially sick and in need of consolidation. In 2018, there were 5,698 banks in the EU, a fall of 30 % compared with 2008, but still too many. The member state with the largest number of banks was Germany (28 % of the EU total), followed by Poland (11 %), Austria (10 %) and Italy (9 %) which means that over half of all EU banks were situated in these four member states.[121]

EF banking policy should strive to encourage fewer but more robust banks and raise the minimum required size for creating new or retaining existing ones. Mergers in the sector would lift the resulting entities' market power and enhance revenues via banking fees. Limits would need to be imposed, however, to avoid ultra-large banks from becoming "too big to fail". Social measures would also be needed to help those who would inevitably lose their jobs due to the mergers and the increasing automation of banking.

4.6. Concluding summary and budgetary aspects

EF economic policies would be based on ten principles supporting entrepreneurship and investment-friendly measures, as well as a knowledge-based production model.

The EF would constitute a single fiscal area with its own taxes, revenues, expenditures and public debts. It would reverse today's trend of ever-growing public borrowing. The EF would exercise fiscal discipline by merging and reducing current EU public debt and eliminating public deficits. In order to boost business, transparency and investors' confidence, it would establish a system of simple and low taxation and tax code. At the same time, public revenues would increase through the best use of public assets, which would be registered by the EF Assets Inventory. Public expenditures would be reduced by eliminating duplicative or non-productive spending.

The EF would establish a full monetary union where the euro would be the only applicable currency. The overarching strategic objectives of EF monetary policy would be to maintain the euro as a hard global reserve currency and to keep inflation lower than, but close to, 2 %.

The EF would establish a banking union under the governance and supervision of a Central Bank. EF banking policy would derive from the main recommendations of the Liikainen report of 2012. Its strategic objectives would focus on reduction of non-performing loans, separation of core banking activities from high-risk trading, reduction of banks' exposure to derivatives and other high risk assets, stricter stress tests and capital requirements and, finally, consolidation of small banks into larger ones.

Over a period of five years the EF would allocate €300 billion to purchase non-performing loans from Europe's banks and transfer them to a "bad-loans bank". This would create a positive economic boost to the entire European economy. In addition, every year it would also put aside €200 for a 'rainy day' sovereign wealth fund with reserves for overcoming difficult financial periods, consisting of cash, equities, bonds, gold and other assets.

Chapter 5

Security governance: Common foreign, defence and security policy

5.1. Common foreign, defence and security governance as pillar of a sovereign state

A sovereign state is by definition the single responsible entity for its foreign affairs, defence and security, including the security of its external borders. A state cannot effectively exercise its powers across its territory and would not be taken seriously internationally if it was not in charge of its own foreign relations, defence and border policy. Therefore, the EF should have its own Foreign Ministry with a full diplomatic service, a Ministry of Defence with its own exclusive military capabilities and its own police, intelligence service and border protection force.

To forge a sovereign federal state with an effective, coherent and consistent external policy and representation, the current EU member states would have to transfer to the EF their seats in the UN's General Assembly and Security Council, their membership in all other international organisations, their military forces (including their nuclear arsenals), diplomatic services, intelligence agencies, embassies and consulates, as well as their border control mechanisms. These transfers could take place gradually in stages, given their sensitivity.

This is surely the most difficult step towards the transition from the EU's current loose structure to the EF, since European armies and foreign services are the symbols of national pride, with a rich and long history. We know it would be difficult for France and the UK to give up their armies, nuclear arsenals and permanent seats on the Security Council. It would be difficult for Spain and Portugal to give up their national embassies in Latin America and hand them over to new EF embassies. It would be hard for Greece, Poland or Finland to give up control of their borders, given the history and importance of those borders today.

However, despite the near-insuperable sensitivities involved, there are strong reasons that argue in favour of that shift:

- The first concerns efficiency. The significant costs of 28 or more separate armies and other security authorities would be spared if all were merged into a single coherent structure. Command and co-ordination of the resulting integrated structure at European level would be much simpler. Substantial savings would be generated by merging national embassies, consulates, intelligence agencies and border services. At the same time this would expand the diplomatic representation of millions of citizens of those EU member states that have no national embassy or consulate in many countries around the world. As a result, the travel, business and study opportunities across the planet for EU citizens as a whole would increase greatly.

- The second reason concerns effectiveness. A common European army would immediately qualify as one of the world's top five armed forces[122] in terms of fire power and personnel. It would include a formidable navy, one of the biggest armies and air forces, and one of the most effective anti-missile and cyber-warfare systems on the planet. Its power projection would be on a global scale, and its deterrent effect immense. None would dare threaten or seize even the tiniest part of the EF's territory, from Cyprus to the Baltic and Arctic regions, without risk of serious cost or casualties.

- A third reason points to the resulting geopolitical, institutional and diplomatic weight of Europe. A joint strong military force would enhance the EF's geopolitical position as a peer equal to the USA, China or Russia. The allure of an EF ambassador representing the world's second biggest economy and military force, and third-largest population, would vastly exceed the prestige and weight of any of the national ambassadors of today's EU member states. Indeed, a joint European army and foreign service would, by dint of their unified policies, be far larger than the sum of their parts, inspiring higher levels of trust and respect from the rest of world. Europe would finally obtain a single face and voice. As a response to Henry Kissinger's famous question, there would finally be a single European president, foreign minister and defence minister to answer the phone in times of need.

- Finally, one could not ignore the advantages of a single European external border linked to a joint European airspace and territorial domain. This unified space would serve as the basis for more coherent policies on immigration, border control, fisheries, exploitation of energy resources and other vital issues.

These joint structures would not necessarily demand full homogeneity, though. EF ambassadors could be selected, for instance, on the basis of their cultural background: francophone ambassadors for the francophone countries of Africa, Spanish-speaking ones for posts in Latin America, and ambassadors from the former Warsaw Pact region for assignment to post-Soviet countries.

In this chapter we explain our proposals for the geopolitical orientation of the EF, its two global strategic objectives, the financial and political viability of a joint defence force and its five strategic priorities, the EF's relations with NATO, the principles and objectives of an EF economic and cultural diplomacy and the creation of a European regional alliance with our larger neighbours (Russia, Ukraine and Turkey).

5.2. EF's global strategic objectives

5.2.1. Becoming a major geopolitical power

The EF's first strategic orientation in terms of global policy would be to attain major geopolitical power by developing its single economic space (the biggest or second-biggest in the world) and to function as a potent international military force (*see below analysis*). It would transform into a peer equal to the USA, Russia and China, and not a junior partner as is the case today. It would be able to protect its territorial integrity and vital interests, while helping ensure global and regional peace. This would be a natural, necessary and achievable development.

It would be natural, because the size of the EF would see it having one of the top three economies and populations on the planet, with an overarching need for its own defence capability. Indeed it would be unnatural, not to mention unwise, for the EF to remain a military dwarf next to Russia, its neighbour with less than one-third of the EU's population and one-tenth of its economy.[123] Geography, demography and wealth matter the most in global politics, and all three elements dictate that Europe must become, once again, a prime power player – this time, however, as a continent and not as the sum of different national states.

It would be also necessary for the EF to ensure its core character. In an uncertain century such as the 21st, there is no guarantee that Europe's interests and values will align with those of the USA, nor it is a given that the USA will remain capable or interested in ensuring Europe's future security. The EF's prosperity and economic development would depend heavily on its ability to set its own geopolitical agenda, from freedom of sea trade to space competition. We cannot remain forever under the constant protection or threat of other big powers that, in the long-term, would undermine the independence of our policy choices.

All this is, ultimately, achievable because the EF would possess the resources, economies of scale and the political framework to transform itself into a geostrategic force – elements that the EU and its individual member states cannot muster today. The EF's military would build upon today's highly developed forces of the UK, France, Germany, Italy, Spain, Poland and others, together with their existing nuclear arsenals. Together, they would merge and develop their technological achievements, research and intelligence into a structure offering much higher power projection.

5.2.2. Promoting a global model of governance based on federalism and humanistic values

As a prime geopolitical force, it would be in the EF's direct interest to support global governance that reflects its own federal model. The EF would work toward a world order that functions on the basis of rules instead of chaos; multilateralism instead of unilateralism; peace versus violence; and negotiations instead of confrontations. Moreover, the EF would bring to the centre of global action the threats we all now face: global warming, food and energy security, health crises and epidemics, and the challenges of artificial intelligence and automation. These can only be confronted via global co-operation, not competition.

The EF should first pursue a re-organisation of the United Nations. Our major objective would be the establishment of a new comprehensive UN Charter – a world constitution with binding provisions that regulate fundamental issues: the maintenance of peace through a global security system; nuclear disarmament and reduction of other arms; the free flow of trade and capital; monetary stability; respect for fundamental human rights and freedoms; secularism and religious freedom; gender equality; sustainable development; high public health standards; the mitigation of climate change; and a functioning system of international justice and enforcement of international rules. The new Charter would, to a large extent, replace various international treaties while incorporating the basic rules and principles of fragmented international law. It would, for instance, absorb the basic provisions of the UN Covenant on Civil and Political Rights, the International Covenant on Economic, Social and Cultural Rights and the United Nations Convention on the Law of the Sea.

The EF would also push for the creation of a global governing body, a "World Council", with enhanced powers to implement the Charter. The World Council would replace the current UN Security Council and be more inclusive. It would feature, as permanent members, all the great powers and regional blocks of the world such as the EF, USA, China, Russia, India, Japan, Mexico, Brazil and the African Union, plus any potential Latin American federation or future regional groupings that might emerge. It would include smaller countries as non-permanent rotating members, from all regions of the planet. The World Council's decisions would be taken by a qualified majority, allowing no veto power for its permanent members or, if so, restricted to very exceptional cases. Such decisions would be further subject to the scrutiny of the UN General Assembly which could veto them by a qualified majority (e.g. three quarters of the total votes) if the Assembly considered that a decision went against humanity's interests.

The Council's decisions would be enforced through economic sanctions, the suspension of certain rights of offending/derelict countries and – where necessary – military action.

All countries, as well as the World Council itself, would be subject to the jurisdiction of a World Court of Justice. The latter would replace the array of UN tribunals currently located in The Hague and elsewhere. Its rulings would be based on the UN Charter and be binding for all the subjects of international law.

We would like to stress how important it is for Europe, whether in its current EU form or as a future EF, to focus its efforts on this international stance. Diplomacy, regulatory frameworks, consensus, free trade and all forms of soft power are the natural tools of European action. They are our strong card and should remain our preferred fields of action.

Regardless of how the UN evolves, the EF would be an active protagonist in all important international fora. It would be a permanent member of the current UN Security Council (replacing the seats of France and the UK), a member of NATO and a major player within all UN bodies such as the International Monetary Fund (IMF), World Bank, World Trade Organisation (WTO) and any other institutions with a global mandate. The EF would participate in regional activities of global importance such as the Asian Development Bank (mainly controlled by Japan and the USA) or the Asian Infrastructure and Development Bank (mainly controlled by China). It would also participate in and, to greatest extent possible, have a say in China's Belt and Road Initiative whose goal is to build a vast transport and trade infrastructure from east Asia to Africa and Europe. And, as mentioned in the previous chapter, the EF would seek to retain the euro as a world reserve currency.

Finally, the EF would reach into its pockets to support international entities that promote its agenda. Many UN agencies are underfunded or face under-funding in the future, which means their development programmes would seriously rely on European assistance. The financial health and consequently credibility of this organisation is hostage to the recurring whims of the politics of its larger donor nations. A characteristic example occurred in October 2019 when UN Secretary-General António Guterres warned that, with a deficit of $230 million, the organization would run out of money by the end of that month.[124] As if that was not enough, the Trump administration directly attacked important UN bodies: in 2019, the U.S. formally quit UNESCO and threatened in 2020 to permanently cut off its funding for the World Health Organization (WHO). Europe must fill in important gaps in the international puzzle of multilateralism to help preserve the system, and especially as other big players, like China, are trying to occupy key UN posts.

5.3. Strategic priorities of EF military defence

5.3.1. Joint defence force: A financially realistic objective

As explained in the previous sections, a joint EF military force is a necessary condition to build a global geopolitical power and defend Europe and its interests. This would require serious financial commitments, a specific strategy and a clear framework of co-operation with NATO, our traditional alliance. The EF's security policy would need to embrace non-military aspects as well, such as research on dual-use military-civilian technologies and the challenges of hybrid warfare.

Financing a viable military would be realistic, given the scale of the EF economy. Assuming that the latter's annual budget would be around €8 trillion, it could annually allocate €300 billion for its military needs, or about 2% of the annual GDP of EU27 plus the UK in 2021 prices. This is an affordable expenditure which compares favourably to that of other major geopolitical powers. In 2020, for example, the U.S. spent $778 billion (3.7 % of GDP), China $252 billion (1.7 %), India $73 billion (2.9 %), France $63 billion (2.1 %), Russia $61 billion (4.3 %), and the UK $59,2 billion (2.2 %).[125]

Money spent on its military would remain largely within the EF's economy by benefiting European contractors, researchers and hundreds of thousands of employees. Moreover, military and civilian technologies go hand-in-hand nowadays: such research would boost non-military users and contribute to new industrial and scientific applications.

The perennial argument surrounding military spending is whether it expands or slows down an economy. That depends, of course, on how it is used. Expenditure on defence research and development has been falling in most European countries since the end of the Cold War and is duplicative due to its lack of co-ordination between the nations. The EU has made a very timid start to get that co-operation in defence going among the member states, both in research and development (R&D) and for defence capability programmes. However it is still lagging far behind the big geopolitical players. In 2017, for instance, the United States spent $55.4 billion on defence R&D, more than four times as much on defence R&D than the rest of the OECD countries combined. The United States spent 23 times the amount spent by the United Kingdom; 36 times the amount spent by Germany; and 39 times the amount spent by France.[126]

The EF would allocate a much bigger budget than the ones of the current EU member states combined, would impose tighter co-ordination and set more ambitious goals. The research, development, production, and marketing of defence material would, to a maximum extent, be limited to within its borders and reserved for its own enterprises. This would be an imperative for federal security but also for the sector's economic viability. Contractors would be strictly scrutinised and subjected to vigorous security clearance procedures. No or very few projects would be opened to geopolitical competitors or their companies. Retaining military expenditure within the European economic space would be a paramount objective.

Military resources would be allocated in the most efficient way possible by funding smart technologies based on artificial intelligence as part of the fourth industrial revolution. For instance, smart missiles or drones launched by simple platforms may be more efficient than developing expensive platforms such as ultra-sophisticated fighters or warships. In 2019, for instance, the technologically disadvantaged Huti rebels of Yemen deployed cheap drones and missiles to destroy critical oil refineries in Saudi Arabia, the region's richest state with the most advanced air defence systems. We do not argue of course that "light" and smart technologies should replace "heavy" ones across the board, but they should complement them and be part of a country's military arsenal, and thus merit investment in them.

5.3.2. The five strategic objectives of EF military defence

EF defence policy would have to be efficient and targeted. Its military doctrine should concentrate on the most important threats, while its resources should be directed to the most cost-effective programmes. We suggest the following five areas of strategic focus: defence of eastern land borders, defence from missile and air force strikes, freedom of vital sea routes, power projection in the European neighbourhood and hybrid and cyber-warfare.

1. *Protection of eastern land and sea borders*

Protection of the EF's eastern borders – from Finland and the Baltic countries down to Greece and Cyprus – would be a top priority. This could be carried out by a permanent stationing of troops along the most vulnerable parts of that frontier. This would strengthen the trust of the EF's eastern constituent states, given how heavily their peoples have suffered from wars, occupations and past oppression.

An adequate number of troops and military forces would have to be deployed in the Baltics and Poland. Russia's historic pattern of invasions would not be repeated with creation of the EF. Moscow's strategic "Zapad" military exercises, held in its Western Military District, Kaliningrad and neighbouring Belarus in 2013 and 2017, were warning signals to Europe against complacency. The EF would pay particular attention to defending the Polish-Lithuanian border, only 104 kilometres long, that connects the Baltics by land to the rest of Central Europe.

A first step in this direction has been NATO's 2016 Enhanced Forward Presence initiative, which deploys four rotating multinational battalion groups across Poland, Lithuania, Latvia and Estonia. These involve more than 4,500 troops led respectively by the UK, Canada, Germany and the United States, and form part of the biggest reinforcement of NATO's collective defense in a generation. However, they fall far short of containing any Russian attack. The four battalions' real purpose is deterrence, serving as "trip-wires", if attacked, that would trigger bigger reinforcements. Whether the latter would be deployed fast enough has yet to be demonstrated. According to war gaming scenarios, the longest it would take Russian forces to reach the outskirts of the Estonian or Latvian capitals is 60 hours, meaning the Western allies would be outgunned and outnumbered unless they could match that on site.[127] The EF would deploy much larger forces of troops, tanks, artillery and air force coverage to make sure that any land invasion from the east would simply be unthinkable. It would do the same on the Finnish border with Russia and along its Baltic territorial waters.

A serious military force would also be deployed along Bulgaria and Greece's borders with Turkey to protect the Balkans against any military threat from the southeast. EF military authorities would also plan for reinforced naval and air assets to protect the EF's territorial waters in the Aegean, east Mediterranean and around the island of Cyprus. The EF would expand its territorial waters to 12 maritime miles, from only 6 miles in Greece today, as would be its sovereign right under international law. It would also ensure the withdrawal of Turkish troops, illegally stationed in northern Cyprus since 1974, and absorb the entire island as part of the EF's sovereign territory, with equal protection for all of its citizens, Greek and Turks. This would be done via a diplomatic and political agreement with Turkey, which itself would have few other options, given the heavy geopolitical size of its federal European interlocutor. Turkey could then define its own Economic Exclusive Zone in the sea together with the EF and our other neighbours in western Asia and north Africa.

2. *Defence against missile and air attacks*

Anti-missile systems must be set up with a clear defensive orientation. To protect its millions of citizens, Europe must assume the responsibility to build a sophisticated shield against enemy rockets or drones. The future is now open to countless scenarios of war and other horrors, and it would be folly to underestimate the offensive capabilities of countries or groups to the east and south of our continent. We must be well-prepared for every scenario that could threaten the safety of our citizens and territorial integrity.

A wide range of missiles could be used against the entire European continent from Russia, Asia and even African countries. These include exo-atmospheric, long-range, and lower-tier short-range rockets and missiles. Though Europe relies mainly on US anti-missile systems, European missile makers are developing a new high-altitude missile interceptor. Involving France, Finland, Italy, The Netherlands, and Spain, it could enter service as early as 2030[128] as is a solid first step toward greater self-reliance in missile defence for Europe.

The best response would be a layered defence combining different types of assets with varying speed, altitude and distance capabilities. The EF would use interoperable, layered systems in different locations that worked together to detect any threat and quickly assess the best way of eliminating it.[129]

3. *Freedom of vital sea lanes*

Currently the French, UK, Italian, German, Spanish and other EU navies have many modern ships ready for deployment to address maritime threats. They consist of fleets of aircraft carriers, ballistic missile submarines, attack submarines, amphibious warfare ships, air-defence destroyers, anti-submarine destroyers, general-purpose and surveillance frigates, and so on. In 2020, the navies of the UK, France and Italy ranked, respectively, 5th, 6th and 9th on the list of the world's most powerful navies (below the USA, China, Russia, and Japan).[130] Combining the EU navies as a joint EF naval force would raise their collective ranking, yielding a formidable sea power.

EF naval forces would be permanently deployed in the Mediterranean, the Baltic Sea, the Black Sea, the Atlantic and the Indian Ocean to ensure that our commercial lanes remain open and safe. The naval forces would fall under European command in co-ordination with our NATO allies and other countries who share interests such as combatting piracy.

The EF would establish a naval base in the Indian Ocean region to ensure the freedom and safety of its critical trade routes which connect Asia, Africa and Europe. China established its first overseas military base in Djibouti, for example, which points to that region's geopolitical significance. Given the gradual melting of the Arctic's ice, a strong European naval base in that region would be necessary too, preferably in Norway, to guarantee freedom of the new sea routes, also crucial for this century's international trade. An Artic base would primarily control the waters of the Barents Sea, which is already dominated by Russia's powerful Northern Fleet, based in Severomorsk. Elsewhere, safeguarding the eastern Mediterranean, close to the Suez Canal, the Middle East, and potentially vast natural gas reserves, would be a strategic priority too. The EF would thus develop a powerful naval base in Cyprus, preferably in the area currently controlled by the UK in Akrotiri and Dhekelia.

4. Power projection in Europe's neighbourhood and beyond

Intervention in regional conflicts is always a hard and delicate choice, for which no successful patterns of planning exist in advance. But it is sometimes a necessary evil: one must bear in mind the notion of the "responsibility to protect" according to which the international community is obliged to protect innocent citizens from criminal brutality of their own government or other forces, if their government fails to do so.

One need only think of the massive suffering that regional conflicts have inflicted on their populations and the impact on Europe's security and immigration policy. Experience since the 1990s has shown that the tragedies of Bosnia, Kosovo, the Caucasus region and Syria could have been averted, or at least mitigated, if a strong mix of diplomacy and military action had been deployed at an early stage.

To reinforce that mix in future, an "EF Rapid Reaction Force" would be established with a solid mandate, adequate resources and viable operational capabilities. It would be based across the federation's Mediterranean region in proximity to neighbouring areas most likely needing intervention, namely North Africa and the Middle East. Its mandate would extend to interventions as a response to any form of organised attacks from those areas, such as raids by terrorists groups (ISIS, Al Qaida, etc.), criminal organisations or other threats that may emerge in future.

5. Hybrid warfare, cyber warfare and intelligence

Security derives not only from military defence. We have entered an era of hybrid warfare where military strategy blends conventional, political and cyber-warfare techniques. Hybrid warfare techniques can produce environmental disasters on the territory of the attacked, disrupt electricity supply or disgorge disinformation campaigns, to name just a few of the tactics. They may involve aggressive financial speculation against strategic financial assets prior to a physical attack. They may even manipulate immigrants and refugees, allowing them to flow into an adversary's territory, as Turkey did in February 2020 along its land border with Greece in the area of Evros, and as Belarus did in the summer of 2021 against Lithuania and Poland.

Disinformation is the ever-evolving tool of hybrid war, not only attacking our democracies but national security as well. According to an Oxford University 2019 report, several sophisticated state actors use computational propaganda for foreign influence operations, among whom the most prominent are China, Russia, Venezuela, Saudi Arabia, India, Iran and Pakistan.[131] They use Facebook and Twitter, in particular, to influence global audiences, with some of these campaigns unfolding during the most sensitive period of the COVID-19 pandemic. Those efforts aim to destabilise European citizens' trust in their governments, demoralizing the public and lowering its confidence in their own state security.

Elsewhere, the EF would have to seriously engage in space military systems, treating satellite technology as a strategic imperative. Americans are rapidly advancing in this area. The U.S. established its Space Force in late 2019 as a special warfare branch of its armed forces. The EF would follow the same path. The mission of its space force would focus on satellite communications, support to nuclear commands, communications and detonation detection, missile warning and space domain awareness. It would also launch many satellites to create a dense network for those missions. Indeed, a plethora of cheap satellites, instead of a few expensive ones as is the case now, would offer strategic depth, better accuracy and less vulnerability to attack. Multiple layers of the platforms would facilitate navigation data, terrestrial monitoring, the detection of hypersonic weapons, and the widest range of defensive or offensive options. Those objectives will be developed by the U.S. in the coming decade, and Europe needs to swiftly catch up.[132]

The EF would need to invest in special forces trained for the encryption of satellite communications and the protection of EF military information technology. It would dedicate resources to guard against "denial of service attacks" where aggressors use digital overloading to render a device or network unavailable. As the "internet of things" advances, those attacks could disrupt things far beyond the military sphere and vital to daily life. They could target, for instance, infrastructure critical for the operation of automated cars, home applications, refrigerators, washing machines, solar panels or medical devices, to name just a few.

The EF would substantially invest in cyber-defence, hiring and training the most qualified people for the task.

The role of artificial intelligence (AI) will be crucial. Europe and NATO started acknowledging it. In 2021, the alliance started writing a new strategy for artificial intelligence and finalised its first cyber-defence policy in several years. At the NATO summit of June 2021 leaders discussed a 'transatlantic technology accelerator' to connect suppliers of cutting-edge military technology investors. But the Secretary General, Mr. Stoltenberg, expressed a serious concern about competition with China: "a country that doesn't share our values" is pulling ahead in key areas like artificial intelligence. "It's not obvious that we will maintain the technological edge ... that was never the case with the Soviet Union during the cold war."[133]

Artificial intelligence will also play a central role in espionage and the collection of intelligence. According to a study by the UK's Royal United Services Institute (RUSI), future enemies could exploit AI to develop "deep fakes" where a computer generates false videos of real people to misguide public opinion and manipulate elections or significant social trends.[134] Artificial intelligence will be absolutely necessary for the intelligence communities to manage huge information volumes and filter what is essential for solid analysis and advice. Therefore, the EF would need to set aside serious funding for investments in advanced technologies for intelligence and counter-intelligence activities, which would complement its cyber-defence efforts.

5.4. Membership of NATO

This text advocates the military emancipation of Europe, but it also acknowledges the need for a close partnership with our allies in all areas that require resources and action at inter-continental scale.

The EF would be full member of NATO, like the majority of the EU's member states today. It would closely work with the USA, Canada and other NATO partner countries in those areas where global interests are at stake. There would be added value in the close co-ordination of nuclear deterrence strategies, anti-missile defence, space and cyber-warfare, anti-piracy and anti-terrorism.

In 2021, NATO counted 30 member countries, the most recent being North Macedonia which joined the alliance in March 2020. This latest accession was important to help contain Russia's influence in the Balkans. In 2019 the allies' collective military expenditure stood at slightly more than one trillion U.S. dollars, or about 2.5 % of their collective annual GDP, while their total military personnel was more than 3.2 million[135] – larger than the population of any of the Baltic states. The EF would maintain these numbers.

Under the maximalistic scenario envisaged by this text, whereby the highest possible number of European countries would join the new federal state, the EF would replace 27 of NATO's current members, meaning that the alliance would merely consist of it, plus the USA, Canada, and Turkey. It would mean that the USA would no longer deal with many different junior European partners, but with an equally powerful and perhaps competitive ally. The very size of the new federal European state would change the balance of powers within NATO, which would need to redefine its priorities.

As a result, Americans might even ask European forces and resources to contribute to the protection of North America, in the way America has done for Europe since the end of World War II. The transatlantic community's overall strategic stance may indeed need some readjustment: instead of containing Russian expansion as its primary goal, NATO would need to take on a more global role to deal with Asia, thus also becoming a "North Pacific" alliance and not only "North Atlantic". Strategy depends on the circumstances of each era. More than 70 years old, NATO's longevity lies in the fact that it has adapted to the challenges of its time. However today, it seems ill-prepared to deal with the increasing military and political power of Russia and China. It has steadily maintained ad-hoc missions in Kosovo (since 1999) or Afghanistan (between 2001 and 2021), but has failed to comprehensively address the large strategic challenges of the 21st century as it did during the Cold War. For instance, NATO has no robust response to China's expansionism in the South China Sea or Russia's invasion of Ukraine, and is still feeling its way for dealing with disinformation campaigns, cyberattacks or other methods of destabilisation.[136] We believe that a strong geopolitical partner such as the EF would contribute far better to a grand strategy than the many small and introverted European states of today.

That said, we need to accept that history is not a static process and that alliances do not last forever. The EF would be a member of NATO only as long as the latter was necessary and willing to serve Europe's geopolitical interests. The isolationist Trump presidency of the U.S. has raised serious doubts about the two continents' converging interests on international stage – doubts already elicited, albeit at a lower level of intensity, by former US President Barack Obama's "pivot to Asia" regional strategy of 2012. The AUKUS security partnership between the U.S., Australia and the United Kingdom, which in September 2021 bypassed France and other EU powers, confirmed further that direction. The EF should not exclude the option of re-examining its position within NATO or seeking other defence partners, if that was key to its interests and values in the future.

5.5. Economic diplomacy

Economic diplomacy is defined in several different ways, depending on its objectives. These usually include access to foreign markets for national businesses, attraction of foreign direct investments to a national territory and influencing international economic and financial rules. Economic diplomacy also involves the use of rewards and sanctions to enhance geopolitical interests or promote values such as human rights or environmental protection. The concept has historically shifted from the narrow scope of business promotion to the wider notion of promoting all major national interests.

Regarding EF economic diplomacy, the key strategic objective would be for the federation to become a major, self-sufficient pillar for an open, globalised system. It would be in the EF's interest to focus its international economic policy on the free movement of trade and capital, given Europe's singular volumes of trade and investment with the rest of the world. The EU is the world's largest trading block, particularly for manufactured goods and services, and is the top trading partner for dozens of countries.[137]

At the same time, however, globalisation has seriously hurt some parts of the European economy due to the ruthless competition by countries of other continents that exploit cheap labour and low environmental and safety requirements. While globalisation can be a positive force for boosting wealth in poorer countries, we also have to make sure that it functions according to fair and just standards.

We would thus support the following strategic objectives for the EF's international economic policy: preserving an open trade and investment system with fair standards, creating appropriate rewards and sanctions to enhance the EF's geopolitical interests, and applying specific economic policy to the European neighborhood.

5.5.1. Maintain an open trade and investment system

The EF's first strategic objective under its economic diplomacy would be the removal of trade and investment barriers at global and regional levels. In the late 2010s and early 2020s, protectionism seemed to be gaining ground, with borders less open than before. The cause lies in several factors, including the rise of national populist governments across the world, introverted U.S. economic policies under the Trump presidency, and the COVID-19 pandemic's destabilising impact. In the longer-term, however, globalisation will probably continue within our century due to the world's growing population, wealth, inter-connection and interdependence. We should not fear globalisation but, instead, try to use it to our benefit. After all, a globalised economic environment is the best for exporting our high quality products, attracting investments and ensuring continued business opportunities for our companies. Just as important: in the next decades, approximately 90 % of global growth will take place outside the current EU's borders and this is a "party" we should not miss.[138] For growth and job creation at home, the EF would have to actively engage with ever-increasing economic activity abroad.

It must be stressed that protectionism works to no one's interests. It makes our small world even smaller and poorer. It blocks countries and their people from new opportunities. Trade wars and the adoption of tariffs and non-tariff measures frequently lead to the closure of enterprises, job losses and missed opportunities to attract investment or to invest abroad. Protectionism leads to fall in demand for goods and services, props up inefficient firms and reduces the opportunities for economy of scale and specialisation vital to so many firms. According to a 2017 study by the World Bank, *"a worldwide increase in tariffs up to legally allowed bound rates, coupled with an increase in the cost of traded services, would* *translate into annual global real income losses of 0.8 percent, or more than US$634 billion, relative to the baseline, after three years. The distortion to the global trading system would be significant and result in an annual decline of global trade of 9 percent, or more than US$2.6 trillion relative to the baseline in 2020*.[139] That analysis remains relevant for all periods, not just for 2017–2020.

The EF would defend and promote at all levels the principles of open trade and investment. It would work closely with its partners to re-design the WTO's rules and principles. It would renegotiate with regional blocks, such as ASEAN and Mercosur, and hammer out bilateral agreements with players big (such as India) or small (such as New Zealand or Angola) to ensure the freest possible move of goods, services and capital. In brief, the EF would strive for a new international economic federalism where people and nations have the possibility to develop their economic potential via trade under common rules. This is the only framework that enables the EF to optimally support its export-oriented business and thus ensure growth at home.

On the other hand, it is indisputable that labour costs in developing countries are much lower than those in Europe, which makes their products far more competitive. Labour protection often falls well below acceptable norms in poor regions of the world, ranging from under-age workers (children), forced labour, exhaustive work hours, bans on trade unions and the right to strike, ultra-low wages or abominable health and safety conditions. Exports from these countries, of course, exploit those factors, with the risk that the price competition could force other countries, including those of Europe, to lower their standards in a "race to the bottom". And developing countries are not the only ones participating in the race. During the EU's – ultimately failed – negotiations with the US to create TTIP ("Transatlantic Trade and Investment Partnership"), there were serious concerns in Brussels about pressure from Washington to push EU to significantly lower its environmental and food safety requirements, for the instance in the case of import into the EU from the US of chicken processed with chlorine.[140]

The EF's main goal in this regard would be to reverse the trend in favour of a "race to the top". This would be in the interest of our firms and economy, and of humanity in general. It would have to be fought on all levels: local, regional, global. The EF would push for higher labour, health and environmental standards in all sectors, especially when drafting international rules.

It would also pursue a rigorous anti-dumping approach at all levels, in line with the WTO's anti-dumping rules (dumping occurs when a party exports a product to a target market at a lower price than it sells the product in its home market, which is often achieved thanks to its lower production costs vis-à-vis the export market). The EF would pursue anti-subsidy policies to block foreign governments from granting financial assistance to companies that export to Europe in order to unfairly capture a share of the latter's market. Anti-dumping and anti-subsidies policies would be linked for a coherent trade defence policy, with the EF using many more investigators and other resources than the EU does today. Big data collection and AI systems would be developed to trace dumping trends and subsidies worldwide much more swiftly and accurately than the situation today.

Such elements would be crucial for the transformative power of the EF to projects its goals to the rest of the world. If we do not succeed in raising the level of international trade and production, we risk losing our moral and economic compass.

It is worth mentioning that, with its huge economy, the EU already has significant regulatory clout that affects business all across the world. The "Brussels effect" has impelled international companies everywhere to apply the EU's rigorous standards on privacy, quality and safety rather than their own national rules, even when the latter are less stringent. They do that to gain access to our large market, and we should continue to press our advantage in that respect.

5.5.2. Use of economic leverage to enhance the EF's geostrategic interests

International economic policy and geopolitics are mutually influential: a strong geopolitical position helps expand a nation's economic interests, while its economic policies can either strengthen or weaken its geopolitical position. The EF must frame its economic diplomacy in harmony with the idea that it is, and must remain, a major geopolitical player.

The EF would be generous toward its geopolitical allies and countries that respect its interests and values. It would offer clear incentives to them regarding mutual investments, development aid, and favourable access for their goods and services produced in, or exported to,

European markets. Those countries would clearly realise the benefits of co-operating with the EF. One historic example is the Marshall plan, that most significant tool of economic diplomacy created by the U.S. for the economic recovery of western Europe in the aftermath of World War II. Between 1948 and 1951, the U.S. allocated $12 billion (equivalent to almost $130 billion in 2020)[141] to the plan. It sparked not only the continent's economic regeneration but planted the seed for its geopolitical rebirth with the beginning of western Europe's integration, the reduction of communist influence and the creation of NATO.[142] It was a brilliant case of economic diplomacy serving the geopolitical interests of the donor in full, as America was able to simultaneously profit from a solid geopolitical partnership on the other side of the Atlantic and a huge export market for its post-war economy. The EF should derive inspiration from it.

It should be noted that today the EU and its member states are, collectively, the world's leading aid donors. And Europe is committed to increasing that contribution by donating at least 0.7 % of its gross national income each year. The EU and its member states are also the biggest financial contributors to climate-change adaptation programmes in developing countries. EU development policy aims to foster the sustainable progress of developing countries, with the primary aim of eradicating poverty.[143] In 2019, the combined development aid from the European Union and its member states reached €75.2 billion, or 55.2 % of global assistance.[144]

The EF would retain the EU's objective of being the planet's largest aid donor, and would annually allocate €100 billion, a third more than current EU commitments. This would focus on helping developing countries create carbon-free circular economies, high levels of education, birth control and the absorption of advanced technologies into their economies. It would set conditions for fair environmental, safety, and labour standards, while promulgating fair access for EF business to their economies.

On the other hand, the EF should not hesitate to use sanctions against countries that threaten its security or violate its core values or international law and peace. They could take many different forms: arms embargos, non-tariff barriers, oil and natural gas sanctions, freezing financial transactions and investments, and so on. Sanctions are more effective if co-ordinated at international level, so the EF would strive to have these imposed by the United Nations or other competent international bodies. Also, sanctions are more fair and effective when targeting those individuals and companies most responsible for a country's misconduct, as opposed to targeting an entire population. Imposing them on the entire oligarchy of a repressive regime would be an example.

The global disinvestment campaign against the former apartheid regime of South Africa offers another way sanctions can effectively support a progressive cause. This campaign by governments and non-governmental organization peaked in the 1980s, forcing the South African regime to launch talks for the abolition of apartheid in the early 1990s. However, and unfortunately, such successes are still rare. According to a study by the Peterson Institute for International Economics, only 35 % of all cases of sanctions imposed by the U.S. between World War I and 1990 produced any positive results for the country's foreign policy goals. For sanctions to work, certain conditions must be met, ideally between two countries with a previous history of friendly relations and trade: the goal must be modest, the target country small, the sanctions imposed quickly and decisively to maximise impact, and the sanctioning country must avoid high costs to itself.[145]

The size and impact of the EF would fulfil many of those conditions to make sanctions more effective than usual, while recognizing that sanctions are usually reciprocal and can hurt the interests of the nation that launches them. However, the EF should be ready to accept retaliation from the other side if so needed. This would be important to gain long-term respect from friends and foes, and for reinforcing its image as a principled global leader.

5.5.3. Economic diplomacy with Europe's neighbourhood

The EF would focus on intensifying its trade and investment links with other parts of the Mediterranean, the Middle East and post-Soviet countries. It is in Europe's direct interest to have prosperous neighbours. Poor ones export criminality, insecurity and extremism. Prosperous neighbours increase business opportunities, investments, and the mutual flow of services, tourists and students. A region of prosperity is usually a region of peace.

There is huge potential for investment in North Africa's agriculture and solar energy. Even larger potential exists in the vast territory of Russia, other post-Soviet republics and Turkey.

EF emphasis would go to energy and food security, technical know-how and high-tech services. It would build on the EU's existing European Neighbourhood Policy, which aims to foster common interests with partner countries to the East and South and a commitment to work jointly in priority areas. Through this policy, the EU offers partner countries greater access to the EU's market, regulatory framework, standards, its agencies and programmes.

The EU has provided support to partners worth over €15 billion during 2014–2020.[146] The EF would devote higher financial, human and diplomatic resources to extend its economic ties with these neighbours compared to the rest of the world. It would annually allocate to them half the amount of total budget for development aid, namely €50 billion out of a global amount of €100 billion.

5.6. Cultural diplomacy

Which has had greater impact on the world: the U.S. military or Hollywood? The English Navy or the English language? French colonisation or French philosophy and literature?

In an increasingly inter-connected world, national cultures have emerged into aspects of a global culture. We have all become a bit American, English, French, Spanish, Brazilian or whatever without even realising or admitting it. Depending on our exposure or interests, we are all influenced by foreign cultures and we have consequently developed our preferences, stereotypes or prejudices towards those nations. Increasingly, we visit those lands as tourists or students, do business with them, consume their products or even join their battles of various kinds.

Culture may serve as the long, soft arm of a nation to the rest of world. A state can exercise its cultural diplomacy in an organised fashion to achieve its political or economic goals abroad, or to strengthen its geopolitical interests and national security. The historic example of "pingpong diplomacy" that marked the thaw in Sino-American relations is characteristic. Here exchanges of table tennis players between the U.S. and China in the early 1970s paved the way for the unprecedent US-China meeting between their leaders in 1972 and thus the beginning of a new era for relations between them, and for global geopolitics.

Cultural diplomacy can contribute to conflict prevention, post-conflict reconciliation or the fight against violent extremism. It can support global campaigns for sustainable development and inclusive growth. It may also generate economic benefits: according to one study, cultural and creative industries represent around 3 % of global GDP, while in the EU alone they account for over 7 million jobs.[147]

Europe has traditionally used the high quality and diversity of its arts and culture to "export" ideas of democracy, freedom of expression, rule of law, environmental protection or gender equality. The EF should continue that tradition in a more organised and systematic fashion. It would develop its own coherent cultural diplomacy to have a transformative impact on people around the world. Its ultimate strategic objective would be the use of European culture and values as a tool to enhance Europe's interests and alliances, and as a tool to help the rest of the world exploit those values in their own interests and thus that of humanity as a whole.

5.6.1. Principles and tools of cultural diplomacy

The European Commission and the EU's High Representative for Foreign Affairs and Security Policy promulgated in 2016 several guiding principles for EU action in the area of international cultural relations, which also seem appropriate for future EF policies.[148] We would like to highlight several, which we consider the most relevant to the EF's objectives: promoting cultural diversity and respect for human rights; fostering mutual respect and inter-cultural dialogue; encouraging a cross-cutting approach to culture that includes (beyond the arts) tourism, education, research and the protection of cultural heritage.

The list of tools in support of cultural diplomacy is long: the arts (film, dance, music, painting, sculpture); language programmes; scientific, educational or other exchanges; creating libraries abroad; the translation of popular European works of literature into non-European languages; broadcasting of news and cultural programmes; religious diplomacy and inter-religious dialogue; promotion of ideas and social policies, such as gender equality or education for all.

The EF would use all of these in their various forms. Culture and arts, as policy, require a creative imagination – and cultural diplomacy should be imaginative as well.

Cultural diplomacy could be exercised abroad or within the EF territory via Europe-based media and institutions, for instance.

5.6.2. Cultural diplomacy practised abroad

The EF would establish "European Civilisation Centres" in foreign countries to promote Europe's culture, values and image. These would host libraries, art exhibitions, seminars and speeches, film sessions, theatre, dance, culinary and other festivals. They would offer training and language courses, art courses and information about European education and opportunities for professional and academic development in Europe. Their message to local people should be clear and optimistic: Europe is a beacon of civilisation, stability, and hope. Come there to get to know us, and we will gladly share mutual ideas, inspiration and opportunities for a brighter life.

We also need to make sure that, when cultural policy is exercised in a foreign country, it should be as inclusive as possible: its design and implementation would have to involve local civil society, educational and cultural institutes, artists, intellectuals and the media. In particular, cultural diplomacy should target young people, as they are more receptive to novel messages and could later prove to be long-term allies for European values and objectives.

Europe's international cultural policy should be standardised but also flexible enough, depending on the nature of the recipient people: Latin American people may be more interested in certain aspects of European culture, while African or Asian might be more interested in others. The EF would be flexible to adapt its policies to the features of each nation.

5.6.3. Cultural diplomacy practised in the EF territory

Cultural diplomacy would also take place domestically. The EF would establish TV and web-channels on its territory in all the most spoken languages of the world, with a focus on European culture and values. International cultural relations would become a standard subject of EF university curricula and research. Specific training programmes would be offered to European business or artists drawn to cultural relations.

International cultural policy, when designed and implemented in the EF territory, should be inclusive as well. It would involve civil society and institutions with experience in international co-operation. It would further involve the embassies and consulates of all foreign countries to explore the most effective channels for co-operation in the arts and education.

5.6.4. Cultural policy vis-à-vis Europe's neighbouring regions

The EF would give special attention to developing cultural ties with its neighbouring regions of North Africa, Middle East and the post-Soviet republics, allocating more resources for its cultural policy towards those countries than others.

Europe's cultural ties to Russians, Ukrainians, Belarussians, Moldovans, Arabs, Turks, Israelis, Georgians, Armenians and other peoples of our "near abroad" are strong, with deep historical roots. The EF would strengthen these ties by fostering a regional policy of dialogue, friendship, and trust. It would send a message of inclusiveness, namely that our common regional interests are much more important than any of our differences. The idea would be to make them feel fortunate to have a powerful neighbour oriented toward peace, freedom and prosperity.

The EF would build its regional cultural policy on a series of projects developed by the EU. We derive inspiration from current or earlier programmes such as the EU's support for the Anna Lindh Foundation in the South Mediterranean; the programme "Young Arab Voices" that deepens the dialogue between young leaders and civil society representatives to develop counter-narratives to violent radicalisation; and the "Community-Led Urban Strategies in Historic Towns" project that seeks to stimulate development by enhancing cultural heritage in towns across Armenia, Belarus, Georgia, Moldova, and Ukraine.[149]

5.7. Strategic Alliance with Europe's three big neighbours

The EF would have a vital interest in creating a partnership with its three biggest European neighbours of Russia, Ukraine and Turkey due to their proximity and importance to our politics, economic activity and security. In doing so, the EF should identify its common strategic interests with all three to reach a joint understanding of what all can and must do together.

Such co-operation should not be viewed as a mere desire, but a necessity. Together, the four actors share more than what divides them. They all face serious competition from the huge Asian economies, which continue to advance on the basis of lower labour and environmental standards. They are all challenged, to different degrees, by the chronically insecure Middle East. They are all secular democracies (Turkey however less than before) that must confront religious intolerance and extremism in various forms. And they are all complementary to each other in terms of trade and economy, because:

- the EF would offer the biggest market in the world, a very large population, advanced industries, high level services, and investment and consumer wealth;
- Russia offers energy resources, heavy industry, metals, minerals and vast space for further development;
- Ukraine has significant agriculture and food production, metals, machinery equipment, transport equipment and chemicals industry;
- Turkey offers the gateway to the East and the Muslim world, together with industrial potential in the areas of textile, manufacturing, mining and food processing.

Joint action and co-ordination by these four powers would turn all into a formidable market of more than 750 million people and a combined GDP of more than €20 trillion in 2021 prices, with unlimited resources and great potential in many areas.

At the time this text's writing, several intractable problems stand in the way: Russia's 2014 annexation of Crimea; the war in Syria; disinformation and other hybrid attacks launched by Russia against Europe; and tensions between Turkey, Greece, Cyprus and the rest of Europe over control of sea areas and migration movements.

What needs to be done to achieve a long-tern understanding? Firstly, a dialogue should commence among the four sides with the aim to identify, as a starting point, their joint strategic interests. A brief proposal is presented here per country:

5.7.1. Russia

A permanent and lasting solution must be found to the presence of Russian or Russia-backed forces in eastern Ukraine, Crimea, Transnistria and Georgia. Russia needs to withdraw from them and offer guarantees that it will respect the territorial integrity of its European neighbours, including all post-Soviet countries. At the same time, Moscow would have to be reassured that EF-Ukrainian relations posed no threat to Russia's vital interests but represented instead an opportunity to boost the economy of the entire area.

Russian capital, workers, exchange students and scientists should be welcome in the EF and Ukraine. The total value of EU-Russian trade was about €175 billion in 2020, higher than the value of Russian trade with any other part of the world. Despite the sanctions imposed on it since the Crimea annexation, Russia remains the fifth trading partner of the EU, while the latter is Russia's first trading partner. As for the origins of imports into Russia, the EU accounted in 2020 for 37 %.[150] The two economies remain vitally interlinked and will continue to do so.

It should be stressed that the heavy geopolitical weight of the EF would more likely extract concessions from Russia and a more reasonable approach towards its weaker post-Soviet neighbours or other European states. As mentioned above, the EF would have world's second biggest defence force; Russia, which traditionally respects power more than international rules, could be expected to treat it with more trepidation and respect than it exercises today toward the EU or Europe's individual countries, whether Germany, France or a post-Brexit UK. As a geopolitical giant, the EF would be able to exert more pressure on Russia for a multiplicity of objectives: ceasing Russia's paramilitary operations in eastern Ukraine, finding a settlement for Transnistria, reducing or even abandoning its disinformation campaigns and cyber-attacks, halting Moscow's energy-based blackmailing, and constructing a more cooperative attitude. It would be much harder for Russia to play European countries against each other, as it does today by hustling, for instance, Hungary, and it would be much easier for Europe to improve its trade, investment and overall business position with that vast and resource-rich country.

Russia must make a realistic strategic choice because, over the long-term, it will have to compete harder against Asia than against Europe. It should thus treat Europe as its most reliable partner and ally. This is the geopolitical destiny of both, and what global competition requires.

5.7.2. Ukraine

Europe should reassure Ukraine about its territorial integrity and offer substantial support for its economic growth. The EF would back direct investments in Ukraine, access for Ukrainian products to the EF market, technical support, and a shared view on agricultural, energy and food production. Ukraine needs great assistance to strengthen its weak institutions and to orchestrate a harmonious co-existence of its two main linguistic groups of Ukrainian and Russian speakers.

A good first step was the EU's 2014 Association Agreement with Kiev. It entered into force in 2017, with the two sides committed to co-operate to help Ukraine converge its economic policy and legislation with that of the EU across a broad range of areas: energy, transportation, industrial co-operation, gradual progress toward visa-free movement of people, consumer protection and cultural co-operation. Much of the agreement covers the Deep and Comprehensive Free Trade Area (DCFTA), which offers Ukraine greater access to EU markets and investments.[151]

The EF would use this agreement as a starting point for its co-operation with Ukraine. Priority would go toward reforming Ukraine's judicial system and supporting its anti-corruption policies. European firms need a safe business environment and a transparent judicial framework in order to operate there. The EU is today Ukraine's largest trading partner, accounting for more than 40 % of its trade. In the recent years it has also been one of its biggest investors. Conversely, however, Ukraine's exports to the EU are not that significant for Europe's economy, as Ukraine accounts for less than 1 % of the EU's total trade. This imbalance would see the EF play its cards, as the stronger partner, in a responsible way.[152]

It is clear that both sides are very valuable to each other in the long-term. The EF would need Ukraine as a partner and buffer towards Russian expansionism. It would also rely on Ukraine's fertile territory for its food security. On the other hand, Ukraine would heavily depend on the EF to safeguard its prosperity, democracy and territorial integrity vis-a-vis Russia. Indeed, the two sides are destined to fight common battles on several fronts, therefore it would be better to do this under a more structured framework.

5.7.3. Turkey

Turkey needs to move closer to Europe; this is becoming more crucial than ever. Turkish citizens should be convinced, like Russians, that their long-term interests lie within a large European space rather than the complex and often bloody political framework of the Middle East.

Europe must help Turkey to gain access to its markets and services. Under conditions, it would grant to Turkey preferential treatment and close investment partnerships. It must also help the country with its burden of hosting of immigrants and refugees from the Middle East and Asia, and to defend itself against radicalism and the problems arising in its immediate neighbourhood.

At the same time, Turkey should understand that any deviation from its agreements with the EF would have serious consequences. Given that waves of immigrants from Asia and Africa are expected to continue over the next decades due to war, poverty or environmental problems, the EF would need to make clear that Turkey could not turn refugees into policy instruments or view Europe as a permanent conduit for endless streams of illegal immigration.

The EF would closely monitor Turkey's human rights record. This is heavily tainted by the current Turkish regime's persecution of its opponents (suspected or real), following the attempted 2016 coup against President Recep Tayyip Erdoğan, and by Turkey's oppression of Kurdish and other ethnic groups. In this respect, the EF would have huge financial leverage: the EU is by far Turkey's number one import and export partner, as well as a significant source of foreign direct investment.[153] Finally, Ankara would have to withdraw its military forces from Cyprus, abolish the "Turkish Republic of Northern Cyprus" and recognise the whole island as part of the EF's sovereign territory.

5.7.4 Assessment: A more universal approach

A more universal approach is needed to foster an enduring alliance with these three countries. The accession of Turkey and Ukraine to the EF under the "Copenhagen criteria" (explained in Chapter 3) would remain as a continuation of EU policy. Even if that process does not work, however, the two countries must be treated as strategic partners in many critical areas.

A comprehensive deal on energy supply must be concluded among all four powers. Ideally, all existing and future pipelines, such as North Stream, Turkish Stream, Trans-Anatolian and others, should be developed in a complementary manner, as long as natural gas is still used as transition fuel on our way to reach carbon neutrality. A healthy and transparent competition between the pipelines and their operators would be welcomed because it would serve the long-term perspectives of all sides involved.

A universal agreement should also be reached on the abolition of visa restrictions and free movement of people within this big European area. Millions of Russian, Ukrainian and Turkish people are young and well qualified to move into the EF and offer their potential. EF citizens should also be encouraged to move into, and work in, Russia, Ukraine and Turkey: these countries are in need of European knowledge, talent and investments. In brief, the people, goods, services and capital of all four powers must remain and grow within this common European space and not drain away elsewhere.

The final step for dialogue should be the creation of a new organisation to co-ordinate the four participants' common strategic interests. An ambitious but accurate name could be "E.STR.AL" (the European Strategic Alliance). Other states, such as Moldova, Belarus and those of the Caucasus region, could join as well. The organisation's remit should cover energy, joint infrastructures, freedom of trade and investments, security, and technological and scientific co-operation. It could build on work already developed by the Organisation for Security and Co-operation in Europe (OSCE), the Energy Charter[154] and other initiatives.

5.8. Concluding summary and budgetary aspects

The EF would set two strategic objectives with regards to its role in the world: to become a major geopolitical power and to achieve a global model of governance on the basis of federalism and humanistic values. This is important to protect its interests and project its power and values at a global stage. It can be better achieved with a joint defence force and foreign policy, which will turn it into a global heavy weight.

The EF would set five strategic priorities for its defence and security: defence of eastern land borders, defence from potential missile and air force strikes, freedom of vital sea routes, intervention in regional conflicts and conduct of hybrid and cyber-warfare. To this end, the EF would annually allocate €300 billion. That expense would be the second highest in the world, trailing only the defence expenditure of the USA., but it would be affordable since it would amount to less than 4 % of annual GDP. The EF would be member of NATO, supplanting that of NATO's European states. This would be a significant step forward for creating the EF federal state as a self-sufficient geopolitical power able to defend its integrity and interests on the basis of its own resources.

In addition, the EF would allocate €320 billion for internal public order and safety, namely federal, state and municipal police forces, border security, intelligence, fire-brigades and all other services necessary for the safety and protection of the broad population. This would correspond to something like 2% of the EF GDP, while, in 2018, the corresponding rate was only 1.7 % for the EU.[155]

The EF would develop its own comprehensive policy of economic diplomacy, with three strategic objectives: maintain an open trade and investment system with fair standards; use of economic leverage to enhance its geostrategic interests; and employ specific economic diplomacy with its neighbourhood.

It would annually allocate €100 billion for investments and development aid to third countries, with a focus on carbon-free and circular economies, advanced technologies, education and health. Half of that amount would be dedicated to its immediate neighbourhood with the goal of surrounding Europe with prosperous and peaceful neighbours.

The EF would develop its own policy on cultural diplomacy to promote European values across the world, and promote its interests and geopolitical position. To that purpose, it would dedicate €10 billion per year, with €4 billion allocated to the establishment and operation of European Cultural Centres in all countries around the world.

The EF would seek to build a sustainable partnership with its three biggest neighbours: Russia, Ukraine and Turkey. This would focus on key issues where interests converge: energy security, food security industrial and technological development and competition with the Asian and other markets. In order to ensure a more strategic framework for the partnership, we propose the creation of the "European Strategic Alliance", E.STR.AL., to develop in a more co-ordinated manner the work of existing organisations and initiatives.

Chapter 6

Socio-cultural governance

6.1. The need for a joint identity and sense of European society

A state cannot be viable in the long-term if its people lack a sense of a common identity and society. Only if citizens share this feeling of participating in something bigger than themselves can they build a real society, state, and vision. This has been achieved with significant success in strong federations, such as the U.S. or Germany. However, the lack of a common identity presents one of the most difficult challenges for the EU today. It would be a similar challenge for the EF tomorrow. As long as Europe is viewed solely as an economic or geopolitical project, it will fail to galvanise its citizens or gain their hearts and minds. A common identity and culture are essential to create the emotional bonds needed to make this vision a solid, functional, and lasting project. The same stands for the shaping of common social policies and attitudes, which largely differ across the EU today.

Europe is perhaps unique with its relatively small geographical space but large diversity of cultures. In 2021 the EU had 27 member states and 24 official languages, plus another 60 indigenous or non-indigenous languages.[156] Moreover, our corner of the world is home to the three main branches of Christianity (Catholic, Protestant and Orthodox), millions of Muslims and many deeply rooted Jewish communities. Leaving such numbers aside, Europe consists of many different cultural blocks with specific traditions, attitudes and values. One could cite a long list of European cultural worlds: Scandinavian, Francophone, Anglo-Saxon, Germanic, Latin Mediterranean, Slavonic, Baltic, Greek, Magyar, Roma, and so on. That list could be further broken down into endless anthropological, ethnic, linguistic or cultural groups.

This text makes the case for a united Europe. So, should we see that immense diversity, with respect to such an objective, as an obstacle or a driving force?

We should not mince words: a common European identity is still a remote target. Most of Europe's inhabitants are emotionally connected to their nationalities and languages rather than to their continent. What is missing is a joint language and political consciousness to bind them together. The average citizen of the USA is above all "American" and secondarily "Californian" or "Floridian". This is not yet the case in Europe, and perhaps it never will be. Language is the main hindrance to a common identity. Language constitutes the agent of thought and self-determination, and thus can function as a strong barrier or bond between people. As long as we lack a single European language, we have to accept that the European project is subject to serious limitations. Moreover, language is not the only divider. There is a long history of conflicts, wars and antagonisms, as well as diverse educational systems, religious beliefs and geographical circumstances that have kept European people entrenched within their own identity groups for centuries. This is a reality that cannot be ignored or disrespected. How, then, should we move forward with such a mosaic?

In our understanding, the issue of identity points to two essential questions.

First, how to assure people across Europe that their new federal state would respect and foster their national and other identities? And second, how to forge a parallel European identity to reinforce the EF, and in what areas?

Concerning the first question, this text proposes the idea of a *union of identities*, namely a federation of nations, cultures, languages, ethnicities and religions that serves mutual respect and interests within the collectivity. People must be convinced that their identities can be best defended within a large and free space based on tolerance and communication rather than closed borders, nationalism or local chauvinism. A minority language spoken across national borders can be better protected within a federal union than within an individual country. A national historic archive can best be developed within a robust European cultural policy rather than within the shrinking national budget of a small state. And national pride could grow, if the respective nation belonged to the strongest federation of nations in the world – the EF.

The EU has long supported projects linked to diversity and identities: all those EU programmes for multilingualism, historic treasures, educational institutions, cultural education and so on. That policy should continue and be reinforced. A federal Europe would persistently communicate the message that identities are best preserved within a common political space where wealth, health, social cohesion and human rights are adequately ensured. A federal Europe must help people realise that nationalism, chauvinism, xenophobia and closed borders have historically destroyed the identities, traditions and cultures of people rather than promoting them.

The EF's constituent states would maintain all the elements considered important for their distinct identities. They could keep their flags, emblems, national anthems, national broadcasters, national academies or national sport teams. They would continue to be the main entities responsible for their history, language, culture, and traditions. Where applicable, they would retain their kings or queens as ceremonial leaders of their nations.

As for the second question: we believe that, gradually over time, a parallel European identity could emerge and grow. There are already some encouraging examples of this. People accept the EU flag as their second one. When they see it flying outside their public buildings next to their national ones, they feel reassured rather than threatened or offended. They also accept the EU logo on signposts outside their local school projects, bridges, roads or hospitals constructed with EU funds. They are also happy to hold an "EU" passport which simultaneously functions as a Belgian, Portuguese or Bulgarian one. This is an EU "identity acquis" which must be appreciated as a major accomplishment of the last decades – and one worth building on.

We should build institutions that help citizens identify themselves with the European idea in a soft and natural manner. Here are three examples. The first would be a European media network to connect Europe's citizens to one another along the lines of *Euronews* and *Eurovision*, which have been a good start. Second, a European research centre with tangible breakthrough-achievements would instil pride in Europe's public; CERN, the European Organisation for Nuclear Research, and ESA, the European Space Agency, are brilliant examples. And, there would be the goal of installing a single EF consulate to replace all national consulates across the world to offer administrative support to all citizens – a possibility excluded today since EU member state retains its exclusive competence in foreign affairs.

Finally, the joint EF citizenship, guaranteeing for those people a common passport, ID card, rights and duties, would be itself a very strong tool towards forming a common identity. It would constitute a strong bond of pride and solidarity in many respects.

Many other similar ideas could be imagined, examples of institutions or projects that would capture the trust and imagination of the EF's citizenry without offending or placing in doubt their other identities. The success of such efforts would gradually build, brick by brick, the sense of a common European belonging that complements national ones: a common European identity that should be seen as an added value and enrichment of one's national or regional identity.

Some ideas in this direction have been discussed in other parts of this text, in particular concerning cultural diplomacy or civic education. This chapter introduces ideas for creating a common framework for social policies to strengthen the common bonds of EF citizens. Belonging to the same social infrastructure makes one feel equal and closer to his or her fellow citizens and their community. These are the areas of social protection, education, health, and programmes that support social cohesion. We elaborate on those topics in the following sections.

6.2. Social protection

Social protection is arguably the most costly, sensitive and complicated part of public policy in all European countries. It involves millions of beneficiaries, dozens of categories of allowances, billions of expenditure, decades of administrative working hours and kilometres of red tape. Experts and non-experts alike have great difficulties grasping the full picture of a country's social protection system. It is hard to follow the debates about which categories of citizens should be entitled to what benefits, which categories should be excluded, and whether such choices would be fair or affordable. In countries with advanced administrations, this is a headache. In many other countries, with messier administrations and poorer resources, it is a nightmare.

Social protection benefits in EU member states today are largely grouped in eight categories: old age (including pensions), sickness/ healthcare, disability, survivors (including survivors' pension), family/

children, unemployment, housing, and social exclusion benefits not else-where classified.[157]

We believe this system is too complicated and consequently unfair. It should be urgently simplified to become fairer and more efficient. We would thus propose a four-tiered model of universal social protection across the EF to replace all existing programmes. This would consist of the following: (a) a universal basic support for every citizen under 65, without exceptions or special conditions; (b) a universal basic pension for every citizen older than 65, without exceptions or special conditions; (c) universal sickness / health care coverage for all, without exceptions or special conditions; and (d) special allowances for people with disabilities

Before entering into the details, some basic figures need explanation. The EU28's population as of 1 January 2019 was approximately 513 mil-lion people. Young and working age people (up to 65 years old) num-bered around 412 million, while those older than 65 numbered some 100 million.[158] In 2018, the last year that data were available for EU-28, expenditure on social protection stood at €3,6 trillion or 26.7 % of GDP of the EU's annual GDP.[159]

6.2.1. Universal basic support

There has been much debate in recent years about the feasibility of allocating a universal basic income ("UBI") from cradle to grave. It aims to ensure a minimum of social cohesion, social justice and a dignified life for all. Among other things, it would be a response to the expected rapid advance of artificial intelligence and automation, which are predicted to increase wealth production but also wipe out millions of human jobs. People should be compensated for that loss through UBI.

There is no experience yet anywhere in the world with the introduc-tion of a permanent general scheme of universal basic income. Some pilot UBI projects have been run but with still inconclusive results. One of them was carried out in Finland by the Helsinki University as Europe's first national, government-backed experiment. It ran during 2017 and 2018 and involved payments of 2,000 randomly selected unemployed people across the country with a regular monthly income of €560, with no obligation to seek a job and no reduction in their payment if they accepted one. It found that that the programme did not do much to encourage recipients into work, but did improve their mental well-being and life satisfaction.

Following the outbreak of the COVID-19 pandemic, the idea gained more attention all over Europe due to the massive closure of businesses and the loss of millions of jobs. Spain began examining the allocation of a basic income to around one million of the country's poorest households as a provisional scheme, with a view to turning it into a permanent programme at a later stage. A similar idea had been expressed by Scotland's first minister, Nicola Sturgeon.[160]

Regarding the EF, we would propose as a first step the allocation of a universal basic support of €300 in 2021 prices for each EF citizen, from birth until the age of 65. It would be directly paid by the EF state budget on the first day of each month. Based on the current demographic figures, this would roughly cost the EF budget €1,440 trillion per year across today's EU-27 plus the UK (400 million people under the age of 65 × 12 months x €300).

This would function as a basic safety net in that €300 would be high enough to prevent someone from sinking into the abyss of destitution. But we also consider this amount low enough to prevent complacency and laziness among its beneficiaries. People should be motivated to work and explore ways to make themselves and their societies richer. We also need to protect the public budget from excessive spending. This is why we call for a universal basic "support" and not "income", because it is not meant to provide full subsistence for everyone.

The universal basic support would replace all social allowances linked to unemployment, social exclusion, family/children protection, the death of a breadwinner in the family and so on. However, it would not replace the equivalent salaries of part-time or full-time work. Practically, this means that a civil servant with a salary of, say, €1000 or an employee in the private sector with the same would receive the €300 on top of their salary.

Our proposal would offer fixed monthly support of €600 for a couple, €900 for a household of three, €1200 for a household of four, and so on. This would offer individuals and families some basic means to move on with their lives and to overcome any temporary reversals in their fortunes.

After a certain period of time, we would support the introduction of a full-scale universal basic income, instead of just a basic support as we do now, provided circumstances allowed – for instance, if large-scale auto-mation generated sufficient wealth to ensure adequate living standards for all members of the society. But we are not there yet.

6.2.2. Universal basic pension

All people aged over 65, regardless of their past or current occupation or wealth status, would be entitled to a universal basic pension of €700 per month in 2021 prices. This would be financed directly by the state budget and not by individual pension funds. It would not depend on previous social contributions by the pensioner or his/her employer; in fact, all obligatory social and pension contributions by employers and employees would be abolished. Based on the current demographic fig-ures, this would cost the EF budget roughly €840 billion per year across today's EU-27 plus the UK (100 million people over the age of 65 × 12 months x €700).

The logic of a universal basic pension rests on the assumption that people over the age of 65 deserve a safe and dignified conclusion to their lives. They are not able to work as hard or as productively as during their younger years, thus they deserve an amount substantially higher than the universal basic support.

A person wishing a pension higher than €700 or a pension earlier than the age of 65, or both, could voluntarily contribute throughout his/her working life to a complementary pension scheme to enhance its pen-sion rights in a proportionate manner. Such a scheme could be offered by the state or by competing schemes organised by regions, trade unions or the private sector. Any person who paid the respective contributions to the private or public scheme during its earlier years could begin receiv-ing a complementary pension at age of, say, 55 or any time thereafter. However it would be forbidden for the state to use public money to bail out any of the funds if it went bankrupt. We need to protect our public finance from the failings of private insurance. In this respect, all private schemes would have to be strictly regulated to avoid risky and speculative behaviour that jeopardised the life-savings of citizens.

6.2.3. Universal health care and sickness allowance

Health care and sickness protection must be simplified and made more transparent. Therefore, we propose a system of universal health protection as part of the overall social protection system. Every EF citizen would be assigned a Personal Health Account at birth for the duration of his/her life. The EF would fund each account with €1,000 per year, starting from birth. This would cover the cost of visits to hospitals, general practitioners and specialists, basic dental care, plus medicine, treatments, and anything else needed for the prevention or treatment of health problems.

Any unused amount at the end of a given year would be carried over and accumulated in the account owner's balance. Thus, a young person would have the possibility to save a lot of money during his/her healthy years that could be accumulated and used for subsequent illness in older age. For instance: a person who spent an annual average of €700 during its first 60 years would accumulate some €18,000 (300 unused euros per year × 60 years), available for subsequent health expenditure. At any rate, the person would continue to receive €1000 per year into their health account until death.

For annual health expenditures higher than €1,000 per year, EF citizens would have to cover the extra costs from their own pocket or via a public or private insurance scheme, as described above for pensions. Such schemes could be run by an EF administration, or national, regional or private organisation.

The funds in a Personal Health Account would be tied to each individual and not transferable to any other account. In case of death, any unused surplus in the account would be returned to the state budget.

In addition to the amount allocated to a Personal Health Account, the EF budget would set aside for society €200 billion per year to cover special health coverage for serious cases involving operations or expensive treatments. This would be allocated to people in need, according to criteria that take into account the severity or urgency of each case and the patient's financial situation. For instance, priority would be given to people of extremely low-income for cancer treatment, urgent operations or treatment of rare diseases.

The universal health protection would thus cost the EF budget approximately €700 billion per year. This would be the combined cost of €500 billion for universal health coverage (500 million people × 1,000 euros) plus €200 billion for special health coverage, as explained above. It would yield a simple, affordable, fair and effective system. It would replace today's subsidised universal health care of the EU member states and would be complemented by the programmes outlined in the next sections, where we propose the creation of a Primary Healthcare Network offering very cheap primary health care at points near to where people live.

It should also be highlighted that several billions of euros would be returned each year to the state budget from the unused amounts of deceased owners of Personal Health Accounts.

The universal health protection we advocate would complete the big picture of social protection, along with universal basic support and a universal basic pension. It would be the financial expression of the idea that health is a basic social right, ensuring that no one is left behind in life due to health problems. It would also stimulate people to be more proactive with their own health care since it would offer them the means to pay for routine annual check-ups, laboratory tests and visits to general practitioners.

6.2.4. Special allowances for people with disabilities

In addition to their universal basic support, pension and health care allowances, people unable to work due to serious disabilities would be entitled to a special monthly disabilities allowance for a dignified life. This would be proportionate to the degree of disability and the financial situation of the beneficiary. For instance, a higher percentage would be reserved for people with serious disabilities, the blind or those restricted exclusively to wheel-chairs.

The EF budget would dedicate an annual amount of €100 billion to that end. This would be disbursed as direct subsidies to those individuals and would also finance investment in rehabilitation centres.

6.2.5. Pros and cons: Universal social protection

Simplifying complicated social welfare systems always sounds like a positive step. But there is a flip-side too: the risk of treating everyone the same, regardless of their needs or potential. The same could happen with the universal social protection system we propose for the EF. There are five main points of potential criticism, but we think each could be effectively addressed by our proposed approach.

(1) *Inequality.* The proposed measures are inherently unfair: the same basic universal support would be received by an unemployed

young person as an economically comfortable citizen. Why would a millionaire, for example, need 300 euros per month while that amount could be allocated to those who truly need it?

Indeed, universal social protection introduces certain injustices. However, injustices occur anyway under Europe's existing social protection systems due to different national frameworks and standards, disparate funding levels, fraud or insufficient statistics. Injustices also flow from political interference in favour of groups with better access than others to political lobbying. There are many scandalous cases in EU member states where certain professionals receive early, high or multiple pensions simply because their trade unions had stronger influence over decision-makers than others. There are also many cases where particular pension funds were bankrupted and consequently rescued by a public budget at the expense of taxpayers or other pension funds. Finally, there are millions of cases where people undeserving of particular social benefits manage to obtain them due to fraudulent evidence or the abuse of vague or unfair criteria. This is an inherently unjust situation that would be terminated by the system proposed here.

It is true that, under our proposal, people of all social classes would receive the same basic support, regardless of their financial situation. On the other hand, we need to acknowledge that nobody can predict what will happen in their life in two, ten or twenty years ahead: people move up and down the social ladder for a wide range of reasons. Some people may be middle class one year and then the lower-income class the next. Think of the millions who saw their social status sink due to the economic crisis of 2008 or as a result of the pandemic of 2020. With a universal basic support scheme, those individuals would have been spared destitution. It is the only way to ensure that the safety net of social protection has no loopholes and no weak spots.

(2) *Uneven value.* The amounts of the universal social protection would not have the same value across the EF's diverse territory. The amounts of €300 for the universal basic support, €700 for the universal basic pension or €1,000 for the universal health coverage would produce very different purchasing power in Paris versus a mountainous Romanian village or a small Spanish town.

The problem of different purchasing powers of salaries would not be new or unique to the EF. That difference is a reality today in all the world's large countries where living standards vary from region to region or city to city. It is not possible to adapt every salary or price of goods to the purchasing power of each local economy. People should select their place of residence according to several factors, including the cost of living of a given area. One could further argue that universal basic support would help poor regions converge towards the richer ones. This would consequently help smooth out the gaps in income purchasing powers across Europe.

(3) *Illiberalism*. Universal basic support is socially unfair and goes against the principles of liberalism: people with no ambitions would become even more complacent. Many would simply withdraw from the production process to lead a life of low expectations at the expense of their fellow citizens still determined to work and create.

In our world view, the system we propose is close to the principles of liberalism. It would redeem business from all social contributions. It would reduce labour costs and thus boost employment rates in many areas. Thanks to its simplicity, it would substantially reduce bureaucratic red tape, judicial disputes and state interventions. It would help alleviate the worries of ambitious people about their daily survival and enable them to pursue their dreams. After all, universal basic support is not meant to introduce a socialist system of wealth re-distribution, but a safety net that stimulates creativity, productivity and freedom of choice. These are all liberal values.

(4) *Inconsistency*. The universal pension limit of age 65 would be very high for vulnerable groups of people who – for whatever reason – would need to leave their work at a younger age. How are they going to cope during those last years before attaining the age of 65?

The universal basic pension aims to ensure that people of non-working age enjoy a dignified life. People younger than 65 are presumed fit for work, therefore they should seek for employment. If suffering from a serious disability, they would be entitled to the disability allowance as proposed above. If wishing to retire earlier, they could opt for a special pension scheme granting them an early pension prior to age 65. In any case, they would be entitled to the universal basic support of 300 euros per month. As said before, that amount might increase if so needed due

to the rise of automation and artificial intelligence and the creation of
the necessary wealth that could sustain a high level of social protection.

(5) *High cost.* The amount of social protection (€3 trillion) is very
high, roughly 42 % of the state budget proposed by this analysis.
Such an approach would introduce a socialist model of general
wealth re-distribution that risks undermining the public budget
and overall economy.

The universal social protection we propose would be affordable and
more predictable: yes, it would cost up to €3 trillion – but less than it did
in 2018, when the last figures for EU-28 became available. A significant
part of this would replace today's costs of allowances linked to unemployment or poverty. It would be part of an EF budget only little higher
than the total public budget today of the EU and all of its member states
combined. In addition, it is reasonable to expect that such a simple and
business-friendly model would contribute to higher wealth production,
more consumption, and higher revenues for the state. It would also help
avoid serious costs to the public budget arising from criminal activity since there would be fewer ways to "game" the system and fewer
health problems across the population by introducing a universal social
safety net.

To sum up, a universal and simple social security system would benefit the entire society. We believe that such a universal social protection
proposal would be simple, transparent, and largely impervious to political lobbying. It would provide for a general safety net that not only
supports individual citizens but also society as whole. It would mitigate
many poverty-related ills such as criminality, drug use, trafficking, pros-
titution, homelessness, suicides, alcoholism, domestic violence, mental
and psychological stress, divorces, extremism, and so on.

One could easily think of families that would stay together thanks
to their guaranteed monthly income instead of suffering the break-ups
that extreme poverty often creates. One could imagine young people
who would be less tempted by gangs and criminality. One could further imagine that homeless people who would no longer be forced to
live on the streets, as they could afford a modest rent or share quarters
with others. Finally, one could think of all those who would experience
lower levels of anxiety and lower rates of mental or stress-related disease.
The lists of potential social benefits is endless. Such a safety net is not
merely about money; it is, above all, about social values, quality of life

and human dignity. It is about our common social pact than no one should be allowed to sink into the abyss of financial desperation. Such solidarity would increase Europe's overall public morale, confidence, and ambition.

6.3. Education

Education is a human right and the bedrock of social progress. One of the main challenges for each society in the 21st century will be the quality and content of its educational system. In the era of knowledge-based economy, education does play the most important role. Its mission is to produce rationally-minded citizens who understand the realities of an ever more complicated world and conceive a good sense of the origins and destinations of their societies. It should also foster skilful human resources that can adapt to the technological developments of the new professional demands.[161]

Today, education in the EU faces several problems. European students are taught different curricula under varying standards of quality. Educational poverty and inequality thrive in many geographic areas and social groups, with a university education less competitive than it used to be. A fresh approach is necessary at European scale, one guided by a new vision. In an increasingly competitive international environment, young Europeans will need to be highly equipped with a solid intellectual background and advanced skills. This will be crucial to all spheres of private, business and public life.

We have identified the following set of strategic objectives for an EF education policy: a common European curriculum for primary and secondary education; reduction of educational poverty and inequality; linking education to the labour markets of the 21st century; and achieving world-class universities and research centres. We elaborate in the following sectors on all of them.

6.3.1. A common European curriculum for primary and secondary education

In federal systems, education traditionally falls to the competence of the federation's constituent parts, namely its states or regions. This would be the same for the diverse composition of the EF. Italian pupils have a particular interest in Italian geography, German pupils in German history, Lithuanian students in their language, and so on. Such interests must be respected and served. Education is a classic example of the application of the principle of subsidiarity, at least with regards to the teaching subjects. This should remain so in the EF.

We also think, however, that in a globalised world a strictly national approach to education would not be enough. Additional elements of a universal education would be needed in several areas such as mathematics or science, which obviously extend beyond national or local identity. As mentioned in the introduction to this chapter, the development of a common European identity would constitute a prime mission and pillar of the EF.

We therefore propose the development of a European curriculum – one that complements national ones. It would be obligatory for all primary and secondary educational institutions across the EF. It would include subjects such as European history and culture, principles of ecological development, humanistic values, "health literacy" or the elements of basic health campaigns as explained in the next section, as well as civic education with a focus on the EF's institutions, values and mission.

The European curriculum would also include mathematics, physics, chemistry, biology, astronomy, geology, natural history and European and global geography – all subjects that rise above national or regional perspectives. This layer of education would reinforce the reading, science and mathematics skills of European pupils and thus our region's competitive position in a highly globalised world. The EF's constituent states would retain their competence over subjects of national history, language, geography, religion, culture and anything else related to the specific aspects of their national and regional identities.

Both the national and European curricula would be taught in the local or national language of the respective pupils. In addition to their native tongue, all EF pupils would learn English, the modern universal language, as well as a third European or other language.

This common European curriculum would be crucial to fostering a sense of joint European identity and belonging. It would be an unprecedented step in our continent's history: all European children, whether living in the mountains of Slovakia, Greek islands, Irish villages or large German cities, would grow up receiving the same basic knowledge and common set of European values. This should be seen as one the most fundamental revolutions of the European project proposed by this text.

6.3.2. Reduction of educational poverty and inequality

Educational poverty is usually defined as those exposed to sub-standard education or failing to enjoy acceptable educational standards.

A 2019 survey of the EU-28 revealed serious levels of underachievement among 15 year-olds: 19.7 % in reading, 22.2 % in mathematics and 20.6 % in science.[162] According to the same survey of 2017,[163] over half of all 15 year-olds with low socio-economic status in Bulgaria, Cyprus, Romania, Greece, Slovakia and Hungary underperformed in mathematics. At primary educational levels, 18 % of students did not learn any foreign languages.

There are also problems of school drop-outs and access to education. Data show that the average drop-out rate for the EU-28 stood at 10.6 % in 2018.[164] There is a high probability that early school-leavers are subsequently either inactive or unemployed, illustrating how educational poverty has long-term and serious personal and societal repercussions. The situation is particularly problematic for students from lower socio-economic backgrounds and minority ethnic groups.

All those problems have been most probably exacerbated due to disruption of schooling during the pandemic of 2020–2021. According to a report of 'Save the Children Italy' in January 2021, 28 % of teenagers aged 14–18 said that at least one classmate had completely disappeared from online lessons. Just before the pandemic, in 2019, a study by Openpolis found that in the regional capital Naples, dropout rates were as high as 19 %. Many teachers worried that some pupils would not return in September 2021.[165]

The situation of teachers also affects educational poverty and inequality. Over 60 % of education expenditure across the EU is devoted to the salaries of education professionals, which are very low in certain EU member states. At the same time, the European teaching force is characterised by a striking gender gap (far more women than men) and shows significant demographic ageing in many countries.[166] Only in a few EU member states is mentoring at the initial stages of the career and continuing professional development compulsory for teachers.[167] Low salaries, excessive workload, high stress and unnecessary administrative burden are factors that typically lower the attractiveness of the teaching profession.

Educational poverty and inequality should thus be treated as serious societal challenges for Europe. It goes a long way toward explaining why the potential talent of many young people across the continent is being wasted, a situation that aggravates and maintains poverty, exclusion, and inequality. This is utterly unfair because children bear no personal responsibility for the failings of their societies. The EF should therefore treat reduction of educational poverty and inequality as one of its main strategic objectives. In this respect, it would adopt a set of measures to ensure higher qualifications and motivation for teachers, investment in school infrastructure, and incentives for school attendance.

All teachers of primary and secondary education in the EF, regardless of their state of residence, would fall under the same salary regime, funded directly by the EF budget. That salary would ensure solid living standards and offer a serious incentive to young people to join the profession. Teachers would enjoy life-long training and mentoring opportunities. Two weeks each year (e.g. at the end of the school year) would be set aside exclusively for their continuing training, mentoring, and consultation. They would also be subjected to regular assessments of their pedagogical skills and subject knowledge.

A specific portion of the EF's education budget would be dedicated to the refurbishment and modernisation of all school buildings to improve their functioning and appeal for both pupils and teachers. It is unacceptable, as is the case in many parts of Europe, to have schools with heating or water problems, ruined toilettes, rudimentary sports facilities or no laboratories. Classroom levels would not exceed 25 pupils. To address these issues, an EF inventory of all primary and secondary schools would be created to better manage current and future school infrastructure.

Every school would offer free or subsidised meals for all children. This would relieve the budgets of lower-income families and encourage poorer children to attend classes instead of dropping out. Schools would offer extra-curricular activities to develop the skills and talents of pupils, thus motivating them to continue their school attendance.

6.3.3. Link education to the labour markets of the 21st century

Many jobs once fundamental to the economy are now being phased out, as new technologies render them obsolete. On the other hand, the need for novel specialisations will emerge from new dynamic sectors. These jobs will require advanced digital and technological skills and a multi-disciplinary background. We are entering a very competitive and globalised working environment where a knowledge-based labour market will be in high demand.

The European educational system should provide a framework for responding to these challenges.

The EF Ministry of Education would establish an "Expert Council on Future Skills" consisting of education experts, representatives of industry, employers and employees. The council would supervise and coordinate the curricula of higher education to adapt them to the emerging needs of labour markets, and engage with employers to develop university curricula and research (examples: use of blockchain, virtual reality, clouds). It would advise on the direction of technical education and the vocational skills to be developed at high school level. Indeed, pupils and students would need to be guided, at the earliest possible stage of their lives, towards the most relevant jobs for their future.

The steering bodies of universities would, for their part, include representatives from industry and professional sectors. This would be instrumental in ensuring that higher education remains relevant to the skills needed by modern enterprise. This approach would be also in line with our proposals in chapter 9 for expert bodies that connect business to education, research and training.

The EF would also lend strong emphasis to the vocational training of young people. It would follow the successful example of Germany, which pursues a dual-vocational training programme. The German system's main characteristic is its co-operation between small and medium-sized companies on one hand and, on the other, publicly funded vocational schools. Trainees typically spend part of each week at a vocational school and at a company, or they may spend longer periods at one before switching to the other. Dual training usually lasts from two to three-and-a-half years. There are around 350 officially recognised training programmes in Germany, so the chances are good that one of them will suit a young person's interests and talents. Employment prospects for students who have completed a dual-vocational training programme are very high. This is one of the reasons why around two-thirds of all students graduating school in Germany go on to start a vocational training programme.[168]

6.3.4. World-class universities and research centres

Higher education and its links to research and innovative business is instrumental for producing highly skilled and qualified citizens.

Europe is no longer setting the pace in the global race for knowledge and talent, while emerging economies are rapidly increasing their investment in higher education. There are approximately 2,700 universities in Europe.[169] Too few of them are recognised as world-class in the global university rankings. According to ShanghaiRanking Consultancy's "Academic Ranking of World Universities", only five of Europe's universities in 2020 were included in the top-20 of the world, of which. only one is in EU-27, and only four EU-27 based universities made it in the top-40.[170] This should be seen as a major warning sign for Europe's competitiveness and overall position in the world.

Europe needs a wide diversity of higher education institutions, but at the same time a co-ordinated re-focus of the institutions' strategic priorities to achieve world class excellence in specific sectors. The EF should provide a new favourable framework in terms of resources, programming, and overall vision.

As in many other policy areas, efficiency of resources and economy of scale would be indisputable advantages compared to the mix of individual EU member states. The EF's robust and sizeable economic framework would ensure better funding of cash-starved universities, better allocation of resources to strategic priorities, and better co-ordination of programmes and research projects.

Resources would stem from the EF's public budget, the budgets of its constituent states as well as partnerships with business, industry or international universities. A minimal fee (e.g. 300 euros per year) would be required for each student. This would support the administrative functioning of each university and would also motivate students to take their studies more seriously and complete them in the swiftest possible fashion.

EF authorities would do strategic planning to re-examine the comparative advantages and purpose of each European university. Such planning would establish education hubs of excellence and determine the conditions and investments needed for each of them. How could we create a European MIT or a European Harvard? Higher education would be instrumental in the accomplishment of almost every objective of this analysis. The EF would thus focus on several measures.

Funding for higher education would be at least €100 billion per year. Institutions would be granted more autonomy to manage their financial resources. Core curricula would be updated by business and research communities. Students would be offered short-term apprenticeships to early connect with real employment. Existing university sectors and departments would be reallocated across Europe to reinforce the weakest universities and, where necessary, merge the latter with stronger ones. A well supported accreditation agency would be established to rank European universities according to widely acceptable standards and increase their incentives to compete for higher performance. This would be crucial to university hiring based on a standard EF-wide assessment and qualification of candidate professors. Direct links would be created between a university's performance versus the size of its student body and the amount of public funding it would receive. Funding sources would be diversified and partnerships would be created with research institutes, businesses and regional authorities.

6.4. Health

Health is a value in itself and a human right. It is commonly seen as the most important aspect of people's lives – more important than money or any other material possession. Every organised society has the obligation to put the good health of citizens at the top of its social agenda – a basic pre-condition for individual and common happiness, prosperity, progress, and overall fulfillment. Every expenditure on health should be seen as both a moral duty το our fellow citizens and a public investment.

The health sector is a significant source of economic expansion and jobs. It offers a high potential for European innovation and growth. In 2019, 7 % of all persons employed and nearly 4 % of the total EU-population worked in the health sector.[171]

The 21st century is setting the scene where health battles will be fought. Climate change is expected to affect global health, for instance, through rising temperatures and increased rainfalls in certain areas. Advancing urbanisation, longer life expectances and antimicrobial resistance will also create the conditions for new, or revived microbial and other diseases in many parts of the world and especially in Europe. Diseases are globalised too: local epidemics can easily turn to pandemics, as it has been the case with HIV/AIDS and COVID-19.

The challenge for our society is to find ways to maintain and capitalise on our health achievements while focusing on new or chronic diseases. We should tackle this together with our international partners and under the auspices of the World Health Organization (WHO). The notion of universal health coverage, as adopted and promoted by WHO, will be instrumental toward this goal. It rests on the idea that *'all people and communities can use the promotive, preventive, curative, rehabilitative and palliative health services they need, of sufficient quality to be effective, while also ensuring that the use of those services does not expose the user to financial hardship'.*[172] It embraces the objectives of equity in access to health services, good quality of health care, and protection of the poor from financial risk when using those services.

Against this background, three strategic objectives have been identified in our analysis for the EF's health policy: strong investment in preventive programmes to avoid later suffering and high health costs; making Europe a global 'health hub'; and achieving a cost-effective health policy. These objectives would be complemented by the universal healthcare protection presented in the previous section of this chapter, as part of the overall social protection system.

6.4.1. Invest in preventive programs to avoid later high health costs and suffering

Health spending is regarded as an investment with significant yields.[173] Investing in disease prevention can reduce costly long-term treatment and prevent dozens of thousands of premature deaths and chronic diseases. We should base our policies on the assumption that one extra public euro spent against smoking or obesity, for instance, would avoid the future costs of 10 or more euros needed to deal with the consequences: heart attacks, many forms of cancer, brain strokes, diabetes, and ulcers, not to mention of course immeasurable psychological pain.

Three major preventive approaches the EF could support are distinguished: creation of a Primary Healthcare Network, the launch of information campaigns to target the root causes of health problems and, finally, the adoption of a set of regulatory initiatives to mainstream health with other policies. Focus should shift from short-term initiatives to long-term investments.

– Primary Healthcare Network

A major argument in favour of the EF's creation would be the economy of scale of its programmes and cost savings derived from merging

27 or more national systems into a single European one. This is why we need a single EF National Health System where all resources would be allocated and distributed in a rational manner across the European continent.

A main pillar of this system would be the creation of basic health care stations to cover the entire EF territory: the Primary Health Care Network. This would aim to create one primary healthcare station per 10,000 people, with none more than 30 kilometres' distant from any EF inhabitant. We estimate this would require a total of 50,000 stations to achieve such a ratio (to cover a total population of 500 million). It would also require an additional few thousand stations to serve the inhabitants of isolated areas such as mountain towns, islands and overseas territories.

Each station would have a standard minimum set of equipment and employ an adequate number of general practitioners, nurses and specialists to offer standard services such as first-level examinations, consultations, medicinal prescriptions, first aid, basic health check-ups and vaccination.

Admittedly, the system might be costly, especially in its initial phase of development. However, it could also turn out to be the most economical solution as it would reduce subsequent direct health costs (hospitalisation, surgeries, emergency care), indirect costs (lost work days, lower productivity, reduction of private income, increase of insurance costs) and a great deal of personal suffering. One should note that, in 2016 alone, 27 % of all patients in the EU went to emergency services because primary care was not available.[174]

– Information campaigns

To achieve an effective health policy, people's personal engagement is of paramount importance. They are the ones ultimately responsible for taking care of themselves and improving their life style. Therefore, targeted campaigns must be launched as part of the EF's overall health prevention policy. We see the need for the following six campaigns, namely to: discourage smoking; counter obesity; fight alcoholism/drug abuse; improve driving safety; promote physical exercise and contact with nature; and improve health literacy. These campaigns would become integral parts of the EF educational system and its civil education policy.

Smoking would be prohibited in all public places, cafes, restaurants and bars, and this prohibition would be strictly and consistently enforced.

It is morally unacceptable to expose millions of non-smokers to the detrimental effects of nicotine. In 2018, 26 % of Europeans smoked, which continues to be the largest single cause of preventable death and disease in the EU. The EF's campaigns would build on the successful examples of the EU's own campaigns, which have helped reduce smoking rates across our continent compared to previous decades.[175] We are inspired by the great success of anti-smoking campaigns in France, for example, where there has been a sharp fall of one million daily smokers in 2017–2018 alone. Measures that contributed to France's success include higher cigarette pricing, campaigns such as the country's national "tobacco-free" month, reimbursements for using tobacco substitutes, and special packaging. Picture warnings of the physical effects of smoking on human body can be very effective in deterring people from that habit.[176]

The EF's campaign against obesity would address the mix of causes and practices that underlie the problem. These involve the quality, quantity and timing of food consumption, lack of exercise, and personal issues of metabolism. Obesity is a serious issue in Europe. In the mid-2010s, the proportion of overweight adults in the EU varied between 54 % in the Netherlands and 68 % in Croatia for men, and 36 % in Italy to 55 % in Malta for women.[177] According to WHO, Europe had the second-highest proportion of overweight or obese people in 2014, behind the Americas.[178] The European public needs to be informed of the complexity of the problem, its horrible consequences for personal health and the means to address its roots.

The campaign against alcohol and drug addiction should take account of the particular sociological variables that come into play. It would focus on regions and social classes where the problem is particularly acute. Drinking patterns and the type of alcohol consumed (wine, beer or spirits) vary significantly from one EU member state to the next. For instance, the alcohol consumption per capita in Sweden and Malta was but one-third of that in the Czech Republic and Hungary in 2018.[179] However, alcohol consumption remains substantial across all EU-member states and is an issue that we must acknowledge as a serious health challenge. Indeed, the EU is the heaviest-drinking region in the world, with over one fifth of its population aged 15 years and above reporting heavy episodic drinking (five or more drinks on an occasion, or 60g of alcohol) at least once a week.[180]

Elsewhere, the EF campaign for driving literacy would be obligatory for all the population, including pedestrians and the drivers of all classes of vehicles. We should keep in mind that, despite recent progresses, 3 % of annual GDP and a significant part of public health costs in Europe are linked to driving accidents. Wearing a motorcycle helmet reduces the risk of death by almost 40 % and the risk of severe injury by more than 70 %. Wearing a seat-belt reduces the risk of fatality for front-seat passengers by 40–50 % and by as much as 75 % for rear-seat passengers. If correctly installed and used, child restraints in vehicles reduce death among infants by approximately 70 %, and for deaths among small children by anywhere between 54 % and 80 %.[181] All such precautionary measures would form part of the campaign. It would also focus on exposing the risks of speeding, driving under the influence of alcohol, driving while distracted by mobile phones, and driving unsafe vehicles.

Another EF campaign would focus on the need for citizens to re-establish contact with nature and do more physical exercise. Exercise provides a wide variety of health benefits: prevention of chronic illnesses and heart disease, positive effects on mood and a strengthening of bones. There is a clear correlation between exercise and cardiorespiratory fitness,[182] with many studies linking increased longevity and well-being to exercise. People must be actively encouraged to commune with nature and to exercise more frequently to rejuvenate body and soul. Regular contact with nature can also help, and EF citizens would be urged to spend more time in woodlands, mountains, parks and doing sports – and thus less time on their sofas.

Finally, an overarching campaign would be launched to improve health and e-health literacy. Health literacy means the ability of individuals to obtain, read, understand, and use healthcare information to make appropriate health decisions and follow instructions for treatment. Moreover, it also refers to the individual's ability to search for, successfully access, comprehend, and appraise desired health information from electronic sources, and apply it on a particular health problem. There is significant room for progress in this area in Europe. A survey in 2016 showed that almost half of the respondents had limited health literacy in eight EU member states (i.e. Austria, Bulgaria, Germany, Greece, Ireland, Netherlands, Poland, and Spain).[183]

People with higher health literacy levels demonstrate healthier behaviour, are more disciplined about treatment and live longer, healthier lives. However, the messages of health literacy and e-health literacy are more complex; they are not as easy or direct to absorb as those of the other five EF health-oriented campaign aspects mentioned above. The EF campaign on health literacy would thus be expanded as widely as possible – across schools, the media, and health centres. They should be conducted on a larger scale and in a more consistent manner than the previously mentioned campaigns which are more familiar with the public.

– Strengthening health standards in other policy areas

The prevention of health problems would be supported by a new set of regulatory acts with strong health relevance in policy areas such as food safety, environmental protection, use of antibiotics or pesticides, and transport.

The EU already has the world's most advanced set of regulations on healthy food, food safety, and environmental protection. The EF would continue that regime. A mix of rules is necessary for strict standards concerning the ingredients of food and drinks, as well as the labelling, advertising, and selling of potentially unhealthy food and products. We need high level standards for the air we breathe, the cars we drive, the water we drink, and anything else relevant to the health and safety of our daily lives. These things matter. There are nearly 400,000 premature deaths every year in the EU-27 and the UK attributed to air pollution, for instance.[184]

Another example of regulatory action lies in road safety rules, which must be approached in a holistic manner. This requires a diverse set of standards governing transport, police intervention, health, education, road users, and the design safety of roads and vehicles.

This of course is easier said than done. We acknowledge it could sometimes be seen as conflicting with our "entrepreneurship-first" principle and the commitment to reduce administrative burdens. Every regulatory measure places some burden on enterprises in order to safeguard the public. In the EF, every measure to protect public health and environment would be based on a cost-benefit analysis, both for the affected businesses and society as a whole. Advances in artificial intelligence and big data processing will make those analyses easier and more effective. Green, safe and non-polluting businesses would be at the heart of EF's production model, as explained in previous chapters. We should thus treat health and environmental protection as a synthesis of both interests: business and societal ones.

The above policy mix of preventive action – Primary Health Network, information campaigns and high regulatory standards – could generate huge social benefits in the mid- and long-term. This is policy that would serve the principles of social liberalism and social ecology, as presented in Chapter 2. It would be grounded in the notion of equal access for all to basic health care, a right to which we are all entitled.

6.4.2. A robust health industry and Europe as a global health hub

A second major strategic objective of the EF's health policy would be the development of Europe as a global health hub. Health is an economic world of its own, as it includes a significant part of other sectors of the EU economy. An indicative list of health-linked sectors contains: insurance; construction (e.g. hospitals and health centres); manufacturing and trade (medicines, medical device, etc.); employment (almost 7 % of total employment in the EU as explained above); services (doctors, nurses, paramedics, etc.); research; transport (e.g. ambulances); medical tourism; advanced technologies (e.g. bioinformatics, robot nurses and surgeons, disease forecasting, computer-assisted diagnosis). It is easy to see how a robust public and private health sector can have multiplier effects on the entire European economy.

Europe should strive to become the top health hub of the planet. As more parts of the world become richer and more populous, demand for prevention and treatment of the 'diseases of affluence' will increase: high blood pressure, type 2 diabetes, osteoporosis, cardiovascular malfunctions, colorectal cancer, acne, gout, and illnesses related to vitamin and mineral deficiencies, just to name a few. The EF would be ready to offer the best services and solutions to people in need across the globe. The cross-cutting idea of creating world-class business hubs, as discussed in other chapters, would have its parallel in the health sector too.

One could imagine the following visionary situation: the existence of several European specialised institutes for cancer treatment, heart operations, brain surgery or other medical interventions that would function as the best in their field. They would become the hub of a new European health industry and the ultimate destination for the world's patients, ensuring the flow of billions of euros into the EF economy each year. This would support countless European suppliers and contractors, creating thousands, perhaps even millions, of jobs.

This vision could be achieved through the provision of the right incentives and specific public-private partnership programmes. The core of such hubs already exists in certain European hospitals which provide cutting-edge medical services. Such hubs would require a horizontal co-ordinated effort because, as previously mentioned, many sectors of the economy would need to be involved, from manufactures of research equipment to travel agencies. The EF authorities would be very supportive of these auxiliary sectors. Switzerland is a model case, where one can find a dense concentration of world-class health centres in several medical fields. Visitors from China, other parts of Asia, Russia, and the Middle East flock to Switzerland because, for them, the quality of their personal health is a priority, despite the cost.[185]

6.4.3. Achieving a cost-efficient health policy

A third strategic health objective refers to the realisation of a cost-efficient policy. Public health is expensive; it is the second largest item of general government expenditure after that of social protection. In 2018, the last year of available collective data for EU-28 member states, total expenditure on health amounted to 7.1 % of their collective GDP.[186] For the EU-27 (without the UK), the government health expenditure amounted to slightly less than €1 trillion.[187]

Health care is a fast-growing expenditure in Europe. According to one study, public expenditure on health care and long-term care by 2060 is expected to increase worldwide by one third.[188] Several causes explain the trend: we are getting more populous, we live longer, medicines and health technology grow more advanced and sophisticated by the year, and we demand higher health standards.

For this reason, we would not treat health expenditure as merely one budget item among others. It should be seen as a major fiscal challenge: if it gets out of hand, it will lead sooner or later to our bankruptcy. We should thus make the efficiency of public health expenditure one of our strategic objectives. We thus believe that several approaches should be followed in the EF.

First, we would focus on more extensive use of e-health. This may involve investment in, and more extensive use of, health information management and networks, electronic health records, tele-medicine services, wearable and portable monitoring systems and health portals. Extensive use of e-health would be based on co-operation between the

EF's constituent states, doctor unions and medical facilities under a European health 'cloud service'. This would help the entire European health world to reap the benefits of big data that would be concentrated and processed through the cloud. It would, as a result, reduce many public and private health costs due to digitalisation and the cloud's economy of scale. Policies that support big data pools, as discussed in chapter 9 on artificial intelligence, and e-health literacy would be crucial in this effort.

The EF would invest in digitalised medical prescriptions to increase transparency, reduce fraud and abuse of the health care system, and render overall costs more rational and predictable.

It would also focus on a more cost-effective use of medicines by setting limits on pricing and the prescription of medicines. It would also facilitate the access of generic drugs, namely medication created to be same as, but cheaper than, existing approved brand-names drugs, while ensuring their proper use and marketing by patients, healthcare staff, and insurers.

Human and material resources would be reallocated in a more rational manner to ensure an even distribution of health staff, especially general practitioners and nurses across EF regions per the needs of their populations. It would further require a more rational concentration of specialised public hospitals and a concentration/merging of public health insurance schemes. The benefits of economy of scale of a much bigger EF health space would be obvious.

Finally, the EF would improve the collection and use of indicators and data. This would support the performance of health systems, and help develop tools to better assess the systems' efficiency.

All these approaches would contribute to a more efficient health system via reduced costs and better results for more people. To reiterate, a focus on prevention would significantly reduce the high health costs caused by serious chronic health problems.

6.5. Social cohesion

Social cohesion is a broad, cross-cutting objective. It could be simply defined as a set of policies to consolidate plurality, and reduce inequality and socioeconomic disparities in the society. It comprises elements such as reduction of disparities of income, wealth and investments, an increase of resilience of social networks and a high level of trust between people, acceptance of diversity, trust in institutions and respect for social rules, bonds of solidarity and civic participation, as well as equal access to basic infrastructure, education, and health. Most of the policy proposals in this analysis aim at social cohesion in one way or another: universal social protection, reduction of educational poverty, reduction of health inequalities, labour rights, integration of immigrants, support of network infrastructure and small and medium-sized enterprises, access to advanced technologies, and an even-handed monetary and banking policy. Each of these has components of inclusion and opportunities for all.

However, the notion of social cohesion, due to its importance for the foundations of an EF, deserves a proper analysis in this section. A lack of social cohesion, combined with a high level of social exclusion, has been the source of turbulent events: the 2011 Arab spring and the collapse of three states (Syria, Libya and Yemen), the 'colour' revolutions in several post-Soviet republics and, of course, the populist movements in the West that have led to the departure of the UK from the EU and the rise of populist illiberal governments such as those of Poland and Hungary.

Many studies demonstrate that the inequality gap is growing across the world, with an ever-larger slice of wealth accumulating to an ever-smaller percentage of people.[189] In 2019 the bank Credit Suisse reported that the richest 1 % of the world owned half of its wealth.[190] At the same period, 109 million people in the EU28 – nearly 22 % of its population – was at risk of poverty or social exclusion.[191]

Social cohesion can vary widely within different areas of a large region. A 2010 study by Bertelsmann Stiftung concluded that the countries of Scandinavia were the leaders in social cohesion, followed by Germany and the small and relatively wealthy central European countries. The below-average category of social cohesion included most of East Europe and some Mediterranean countries, while Latvia, Lithuania and the Bakans scored the lowest points.[192]

Given that EF society would be big, complex and versatile, it would need several diverse approaches to address its different forms of inequality. Social cohesion demands the involvement of every part of the public sector. Several solutions are proposed: (1) a managerial one, based on comprehensive data collection to identify social inequalities arising in the EF; (2) a financial one, allocating the means to support the people most in need; and (3) an institutional one, namely ensuring a framework for inclusive participation of citizens in social programmes, including special treatment of prisoners S Finally, special attention should be given to the US "Great Society" programme of the 1960s, which could serve as inspiration for similar initiatives in the EF.

6.5.1. The managerial approach: Data collection through the Social Monitor

Thanks to advances in social science and statistics, many surveys and databases have been developed in recent decades that map the social landscapes of regions, states and groups of states. One only has to look at the websites of Eurostat (the EU's statistical wing), the OECD (Organisation for Economic Cooperation and Development) or the United Nations Human Development Index[193] to understand the depth and potential of these tools. The EF would build on that stock of knowledge to establish its own database, the "Social Monitor".

The Social Monitor's mission would be to generate a clear and complete picture of the state of social cohesion across the EF, and to help policy makers frame the most efficient initiatives. It would present a comprehensive volume of data and indicators ranging from objectives statistics, such as GDP per region, employment rates, property ownership, criminality rates or car accidents, to more subjective ones such as values, perceptions or behavioural patterns.

The data would be comparable, widely available, and of the highest possible quality. It would also be correlated with the right methodologies to identify where the real problems of social inequalities exist. Here are some examples of problems it could highlight: what are the social groups or regions with the lowest percentage of home ownership? Which people, and where, smoke the most and why? What are regions with the highest rates of violent criminality and why? And in which areas are drug addiction, alcoholism or suicides most prevalent? In brief, it would function as a first-line "red-alert" mechanism to signal the biggest extant or growing social problems across the EF, and thus provide the justification for new social policies.

The Social Monitor would employ specialists and researchers on a full-time basis to offer the best service to policy makers. Substantial resources would be set aside each year for its fully-fledged functioning. It would thus operate as a genuinely vital tool of social policy, and not as yet another expensive academic exercise.

6.5.2. The financial approach: Material support and housing projects

The Social Monitor would identify the first steps needed for social cohesion by offering as accurate a picture as possible about social inequalities. The EF authorities would then need to decide how to prioritise the problems and how best to solve them via targeted projects.

Given the huge array of possible interventions across all sectors of society, we are not in position to make comprehensive proposals in this text. Specific policies of social cohesion respond to the most acute needs, as diagnosed at the time. We could, however, offer examples of projects that would address specific problems such as extra funding for sub-standard schools; the creation of cultural centres in remote or underdeveloped regions; special training on advanced technologies for unemployed youth or small enterprises; tailored infrastructure for poor communities to produce their own low carbon energy sources; or better policing, education and consultation in areas of high criminality involving young people.

Some good examples of social cohesion projects already applied in the EU are worth mentioning here. In Sweden's Norra Norrland region, the EU financed 163 training projects for the construction sector using wood and wood products. Overall, almost 40,000 people and 1,800 firms in the region participated. In the Södra region of the same country, EU funding helped to create eight new educational establishments and expand the provision of distance learning courses. This led to the creation of more than 77,000 new jobs, involving 22 new businesses and skills training for over 20,000 men and 18,000 women.[194]

Another example of a very targeted project involves Slovakia, where a new community centre in the village of Širkovce, in the the country's Banská Bystrica region, was created to provide educational, health, and leisure activities to marginalised Roma communities. The state-of-the-art facility provides a range of educational, health, and leisure activities – a significant boost to quality of life for these traditionally marginalised people. The project also strengthened social cohesion between the Roma and other Širkovce residents.[195]

Finally, an impressive example of social cohesion programmes at national level unfolded in Spain during 2007–2013. There, a total allocation of € 355 billion from the EU's Cohesion Policy led to the creation of around 58,000 jobs, support for more than 43,000 small businesses, co-financing of almost 30,000 research and development projects, access to broadband for an additional 1.3 million people, and water projects bringing service to 1.7 million people and improved waste water management systems for 2.2 million citizens. By the end of 2013, 6.6 million unemployed people participated in programmes to improve their employability. In addition, 3.6 million young people aged between 15 and 24 years participated in education or training courses dedicated to skills upgrade and prevent early school drop outs.[196]

All these examples demonstrate how valuable such projects can be and the opportunities they can offer to society's less privileged members. The EF would earmark €120 billion from its annual budget for social and territorial cohesion projects. This could address many problems in underdeveloped areas or within underprivileged groups. As a measure of comparison, we note that EU funding for regional and cohesion policy in 2014–2020 amounted to €351.8 billion, or less than €60 billion per year.[197]

6.5.2. Housing projects for the have-nots

Of key importance in the social cohesion debate is the matter of private housing. Private property is the bedrock of personal wealth, fulfillment, and social status. And it is a handmaiden to liberty: one can use his/her private property as a mortgage to access financing for their business, generate income or to climb up the social ladder. Around 30 % of EU citizens did not reside in their own property in 2017,[198] which equals approximately 150 million people. Some of them are relatively well-off and prefer rent as a choice. However, many of them are simply poor and can only dream of having their own roof over their head. They should be given a chance to realise that dream. This is becoming ever more acute due to the growth of Airbnb and other platforms of the "share-economy" in urban areas that removes available housing stock for those who need it. In 2019, for instance, there were 77,000 listings of Airbnb in London, 60,000 in Paris and 30,000 in Rome.[199] Despite the temporary COVID-19 disruption, this trend could later continue across many large and small cities in Europe. They could generate a shortage of ordinary rental opportunities, while making those that do exist less affordable for low or middle-income families.

In 2019, the European Economic and Social Committee (EESC) called for more robust EU housing policies, calling on the EU to adopt urgent common measures in sector. Noting that Europe was experiencing a 'housing crisis', the Committee argued that policy at European level must make affordable residences available to all Europeans. "The real danger of excessive housing costs no longer affects the most disadvantaged only, but also an ever-growing part of the rest of the population."[200]

The EF would thus support the allocation of 500,000 housing units per year to low-income people who lack their own property or who own properties of negligible value. Based on a price of €150,000 per housing unit (price of a modest apartment in the EU) as a reasonable metric, this policy choice would require annual expenditure of €75 billion. The allocation of those properties to the beneficiaries would be carried out on the basis of specific rates per region, gender, age, family situation and other criteria. It would also be subject to certain conditions: beneficiaries would be banned from selling their property for a certain minimum period of time (e.g. two years) to prevent price speculation. They would also have to pay back a portion of the value (e.g. 30 %) over time to ensure their commitment to the property and a sense of responsibility and accountability.

The programme would further require the proper infrastructure of statistical programmes and inspectors to assess the market values of real estate assets and beneficiaries' property status. In this respect, artificial intelligence, digitation of land registries and deep learning tools would be a valuable asset. It would also cover general housing and community amenities, including housing development, community development, street lighting, research, and other costs.

It is an endeavour worth pursuing. Within 10 years, it would lead to the allocation of private properties to 5 million households (around 10 million people, or 2 % of the EU27 plus the UK population). Such an effort would exert a dramatically positive impact on many people and their communities, while the cost would be affordable for the EF budget.[201] Many of Europe's "excluded" would be finally "included": by getting their own house, they would integrate better into European society. It would be easier for them to establish businesses, families, and have stable roots. And they would be more likely to develop a pro-European identity and more friendly attitude to its institutions. This policy would also link coherently – in terms of cost and geographic feasibility – with the demographic goal of reaching 600 million population for the EF, as explained in the next chapter.

6.5.3. The institutional approach: Inclusive participation of the citizens

The process of policy making is as important as the policies themselves for building social cohesion. It should incorporate the views of all stakeholders, from authorities and civil society to final beneficiaries. Giving historically excluded stakeholders the proper means to express their concerns is critical to the creation of a coherent society

Civic participation and political feedback for designing and implementing programmes of social cohesion are central to "political cohesion" between the different levels of administration, and different social classes. They also increase mutual confidence among stakeholders.

Let's take the example of the construction of a hospital in a poor, remote area of Europe. The EF authorities would make sure that, before this project is launched, its beneficiaries would be thoroughly consulted. Among those beneficiaries one could imagine local authorities, their citizens, the project's workers, land owners around the hospital and, above all, the patients. All would be asked to identify the major health needs of their local societies. Why do they need a hospital? Does the particular region suffer from higher rates of certain health problems compared to other regions? What about the size and the overall mission of the hospital? Stakeholders would also be asked about the alternatives: would it be better to construct more but smaller centres of first-level health care, instead of one big hospital?

The needs of local societies should be voiced and heard at the very first stages of such projects (the issue of democratic engagement, public consultation, and public participation has been reviewed in more detail in Chapter 3)

6.5.4. Treatment of prisoners: Care for the down and out

A special case for inclusive citizens participation refers to the treatment of prisoners. Nelson Mandela – perhaps the most famous long-term prisoner in history – made a highly inspirational and accurate statement: *"It is said that no one truly knows a nation until one has been inside its jails. A nation should not be judged by how it treats its highest citizens, but its lowest ones."*

It is difficult to disagree with that assessment. Prisons are the mirrors of our civilisation. The quality of prisoners' lives should be seen as a society's perception of dignity of life in general. Unfortunately, in many parts of Europe prisons remain a source of "social infection". They incubate all kinds of vices –violence, criminality, drug use, gangs – as well as physical and mental problems. They cause much suffering to inmates and their families. In several EU member states they function as revolving doors where the rates of recidivism and re-imprisonment can exceed 50 % during the first five years after an inmate's release.[202] Some people enter prison as minor criminals but exit them professors in crime.

In 2013, for example, the European Prison Observatory carried out two studies of the prison conditions in Europe.[203] Both found that many of the European Prison Rules, a recommendation of the Council of Europe, were not widely respected in a number of EU member states. Inmates were documented to be living in inadequate space, with little or no privacy. They were frequently exposed to contact with gangs, emotional pressure, and physical violence. Hygienic standards were often breached, with erratic access to showers and a lack of hot water, while sanitary facilities often afforded no privacy. Healthcare services also tended to be sub-standard. The number of specialists working in prisons was found to be insufficient, often leading to long delays in the provision of urgent services. Vocational training was also insufficient, while opportunities for meaningful work were very limited and often far from useful for reintegration purposes.[204]

Moreover, overcrowding remains a serious problem. European prisons are, on average, close to full capacity, with inmates having occupied, on average, more than 9 of 10 available places in 2016, according to the Council of Europe's Annual Penal Statistics report. Thirteen of 47 prison administrations reported having more inmates than places to host them. The highest levels of overcrowding were observed in North Macedonia (132 prisoners per 100 places available), Hungary (132), Cyprus (127), Belgium (120), France (117), Portugal (109), Italy (109), Serbia (109), Albania (108), the Czech Republic (108), Romania (106) and Turkey (103).[205]

The EF would strictly apply the European Prison Rules, which ensure high standards for health, education, hygiene, legal advice, nutrition, recreation, discipline, and other aspects of prison life. The rules also contain provisions for the training of prison staff, their conduct, and qualifications. If implemented properly, this would create the right framework for a better penitentiary system.

In this respect, the EF would allocate serious resources to make sure that prisoners live under humane conditions and have the chance to become creative members of society. New state-of-the-art prisons would be built in various EF constituent states. Indeed, modern new prisons must be constructed to replace the overcrowded cages that we euphemistically call "correctional" centres. As mentioned earlier, alternative penalties to reduce prison population would be used in more frequent and targeted ways, including measures such as house arrest, community service or focused treatment of behavioural problems. The EF prison policy would be largely inspired by the Scandinavian penitentiary model which ensures the highest standards for inmates' education and their smooth return to society.

Every prisoner would occupy his/her private cell with adequate space, and have the opportunity to develop new skills and knowledge. Indeed, there would be great emphasis on developing prisoners' professional qualifications, supplemented by psychological support to help their social reintegration after release from prison. These programmes would focus on changing behaviour and attitudes, including anger management or relapse prevention. Unfortunately, much prison time is wasted on either doing nothing or on activities that are irrelevant, even detrimental, to future rehabilitation. One of them is drug use.

EF reintegration programmes would include outdoor contacts, opportunities for education and vocational training, physical and mental health care, drug dependence treatment, and efforts to change behaviour and attitudes.[206]

Social cohesion in the EF would reach virtually all layers of its society, and especially the ones who have been suspended for some time from their participation in its functioning. An annual budget of €20 billion would be allocated to a humane penitentiary system in the EF.

6.5.5. Case study: LBJ's Great Society programme

For purposes of our argument about social cohesion, it is worth turning to the past to pay tribute to perhaps the western world's greatest experiment in that area: the "Great Society" programme of US President Lyndon B. Johnson during the 1960s.

Johnson launched his domestic Great Society initiative in 1964–1965. Its main goal was to eliminate poverty and racial injustice across the United States. It involved new major spending initiatives in education, medical care, urban renewal, rural poverty and transportation. It covered landmark programmes and legislation such as the legendary US Civil Rights Act, Medicaid, Medicare, the "War on Poverty" programme, the Economic Opportunity Act, several education acts, and the creation of the Housing and Urban Development agency. According to Joseph A. Califano Jr., advisor to Johnson, "*from 1963, when Lyndon Johnson took office, until 1970, as the impact of his Great Society programs were felt, the portion of Americans living below the poverty line dropped from 22.2 percent to 12.6 percent, the most dramatic decline over such a brief period in this century.*"[207]

That was another era. We believe, though, that the EF policy makers in future – and the EU member states policy makers today – should derive inspiration from that programme. It is characteristic of how the mix of political determination, new institutions, and financial commitments can transform large parts of society at an unprecedented scale and pace. We should all see it as a case study of a society that was thirsty for justice and change.

6.6. Concluding summary and budgetary aspects

The EF would introduce a truly universal system of social protection, ensuring basic financial support and health care support for all. It would consist of a universal basic support for each person, a universal basic pension for all over 65, universal health protection and special allowances for people with disabilities. All other allowances, such as unemployment or special poverty-related subsidies, would be abolished. This system would offer a truly simple and universal social protection without loopholes and tricks.

The EF would pursue four strategic objectives to fulfill the educational needs of a united Europe in a globalised world: the adoption of common European curricula for the primary and secondary education; a reduction of educational poverty and inequality; linking education to the labour demands of the 21st century, and achieving world class universities and research centres.

EF health policy would pursue three strategic objectives: investment in prevention, making Europe a global health hub, and implementing a cost-efficient health budget. A preventive approach would be based on creating a Primary Healthcare Network, twinned with six information campaigns addressing the root causes of health problems and the adoption of appropriate regulatory standards.

The EF would need to ensure that its citizens and regions converge toward a harmonious and inclusive model of economic development. Social cohesion is an important condition for the very existence of a sovereign state and the people's trust in it. The most effective tools to identity the main problems of inequality are needed. These would be achieved through the establishment of the Social Monitor. Vigorous financial support through targeted interventions would be needed to rectify identified problems – financial support that would be much higher than that of the EU's Cohesion Fund and Social Fund combined. A major housing programme would make available private properties each year for hundreds of thousands of people, offering them a chance for a new beginning in their lives.

A total cost of almost €3.080 trillion is estimated and broken down as follows:

- €1,440 billion for a universal basic support
- €840 billion for a universal basic pension
- €500 billion for universal health protection
- €200 billion for special health coverage of serious health problems
- €100 billion for special allowances for people with disabilities.

In addition, another €400 billion would be allocated to health infrastructure, and especially medical products, appliances and equipment, outpatient services, hospital services, public health services, research and development, the six health educational campaigns, promotion of world class health hubs, administrative costs, and other outlays for materials and other expenditures. That cost would include €100 billion for the National Healthcare Network.

This means that the total health expenditure would amount to €900 billion, if added to the universal health protection. This would be affordable. In 2018, for instance, government expenditure by EU28 on health totaled €944 billion.[208]

As for education, general government expenditure totaled €624 billion in the EU in 2018.[209] In the EF, that would rise to €750 billion. The funding would focus on developing common curricula, reducing education poverty, refurbishing or building new schools, subsidising free school meals, offering good teacher salaries and training programmes, and offering vocational training and more funding for higher education.

Finally, EF Social cohesion policy would require €200 billion per year. This would consist of €75 billion for its social cohesion programmes, €75 billion for the allocation of affordable housing units to 500,000 households, €20 billion for a more humane penitentiary system and €30 billion for other housing and community amenities such as community development, water supply, street lighting, research, and related costs.

Part III

MAJOR POLICY SECTORS OF THE NEW EUROPEAN FEDERATION

The third part of our analysis focuses on a number of more specific policies, which would be essential for the federation's progress and survival. They intend to offer some answers to the five existential challenges that were identified in the first chapter. These concern the topics and immigration and demographic policy, agriculture and food policy, production and new technologies, and finally energy and circular economy.

Chapter 7

Immigration and demographic policy

In Chapter 1 we identified demographic stagnation as one of Europe's existential threats today. It would be imperative that we dedicate special resources and political planning to reversing that trend. We must ensure that Europe becomes more populous and younger. An important part of this policy would be the topic of immigration into Europe: this trend continues unabated and raises important financial, security, social and cultural issues. This chapter deals with immigration and demographic policy. It lays out the strategic direction the EF should follow in the 21st century.

7.1. Immigration policy

7.1.1. Introduction: The context

Since the 1990s a constant flow of immigrants and refugees, mainly from Asia, Africa and post-Soviet republics, has headed toward Europe. This rose to unprecedented levels after the Syrian war exploded in 2011. Moreover, the devastating impact of climate change on many countries will add untold scores of 'environmental refugees' to other immigrants and refugees seeking to escape poverty, conflicts or repressive regimes.

Many in Europe see the massive influx of newcomers as a crisis and threat. It is difficult to wholly disagree with that point of view. In 2015, more than one million refugees arrived in the EU from Syria alone, putting an enormous strain on Europe's social welfare, the Schengen system, and the EU's political unity. The massive arrivals sparked a string of xenophobic and populist movements. They were used as political leverage for the rise or consolidation of illiberal and populist governments in member states such as Poland, Hungary, Austria and Italy. As a result, central European countries closed the "Balkan corridor" in 2016, leaving tens of thousands of refugees or immigrants stuck in Greece ever since.

However, these arrivals are less problematic than popularly perceived. Even if 20 million immigrants were to flood into the EU-27 and the UK over 10 years, that could be efficiently handled by a union of 500-plus million people. It is the equivalent of a town of 5,000 receiving 200 new residents. Could they be integrated into the town within 10 years? The answer is a definite yes, provided that the right structures and political will exist.

That example looks simplistic, of course, because immigrants would probably cluster in specific quarters of our imaginary townscape, just as they prefer to do – across the European landscape – in Germany or other wealthy EU member states today. But our example nonetheless offers a guiding framework. Receiving people should be seen as a manageable task. It is an opportunity rather than a crisis. Immigrants can boost declining local economies, strengthen the size of populations and rejuvenate regions. They can reanimate empty residences, fields, shops and factories which would otherwise lie deserted. According to one study, immigrants in advanced economies can be expected to increase output and productivity. A one-percentage point increase in the inflow of immigrant workers also brings a diversity of skill sets, which complement each other and increase productivity. Even a modest increase of productivity from immigration benefits the average income of the native residents.[210]

Most immigrants are young and willing to work hard and train to move from the category of "unskilled" to "skilled" works. The sooner they start working, the sooner they will pay taxes, integrate into society, and boost our economy and population.

At the beginning of 2019, 21.8 million people (4.9 %) of the 446.8 million people living in the EU-27 were non-EU-27 citizens, while 2.4 million immigrants entered the EU27 from abroad in 2018.[211] The number of non-EU citizens illegally present in the EU stood at almost one million in 2016.[212]

National ad-hoc approaches to immigration should be abandoned and a more coherent policy at the federal European level should be drawn up. In 2021, immigration was still under the control of each EU member state, producing very diverse strategies due to their different economic needs, strengths, cultures, and geographic locations. The famous 'Dublin regime', which regulates how asylum is granted to refugees, rests on national versus EU competence, thus failing to establish a truly pan-European policy. It unfairly assigns a heavy burden to the first receivers of refugees – countries such as Greece or Italy. In 2020, the EU began deliberating a new pact on migration and asylum to introduce a more consistent approach at European level, but the eventual outcome is fraught with uncertainty.

Contrary to the current situation, the EF would need to develop its own immigration policy based on two strategic principles: organised reception of two million "invited" immigrants per year all across Europe, and a consistent approach for dealing with human traffickers and un-invited immigrants.

7.1.2. Reception of two million new immigrants per year

Immigration must be organised, legal, and controlled. This is important for society's ability to absorb newcomers, and for the immigrants themselves to find a hospitable new home with decent living standards and opportunities for a better life. To that end, the EF would create a European Immigration Authority as the main body to manage the selection, arrival and settlement of immigrants. It would be funded and controlled by the EF government and accountable to the EF parliament. It would have enhanced co-ordination powers and, where necessary, executive powers to achieve the overall objectives of the EF's immigration strategy.

The EF would define the number of officially accepted new arrivals each year, namely around 2,000,000 immigrants, which corresponds to only 0.4 % of the EU27 and the UK's current population. This would be high enough to address Europe's demographic and labour needs, but also low enough to ensure its ability to smoothly absorb the numbers.

Immigration permits would be issued on the basis of four justifications: work, study, family reunions and humanitarian grounds.

– Work permits

The annual number of work permits would be 700,000.

They would be issued for those seeking employment in areas where EF society had the biggest need. The EF would prioritise the arrival of highly skilled migrants according to the skills and competences required as Europe's working age population declines. On the other hand, large segments of society, from small business to service industries, will further need many unskilled workers. Therefore, a balance between skilled and unskilled workers would be the goal.

A strict 'points-based' system, as the one being planned for the post-Brexit UK[213] to assess the value of willing immigrant before letting them into the country, is not favoured. This could lead to arbitrary criteria and decisions. On the other hand, the labour market has to be rational. This means that, depending on its needs and timing, the EF could open its doors more widely to immigrants with particular skills or knowledge (e.g. medical assistants or mechanics) than others. Flexibility should be the norm, guaranteeing that Europe and its immigrants offer mutually practical solutions.

– Student permits

The EF should welcome young people across the world who want to come to Europe for study and research purposes. They could be granted subsequent work permits, under specific conditions, in order for Europe to profit from their talents. Many of them would later become scientists or qualified professionals. It would be a loss if they left our continent to offer their services elsewhere.

As noted in other chapters, the battles of the new global economic landscape will be fought in the fields of advanced technologies and research. EF universities and embassies would pursue contacts with universities and education authorities across the world to target the most talented candidates. The EF's embassies and universities would carry out a promotional campaign in countries of origin. A generous scholarship programme would be developed to facilitate candidates' integration into European academic life. Procedures for granting student visas and residents permits would be swift and simple. English-speaking courses would be increased to help the foreign students. To subsequently retain them, the EF constituent states would offer national language courses, opportunities for housing, and guidance on local employment opportunities.

A total of 500,000 study permits would be designated for this category of immigrants, which corresponds roughly to the EU's number of permits issued to non-EU students in the 2010s. The most popular studying destinations were the UK, Germany and France, while the majority of students came from the U.S., China, and India.[214] EF policies would seek to diversify both the destinations and origins of international students, however.

– Family reunion permits

The EF would issue up to 700,000 permits for family reunions of set-
tled immigrants with their first-degree relatives. This would be important to ensure the wellbeing of immigrants and their easier integration
into EF society. Family reunions were actually the main reason for first-
residence permits being issued in the EU in 2018 (915,000 first-residence
permits).[215] For the EF, this number would be reduced, as part of the
lower total number of legally invited immigrants (i.e., from 2,4 million
today in the EU to 2 million in the EF). However, a certain flexibility
should be allowed for immigration flows to vary each year.

– Humanitarian permits

As for humanitarian-related immigration, the EF would offer the
opportunity for a new life to people coming from failed states or those
suffering extreme poverty or hunger. Emphasis would go to those countries most affected by climate change or where no institutions exist to
meet a population's elementary needs. As an example, one thinks of the
countries hit by the massive tsunami of December 2004. The annual
number of these permits would be 100,000 per year, particularly for
young people.

The total two million newcomers we propose per year for all four
categories is reserved for legally invited immigrants. We should take
into account, though, the need to accept possible additional arrivals of
refugees at certain times, depending on wars or other developments in
regions near Europe. The number of such refugees could fluctuate highly
from one year to the next. For that reason, we should set aside some
'reserve seats' in our immigration strategy for them too.

All such immigration permits would, as much as possible, adhere to
geographic quotas to represent, in a proportional manner, all the world's
continents and regions. Candidate immigrants would be selected according to specific criteria and quotas by age, skills, and family situation.
The EF should offer a balanced access to people from across the globe,
without discrimination or preferences of origin. The question, of course,
is whether this would be feasible since reality has shown that the bulk
of immigrants and refugees tend to come from the same regions. Even
so, an organised and orderly reception of immigrants could be feasibly

managed: indeed, such an EF approach would be much more realistic than Europe's fragmented approach based on national ad-hoc policies.

All new immigrants to the EF would receive a monthly subsidy for the first two years after their arrival to help settle in and ease their transition to work and society. We would propose €700 per month in 2021 prices, enough to provide a dignified life. The total amount thus allocated annually for 4 million people (2 million for the first year and another 2 million for their second year in the EF) would be nearly €34 billion. In addition, every student would receive an average scholarship of €3,000 per year. The EF would have to set strict limits, however, on how often a failing immigrant student could repeat his/her year at university.

After several years of their life and work in the EF, immigrants would be granted EF citizenship, provided they fulfilled criteria regarding their proper integration. They would need to prove a good knowledge of at least one EF language, their acquaintance with local culture and history, and a good citizen record (e.g. without criminal offences). Immigrant children born in the EF would be granted citizenship after a consecutive residence in the federation of around 12 years.

All EF constituent states and regions, without exception, would be responsible for the first reception of arriving immigrants and their settlement. The European Immigration Authority would assign to each of those states and regions a specific number of newly arrived immigrants according to proportionate quotas. Those could be set per population and GDP of each constituent state and region. In the case of immigration permits for studies and research, the quotas would be assigned per university or research institution.

Immigrants would be obliged to register locally and reside during their first two years in the region of their first settlement. This would be important to avoid the overloading of certain regions by newcomers and give time to the immigrants and local authorities to examine their situation and accommodate their needs. They could, however, move to another constituent state or region with the latter's consent and at the expense of the first state or region of residence. Under such a scheme, regions could exchange resources to make consensual transfers fairer and easier. After the two-year period, immigrants would be free to decide where to put down permanent roots in the EF, with no more restraints.

The necessary infrastructure would be created or deployed in each EF region to ensure the arrivals' first accommodation, health, education and social welfare services. Paperwork for the admission of immigrants into productive life would be a quick "one-stop" procedure. Access to language and cultural courses, training programmes and full health and educational benefits would be ensured. Information networks between authorities, employers, and immigrants would offer the best employment options for all – employers and immigrants. Their swift integration would also keep many away from criminality and radicalisation.

Germany has proven a relatively successful example of immigrants' integration during the 2010s. According to a 2018 study of VHW (Bundesverband Wohnen und Stadtentwicklung), a German association – and in contrast to 10 years earlier – immigrants showed a stronger desire for upward mobility, a stronger bond to the country, better command of the language, and less religiosity. The study examined the values, attitudes and everyday needs of over 2,000 immigrants and refugees. On the other hand, two-thirds of the respondents claimed that they experienced discrimination in Germany, and there was a greater sense they were disadvantaged in the labour and housing market.[216] As Germany is one of the wealthiest and best organised countries in Europe, it would be safe to assume that the situation of immigrants is the same or worse in many other parts of the continent.

In sum, Europe has a moral duty, as well as a demographic and economic interest, to receive people from all over the world. It is imperative to accommodate their needs, make them part of our productive economy, and offer them opportunities to thrive in our continent. This entails risks of course: some of them will become criminals, radicalised or disrespectful of our values and rules. But experience has proven that such individuals are very few in number. The easier newcomers are accepted by European society, the more the risks will be mitigated or eliminated. In the long-term, immigrants need Europe as much as Europe will need them. Their integration into our societies should become our strategic, demographic, economic, and humanitarian priority.

7.1.3. A consistent policy on non-invited immigrants: Refugees, economic immigrants and traffickers

As reality has shown, immigration cannot always be an easily organised or controlled project. Europe has long land borders and coastlines and is an attractive destination thanks to its prosperity. It is therefore experiencing many thousands of uninvited people per year. A consistent and principled policy is thus needed for dealing with them.

A first step would be to improve the guarding of our borders to the crossings of non-invited visitors. A European Border and Coast Guard would be set up and fully equipped to deter these illegal border entries. It would be supported by advanced surveillance, drones, satellites, and automated systems to prevent illegal entries at an early stage without putting lives in risk in the sea waters.

In case of asylum seekers – persons typically not invited – the EF would strictly follow the rules and procedures of international conventions, in close co-operation with the UNHCR (United Nations High Commissioner for Refugees). Those procedures are necessary to determine a refugee's status and whether to grant them asylum or not, and for how long. In co-operation with the relevant neighbouring countries, the EF would aim to establish pre-screening camps on their coasts (e.g. in Turkey, Libya or Morocco) to determine in advance the persons' status and facilitate their entry into the EF in a more systematic and safe manner. Every asylum claim would be processed quickly, meaning that a large number of employees, facilities and equipment would be assigned to this purpose. All persons not found eligible for asylum would be immediately returned to their place of origin or other venues, and released with enough money (for instance €1,000) and, if necessary, temporary papers to find their way back home. This would be done in co-ordination with the respective foreign countries. Any person illegally entering the EF for a second time would simply be deported with no such benefits.

Deportation and voluntary repatriation are usually expensive, so EF authorities would seek access to relatively cheap chartered flights or vessels contracted expressly for that purpose. Deportations in general have not proven feasible: on average, approximately 370,000 applications are rejected each year but only about one-third of the total is actually expelled from the EU.[217]

The EF would adopt a very clear stance against trafficking to send an unequivocal and discouraging message to all sides involved. In many parts of the world, and especially in Africa, there are advertisements from recruiters that deceive people into pay steep fees for the chance of being conveyed to Europe. The EF would employ a large force of anti-trafficking vessels and security officers in the Mediterranean and land borders with Turkey and post-Soviet republics. It would actively seek and intercept illegal boats, board them, remove all passengers and sink the boats. It would take all rescued passengers to specially designated locations, under humanitarian treatment, to be kept there until the traffickers amongst them are identified.

EF authorities would imprison all identified traffickers. Their arrest would be publicised in the countries of origin via posters, leaflets, the Internet, and TV. The EF would further charge governments of countries of origin for the cost of anti-smuggling and immigrant repatriation operations concerning the number of their nationals rescued and, if necessary, recuperate the cost by reducing the EF's foreign aid to those countries. Finally, it would impose sanctions and cut all aid to persistently non-compliant governments. This would be a tough and initially costly approach, but it would bear fruit in the mid- and long-term. Once the world understood the EF's determination to halt the disgraceful phenomenon of trafficking and immigrants' abuse, it would eventually fade away or shift elsewhere.

Finally, the EF would send strong signals to countries that actively promote emigration of their own citizens to Europe, in order to get their remittances in return and solve their own problems of overpopulation. The EF would remind them of financial consequences, in case they do not prevent this phenomenon, reduced aid and serious constraints in the sending of remittances.

The EF would also use positive incentives. It would co-operate with its neighbouring countries of North Africa, Middle East and post-Soviet republics to stem their flows of illegal immigration, offering financial assistance and training to that end. The example of co-operation between the Italian and Libyan coastguards and border services, despite some setbacks and flaws, offers a good precedent. In 2020, for instance, the EU Emergency Trust Fund for Africa delivered to Libya 30 vehicles as part of the EU border management programmes in that country.[218] The EU also set up its EU Facility for Refugees in Turkey, which offered significant financial support to prevent their uncontrolled movements into the EU territory.

7.2. Demographic policy

7.2.1. Introduction

As explained in Chapter 1, the EU suffers demographic stagnation. It is worth stressing here that, despite some ups and downs per region and era, the overall average birth rate remains lower than 2 per woman, which is the minimum figure for one generation to replace itself. If Europe remains demographically stagnant, it risks entering an era of financial and geopolitical weakness, and irrelevance.

The logic is simple: the fewer we are, the weaker we become; the more, the stronger. It is thus imperative that a European demographic policy is adopted, funded and implemented as an urgent priority. It would require a substantial allocation of resources and, if needed, at the expense of other policies. Like all investments, it would entail short-term costs but with long-term benefits.

EF demographic policy would set clear targets for a harmonious increase of the population across its territory, achieving an average of at least 2,1 births per woman and thus positive population growth. Each constituent state and region would strive for a positive growth rate. At the macro-level, we would like to see the EF's population climbing from its current 500 million people, of EU27 and the UK, to around 600 million by the end of the 21st century. This would be crucial to stay apace with the rest of the planet. At the same time, it would support global efforts to control population growth, especially in poor and overcrowded regions. It would make sure that demographic growth in Europe was coupled with measures to mitigate its inevitable economic and environmental burdens. For example, we must deal with the additional 100 million kilograms of daily municipal garbage that would be produced by the larger envisioned population (i.e., an estimated 1 kg per person). Many proposals suggested in Chapter 10 on sustainable development would be relevant in this respect.

Such measures, even if costly, would be vital. They would constitute a complex cross-cutting exercise, affecting all social and growth-oriented policies explained in the other chapters of this analysis. One could even argue that most of the issues about growth and social policies discussed relate to the improvement of our demographic situation.

Still institutions and measures specifically focused on the demographic challenges are required.

7.2.2. A set of decisive measures

A European Demographic Authority (EDA) would be created. It would be the central authority to design and assess implementation of the federation's demographic policy. Its mission would be to identify the roots of our demographic stagnation and frame solutions. It would be granted certain executive powers regarding, for instance, the allocation of funds or the co-ordination of other state services with demographic aspects (education, health, social welfare, etc.). The EDA would be supervised by the federal government and accountable to its parliament, to whom it would report once per year.

In parallel, a European Demographic Fund (EDF) would support the EDA and its policies. We would propose an annual budget of €60 billion, financed partly by VAT or other taxes levied on activities that impose high social or environmental costs, such as tobacco or fossil fuel consumption.

The EDA would be directly responsible for a wide spectrum of measures, potentially costly but decisive for Europe's future prosperity, the most important being:

– *Allowances for families of three children or more*

Expanding from a second to third child is nowadays the "extra mile" for many European families due to contemporary way of life and also the ensuing economic costs. The EF would assist them to go the extra mile.

In 2015, 5.1 million children were born in the EU28. Just 18.1 % of all live births in 2015 involved a third, fourth or subsequent child.[219] The EF would aim to increase those rates.

A generous allowance of €5,000 would be granted to pairs of parents for the birth of each child beyond their first two children. Moreover, with the birth of a family's third child, all its children would be allocated an additional €200 per month per child until the age of 18. This would come on top of the universal basic support of 300 euros per child and adult, as described in Chapter 6. A similar policy was adopted in 2020 by the Hungarian government, which offered married couples a 10 million-forint (€30,600) loan with no obligation to repay it if they have three children. In spite of the rhetoric of national chauvinism of the Orban government behind the measure, its impact will be interesting to observe.

It should be clarified however that such measures would only apply to EF citizens and long-term residents. They would not immediately apply to newly arrived immigrants, who could only benefit after a significant "cooling off" period of several years of residency and after they integrate with their region's culture and language. This would prevent newcomers from abusing the EF's welfare system.

– Universal free pre-school child care

Working persons, and especially women, would need assurance that their children receive proper care in their first years to avoid the family-or-career dilemma for parents.

The EF would financially support a universal network of free pre-school care centres. These would consist of spacious, safe, and clean facilities where all children would spend time while their parents are at work. This could end many parents' hesitations about whether to have more children or not. It is estimated that such an approach to child-care reform increased Germany's fertility rates in the 2010s. According to its Federal Institute for Population Research, the most important cause of the trend was the country's childcare reforms. Tripling the number of childcare places over 15 years helped women combine work and family, and raised fertility rates, even factored out the impact of immigration.[220]

The EDA would map Europe's available pre-school child-care facilities to identify gaps. It would, as a priority, oversee the establishment of new childcare centres or expand and refurbish existing ones as needed. Approximately €20 billion would be allocated by the EDF each year for that goal.

– Paid maternity leave of six months

Under the current EU legislation,[221] women have the right to a minimum of three months of maternity leave, of which at least two weeks are compulsory. In the EF, maternity paid leave would be expanded to a standard six months and allocated evenly, or in other proportions according to the mother's wish, before and after birth. Paternity leave, for fathers too, would also be ensured and prolonged compared to the existing status quo.[222]

Those measures should be effective. According to a study by Sydney University, for every three women intending to have more children, access to paid maternity leave schemes increases the total number of children they wish to have by one.[223] Moreover, paid maternity leave increases their link to the labour force, and has positive health effects for mothers and children.

– *Facilitation of adoptions*

Adopting children should also be encouraged by EF policy. The rules would be as flexible as possible to enable parents to have a new child. Today the eligibility criteria adopting parents must meet vary greatly from one EU member state to another, such as the minimum or maximum age. There are also different standards whether tentative parents are heterosexual, homosexual or single. Different approaches also exist for the information made available to adoptees and birth parents, for consultation of the child and for parental and child consent. For instance, all the EU member states give adopted children access to their data, though the age at which they may have that varies from 12 in Belgium to 14 in Austria and Lithuania, and up to 25 in Italy.[224]

In 2006, a Eurobarometer survey showed that, on average, 76 % of Europeans supported EU involvement in facilitating adoptions between Member States. In this respect, all the rules would be harmonised across the EF, in the least restrictive possible manner for adoptions.

This would also involve adoptions of children from foreign countries, in full compliance with international rules.[225] Common procedures would be defined with foreign countries to make them as transparent as possible. According to current data, top 10 countries offering children for adoption in the EU are, is descending order: Russia, Ethiopia, China, Colombia, Vietnam, Ukraine, Haiti, Brazil, India, and Kazakhstan.[226]

– *Access to fertility centres*

Problems of fertility cause a great deal of personal unhappiness, aside from contributing to demographic deficits. The good news is that biotechnology and medicine are advancing: conception and birth of children are going to become much easier as science evolves. This will hopefully become cheaper too. At any rate, the EF would financially support couples willing to bring children into their lives and society. It would not cap the cycles of assisted fertilisation that a woman could have, nor it would impose an age limit: as reproduction technology advances, all opportunities should be used to ensure parenthood for as many people as possible. The EF would all the more embrace that approach because marriages occur nowadays at a later age. Consequently the same happens with childbirth.

The EDA would earmark €10 billion per year as a special subsidy to help low-income couples with difficulties to afford fertility treatment.

– Immigration policy as a variable of demographic policy

In the previous section of this chapter, admission of approximately two million immigrants per year into the EF was proposed. If that figure was implemented consistently, a total of 160 million new people would arrive in the EF between 2022 and the end of the century. Not all would stay in Europe. However, a significant portion would become EF citizens, producing more EF citizens in the future and thus contributing significantly to our continent's demographic growth. It should be stressed that immigrants in Europe lower the average age of the total population: in early 2019, the median age of the EU27 population stood at 43.7 years, while only the year before, in 2018, the average age of immigrants was 29.2 years.[227] This means a lot for the rebalancing of our demographic pyramid.

– Public information campaigns

Adopting the above measures would not be enough; we would also need an active and aware public. The EF would support regular and consistent information campaigns across the entire spectrum of mass communication, from traditional media and the internet to posters in public places. Campaigns would inform people about the EF's available financial and institutional support for parents and children, the risks of demographic decline, and the societal value of achieving a new demographic boom.

Such measures would not be sufficient on their own, though. Demographic policy is a multi-faceted challenge. It can only succeed if there is genuine political commitment at all levels of government and across all areas of social policy. But it would be worth the effort. Its success would generate invaluable results: healthier public finances, more stable pension systems, a wider productive base and a stronger economy, not to mention a more dynamic society of younger and talented workers for the future.

7.3. Concluding summary and budgetary issues

Europe should develop a coherent immigration and demographic strategy to stimulate increased mobility and a bigger population in the 21st century.

The EF would establish a European Immigration Authority to design and implement EF immigration policy. It would officially receive two million immigrants per year for the purpose of work, study, humanitarian assistance, or family reunions. Conditions would be defined for their rapid integration, education, and employment, and to put down firm roots in their new home. All regions and states would be responsible to receive them in proportionate rates. As for non-invited immigrants, asylum seekers would enjoy accelerated procedures to determine their refugee status. Anyone non-eligible would be swiftly deported, under humane conditions, to the country of origin. A strict approach would be also levied against traffickers of human beings.

The EF would define its demographic boost as a strategic target, with the overall aim of reaching a population of approximately 600 million by the end of the century. Its policy would consist of generous allowances for families of three children and more, universal free pre-school childcare, paid maternity leave of six months, support for adoptions, access to fertility centres and prenatal care, an inclusive immigration policy, and, finally, public information campaigns.

The annual budget of EF immigration policy would amount to €60 billion. This would include the costs of subsidies for the first two years of new immigrants' residency in Europe, scholarships for students, and for basic housing needs for first-time settlers, language and vocational training and costs for the repatriation of non-invited immigrants and the accommodation of refugees.

The overall cost to the EF budget for this demographic policy would reach €120 billion per year, split between 60 billion for support to individuals and social programmes, and another 60 billion for the economic and environmental strains caused by the expected population increase.

Chapter 8
Agriculture and food policy

8.1. Introduction: The big challenges for European agriculture and food security

Agriculture and food security in the 21st century will be globally affected by three long-term trends: global warming, an expanding world population, and increasing demand for meat and dairy products.

As mentioned in the first chapter of this text, global warming and its risks to our food security are existential challenges for Europe and the entire world. The rise of global temperatures is likely to increase the number of undernourished people by the millions. It is also expected to affect southern Europe dramatically, with prolonged periods of drought, desertification in certain areas, and crop failures. Declining water supplies in this region are predicted to push down agriculture and food production. Global population is projected to increase by about 1,5 billion people by 2050, compared to today. That increase will be accompanied by a rise in living standards across the world and a greater demand for diets rich in meat and dairy products. More crops and water will be needed to feed animals and more land set aside for that purpose.

What do those trends mean for Europe's agriculture and food security in the 21st century? Some basic figures offer some idea. European agri-food production today is one of the shrinking, but still important, EU economic sectors. While there were 10.5 million agricultural holdings in the EU in 2016, farm numbers have been in steep decline for years,[228] with about 9.7 million people working in the sector across the EU for that year. Meanwhile, another 44 million jobs in the same year were active in food processing, retailing and food services – all dependent on agriculture.[229] The EU is, roughly, a net importer of raw agricultural material (cereals, fodder plants, fruits, vegetables, beans, coffee, seeds, trees, etc.) and a net exporter of meat and animal products, processed food, and drinks. In total, the EU-27 imported 153 million tonnes of agricultural products in 2019 and exported 134 million tonnes.[230]

There are reasons to be worried. The rest of the world is going to become richer and more populous. It will consequently retain for its own consumption the agricultural material that it produces. It is thus likely to export fewer, but more expensive, commodities to Europe. Moreover, the current trade deficit of raw agricultural materials is set to widen further. The consequence is that Europe will need to become more food sufficient. Yet its limited geographical space and future scarcity of water and other resources caused by global warming could make that goal difficult. Moreover, it will need to develop farming policies that are more climate-friendly, and this is possible. For instance, an analysis by the European Commission shows that by 2050 the agriculture sector can reduce its non-CO_2 emissions (e.g. methane) by up to 49 % compared to 1990.[231]

Several strategic directions are suggested of how the EF agricultural and food policy should develop in the course of this century to ensure that the federation avoids food and water crises, while moving to a more sustainable future. These are: (1) to embark on a new "green revolution" to increase agricultural production and food sufficiency; (2) rationalise the use of water for agriculture; (3) reduce consumption of meat and dairy products; (4) reduce food waste; (5) increase the share of organic farming in the overall sector; and (6) ensure Europe's access to foreign agricultural land and food production. These objectives are examined based on the principle of ecological development. But first it would be useful to explain the EU's current strategy for a more viable agricultural and food policy – the 'Farm to Fork'.

8.2. The EU Farm to Fork strategy

As part of the European Green Deal, the European Commission launched in 2019 its 'Farm to Fork' strategy based on food sustainability and support for food producers. With an eye to achieving a climate friendly policy, it strives to increase food production efficiency, while not increasing the price or lowering the quality of the goods. According to the European Commission, the Farm to Fork Strategy should accelerate Europe's transition to a sustainable food system with a neutral or positive impact on the environment, help mitigate climate change and adapt to its impacts, reverse the loss of biodiversity, ensure food security, nutrition and public health, and preserve the affordability of food.[232]

The programme includes targets for 2030 such as making 25 % of EU agriculture organic, cutting the use of pesticides by half, reducing the use of fertilizers by 20 % and that of antimicrobials by 50 %, and slashing food waste by 50 %. The strategy calls for setting aside €10 billion for the period until then, for research and development to support these goals.[233]

As a first step, the strategy proposes a legislative framework for sustainable food systems to enable the strategy's implementation. It was updated in 2020 by including a contingency plan for ensuring food supply and food security, based on the lessons learnt from the COVID-19 pandemic. The EU will also support the global transition to sustainable agri-food systems through its trade policies and international co-operation instruments.

The EF would build many of its agricultural and food policies on the EU's 'Farm to Fork' programme through the following objectives:

8.3. The EF strategic agriculture and food policy objectives

8.3.1. Embark on a new "green revolution" to increase agricultural production and food security

The green revolution historically refers to a set of new farming practices during 1940–1970 that increased agricultural production worldwide. It is credited with saving hundreds of millions of people from starvation. It involved the development of high-yielding varieties of crops, the modernisation of farming techniques, an expansion of irrigation, and very wide use of hybridised seeds, synthetic fertilizers, and pesticides.[234]

Now that both world's population and environmental threats are rapidly expanding, Europe needs to position itself at the centre of a very different green revolution. Its agriculture must be modernised to embrace a whole new set of techniques that simultaneously increase farming efficiency while properly husbanding our natural resources with minimal harm to the environment.[235] This radical departure from the "old" green revolution should include:

- Precision agriculture or satellite farming: this is a set of management techniques based on observing, measuring, and responding to inter- and intra-field variability in crops. The goal here would be to optimise returns on inputs while preserving resources, as enabled by GPS (Global Positioning System).

– Crops sensors: rather than prescribing blanket field fertilisation before application, high-resolution crop sensors would apprise farmers of the exact amounts needed, and where. Optical sensors or drones would analyse crop health by infra-red light and other means.

– Rapid-iteration selective breeding: this is the breeding of new varieties where the end-result is analysed quantitatively and improvements are generated algorithmically.

– Robotic farm swarms: the technology of using agri-bots with thousands of microscopic sensors to monitor, predict, cultivate, and harvest crops, with little or no human intervention needed.

– Closed ecological systems: ecosystems that rely only on matter exchanged within their environment by processing waste products into oxygen, food, and water to support their production.

– Vertical farming: the extension of agriculture into urban areas by cultivating plant or animal life within high buildings. The advantages would include year-round crop production, urban food autonomy, and reduced transport costs.

– Synthetic biology: biotechnologies that would build and remediate biological systems via engineering principles for the design and assemblage of biological components. Through such intervention, organisms could produce substances such as medicines or fuel, or be structured to sensing changes in the environment.

– Aquaponics: the cultivation of plants and aquatic animals in a recirculating environment characterized by tight synthesis between plants and fish, with each side excreting waste that is converted to nutrients or food used by the other. This is combined with a purification of the water as plants absorb the nutrients produced by the fish.

These are just a few examples. Many similar scientific techniques are under development, of which some should become financially viable during the 2020s. The EF would focus its funding and research on the integration of these techniques into Europe's wider agricultural production. The above-cited figure of €10 billion as part of the EU's Farm to Fork strategy – covering a 10-year period – would, under the EF, become an annual expenditure: sustainable agriculture is that important. The money would be used to swiftly train farmers to adopt the new techniques, and to support agricultural schools and universities to study and further develop the technology. Indeed, the EF's entire agricultural policy would be based on the new revolutionary tools to generate higher yields and a lower burden on our natural environment.

8.3.2. Rationalise water use

Due to climate change and the risks of higher temperatures in Europe, a significant part of the continent is expected to suffer from water scarcity. Nearly 45 % of total water extraction in Europe is used today for agriculture, with southern European countries using two-thirds of their extraction for that end. In northern member states, levels of water use in agriculture are lower, though irrigation still accounts for more than 30 % in some areas.[236]

The EF would, by all possible means, finance and support advanced methods to reduce wasteful uses of water. A first measure would target the use of irrigation systems, which would be optimised to provide water only when and where necessary. Soil moisture would be directly measured to determine the exact needs of individual crops. Drip irrigation methods would be used to ensure that water reaches a plant's roots without leaking into surrounding soil. Ground cover fabrics would be used to reduce evapotranspiration.

EF farmers would be trained and guided toward enhanced water retention in the soil via methods such as residue management, conservation tillage, contouring, and field levelling. Those would significantly reduce the amount of water applied to agricultural fields.[237]

The EF would also make sure that water use would be appropriately priced if it exceeded particular thresholds. The goal would be to ensure a full cost recovery of water while creating incentives to use it efficiently.

Finally, the EF would lend full support to water-efficient production, while gradually abandoning the production of water intensive crops such as cotton or rice, particularly in areas threatened by water scarcity and desertification.

8.3.3. Reduce consumption of meat and dairy products

Today we eat more than twice as much meat per capita compared to 50 years ago.[238]

Livestock breeding and meat production exert enormous pressure on our planet's natural environment, requiring disproportionate amounts of water compared to the production of plant food. For example, the production of one kilogram each of pork and mutton requires, respectively, 6,000 and 10,000 litres of water, while to get a kilogram of beef demands a whopping 15,000 litres. By contrast, one needs only 1,600 litres of water to produce a kilogram of bread. Even a thirsty crop, such as rice, needs only 2,500 litres to produce one kilogram of the grain. These figures fall far below those required for meat production.[239]

Millions of hectares of agricultural land are used for the production of animal feed instead of human food; consequently huge forest areas are destroyed each year for that purpose. Waterways are polluted with thousands of tonnes of nitrates leaking from animal farms, while livestock breeding emits a significant amount of methane, a potent greenhouse gas that aggravates global warming. Meanwhile, the excessive use of antibiotics on farm animals causes microbial resistance, with adverse effects on human health too. Moreover, intensive livestock breeding is usually carried out under cruel conditions causing unnecessary and unacceptable suffering to billions of animals.

Europeans should switch to a diet with lower amounts of meat and dairy products. However, the argument is not for a total switch to a vegetarian or vegan diet, as that is neither realistic nor desirable. Animal breeding and consumption of animal products have been part of human history and nature, and should not be abolished. Meat, cheese, butter or honey are both delicious and necessary for our well-being. However, the consumption of those products could be moderated.

The benefits of such a switch would be numerous for our and other societies across the world. Reducing the consumption of meat and animal products would significantly improve the quality of water, soil, air and other natural resources. Vast tracts of forest would be spared. Human and animal diseases linked to intensive animal breeding would fall. Household finances would improve, as people would pay less for plant food than expensive meat. Europe's economy would benefit from reduced imports of animal feed and products, and their replacement by local, less intensive plant food production. Finally, much animal suffering would be avoided – a major ethical achievement for our civilisation.

To achieve this objective, the EF would adopt a package of measures to reduce livestock breeding and the promotion of plant food. It would first launch a vigorous campaign to encourage people to consume less meat or dairy products while persuading them to introduce a greater proportion of plant food into their diet. The campaign would explain the benefits for our agriculture, health and economy of such a switch, and the avoided adverse effects of intensive animal breeding. This promotional effort could be folded into the EF's campaign against obesity, as discussed in Chapter 6's health policies.

The EF would also promote the research, production and consumption of cultured or laboratory meat, also known as "in vitro meat", which is grown in cell culture via tissue engineering techniques. It has not yet been commercialised, mainly due to the challenges of scaling and cost. Its production, however, is expected to become financially viable during the 2020s or 2030s. It is worth mentioning that in 2020, the average cost of producing a kilogram of that cultured meat was about €100, significantly lower than the $800 cited the previous year by the Israeli biotech company, Future Meat Technologies. According to one-perhaps over-optimistic vegan estimation, the cost was projected to fall to only €10 by the next years.[240] Even if those figures seem exaggerated, it is a sure fact this new technology will become much more affordable soon.

A more controversial measure would be the additional taxation of animal products. This would not be an easy choice as it would hurt low-income households and by opposed by a large part of the population. On the other hand, it would definitely be effective. We could perhaps explore a step-by-step approach, starting with the taxation of more expensive and less popular types of meat. The taxation could then gradually expand to broader categories of animal products, as social acceptance evolves. Such discussions have already started in EU member states with an ecological tradition such as Denmark, Sweden or Germany.

8.3.4. Reduce food waste and rationalise our food consumption

Europe is a region of food affluence. We produce, import and consume more food than we need. Around 88 million tonnes of food (or

20 % of the total food produced) are wasted annually in the EU, with associated costs estimated at €143 billion.[241] We also eat too much: more than half of the EU27, plus the UK, adult population is overweight.[242] A scenario of food shortages, malnutrition or even famine in Europe sounds like science fiction today. However, we should not exclude it in the future. We need to opt for the strategic choice of reducing but improving our food consumption – this will be very important for our health, environment, and food security in a time of overpopulation and adverse climate conditions.

A big part of the responsibility to reduce food waste lies with producers, traders, and households. There is little that a government can do if these economic partners do not change their habits. The EF would thus actively pursue action at all levels, starting with farming fields and thence to shops, homes and landfills of garbage.

The EF would first invest in the reduction of harvest losses by helping farmers improve their timing, techniques, and equipment. It would pursue the development of markets for products that do not normally make it into the food chain. For instance, in some places, entrepreneurs have spotted opportunities for gleaning, or collecting leftover crops, from farmers' fields after they have been commercially harvested.

The EF would engage the public in a wide effort to rationalise its food consumption and restrict it to necessary levels. People would be informed about Europe's huge amounts of wasted food and how to adapt habits for a more efficient approach. Consumers would be informed about the importance of reducing food waste and using simple practices to achieve this: planning weekly menus, purchasing according to strict shopping lists or making better use of leftovers. That initiative would be part of the larger campaign against obesity, as described in Chapter 6.

EF authorities would organise a more coherent system for redistributing safe surplus food to those in need. One factor that deters companies from donating food surpluses is the risk of liability in case of intoxication, illness or other injury. In this respect, the EF would introduce tax incentives to encourage food donation, along with relevant liability protection for donors.

The EF would also promote the integration of food-saving policies with business activities. Businesses with a large 'food footprint', such as cafeterias and restaurants, would be encouraged to conduct food waste audits to determine how and why they waste food. A voluntary EF label would be promoted to certify business as "resource economical" on the basis of those audits.[243]

As an alternative, the EF would promote schemes to increase the amount of food waste that ends up in composting or anaerobic digestion facilities, where it is broken down and converted into gases. This is another way to create renewable energy.

8.3.5. Increase the proportion of organic farming

Organic farming aims for sustainability and biological diversity, while excluding the use of synthetic pesticides, antibiotics, synthetic fertilizers and growth hormones. Typical organic farming practices exploit on-site resources such as livestock manure for fertilizer or feed produced on the farm. They choose plant and animal species that are resistant to disease. They also focus on raising livestock in free-range, open-air systems and providing them with organic feed.[244]

In 2018, a total of 13.4 million hectares was cultivated as organic in the EU, representing approximately 7.5 % of all its utilised agricultural space.[245] The 'organic area' was cultivated by almost 185,000 farmers, while a total of approximately 300,000 organic operators (namely farmers, as well as processors and importers) were registered.[246]

Organic farming is viewed as a more demanding choice both for producers and consumers. Organic products often take longer to produce and often need more work. They are processed and distributed on a smaller scale and subject to specific controls and certification. Those burdens translate into higher prices for the consumer. Studies suggest that, with respect to land use, organic farms tend to achieve a lower production per surface unit than conventional farms. However, this difference can partly be attributed to the fact that organic farms in Europe are often located in less favourable environments. A strategic question here is: should European agriculture follow the path of organic farming, given its lower productivity and higher cost? Could it adequately and acceptably address our future's existential challenge to food security?

The global debate is not conclusive. While some experts believe that organic farming is our best hope for the future, others argue that it is unrealistic to expect the practice to feed so many people in Europe's limited agricultural territory. One argument is that the gap in yield from organic production is not, in fact, a real obstacle to feeding the world because we currently grow far more food than is necessary. By reducing food waste and prioritising crops for human food rather than for animal feed, organic production could offer adequate solutions, even with slightly lower yields. The EF should support organic farming as a parallel option alongside the improved techniques for conventional farming, as proposed above. Organic farming should be a complementary part -although yet a major one- of our agricultural strategy to reduce pressure on the environment, diversify food production, and improve quality of life.

The EF would thus aim to increase organic farming to at least 25 %, if not more, of Europe's overall agricultural production. At this level the advantages of scale would enter the picture, thus making this type of farming more productive and less costly. Elsewhere, more public resources would be dedicated to research to improve the productivity of organic farming, while its benefits would be taught in basic school curricula and promoted through public campaigns.

Finally, during the initial phase of the respective programmes, the EF would apply targeted subsidies to ensure that organic products were affordable for the final consumers.

These are objectives worth pursuing. Reaching a level of 25 % for organic farming would engender multiple benefits for European society: lower dependency on imported oil, which is a prime component of synthetic fertilizers; lower exposure to synthetic pesticides that threaten public health and ecosystems; cleaner water sources and soil; fewer health problems linked to microbial antibiotic resistance; and a society living in greater harmony with nature.

8.3.6. Ensure access to foreign agricultural land and food production

Europe is a relatively small and densely populated space. Even if it succeeds in attaining much higher agricultural production, it would also need foreign lands to secure its food sufficiency.

The EF would first ensure access to the production of Ukraine and Russia, its two big neighbours with significant agricultural capacities. They are both famous for their fertile "black earth" areas, and are leading global producers of critical crops such as wheat, maize, buckwheat, barley, and rye.[247] Access to their production could be ensured through special trade and investment agreements (as discussed under the 'European Strategic Alliance' in Chapter 5). Ukraine's accession to the EF at some point later in the century would, of course, be welcomed from the perspective of European food security.

The EF would also focus on strategic partnerships with Africa and the nearer regions of Asia. It would offer the necessary investment and technical assistance, while African and Asian countries would offer privileged access for European food companies to their resources. This could include long-term leasing of land, joint ventures on food production, and favourable trade arrangements. It should be noted that Chinese land acquisitions in Africa have already boomed, especially since the international food-price crises of 2007–2008.[248] Similar policies in Africa are followed by countries such as Saudi Arabia and India.

The EF would avoid the notorious policy of "land grabs", namely taking over the agricultural land of poor countries to produce food against the interests of local landowners and producers. It would ensure that, under its partnerships, the host country would receive substantial assistance to improve its agricultural methods, use valuable resources more efficiently, reduce its greenhouse gas emissions and increase agricultural yields. The EF would help its partners catch up with the new green revolution, as elaborated above. Those countries will need European knowledge and money as much as Europe will need their resources and food.

In that respect, EF authorities would activate the tools of economic diplomacy to promote European agri-food businesses in the other continents. It would help them enter overseas production and the international marketing world. It would play a co-ordinating role to link European agri-food entities with governments and business in partner countries, including tools to fund the initial stage of their expansion overseas. The EF's specialised banks (described in Chapter 4) would fund the leasing of land, technology transfers and other aspects linked to foreign investment. Private banks would be encouraged to include food security partnerships in their lending portfolios.

8.4. Concluding summary and budgetary aspects

The EF would invest in a new model of agricultural production and food policy to address the threats of climate change, overpopulation, and potential food insecurity. It would embrace the Farm to Fork strategy the EU is currently developing under the European Green Deal. The EF would focus on a swift adoption of new agricultural technologies, a reduction in water use, lower consumption of meat and dairy products, reduced food waste, expanded organic production, and access to the agricultural and food production of other fertile countries. The overall objectives would be to ensure food security for the European population, respect for nature and a mitigation of global warming.

The EU28 budget for the Common Agricultural Policy (CAP) accounted for almost €50 billion[249] in 2019, representing less than 0.4 % of their collective annual GDP. The EF would increase that to 1 % of annual GDP, or around €140 billion per year. This would be a serious signal of our commitment to all the above strategic objectives. A large part of that amount would be allocated to support the necessary policies, such as: the integration of new technologies in Europe's agricultural production; extensive training of farmers to adopt those techniques; research to improve the yields and efficiency of organic farming; widespread campaigns in favour of organic production and the reduction of food waste and meat consumption; investment in water efficiency and in the agricultural areas of other continents to ensure access to their production; and targeted subsidies to support production cutting across all these areas.

Chapter 9

Enterprises, industry and employment during the fourth industrial revolution

9.1. The fourth industrial revolution and a new world of disruptions and opportunities

JP Morgan Chase is one of the largest employers in the US banking sector, with more than 250,000 employees in 2019.[250] Previously, its workforce collectively spent 360,000 hours each year to deal with commercial-loan agreements. In 2016, however, the company began implementing a programme called COIN ("Contract Intelligence"). COIN uses a machine-learning system, supported by a cloud network. Apart from cutting the time it takes to review documents, COIN has also helped the bank to decrease human-error mistakes linked to the processing of some 12,000 new contracts each year.[251] Thousands of human job positions connected to those contracts are expected to be lost or transferred to other departments across the bank.

JP Morgan's new programme is just one example of what is coming. Estimates of how many jobs today will be lost by mid-century vary from one quarter to fully one half, due to the impact of artificial intelligence and automation. This will affect all economically developed countries, but even more so developing ones since any extensive use of robots would erode their traditional labour-cost advantage.[252] A radical new era is dawning.

Ours is the third consecutive century of breathtaking technological progress. What started in the 19th century with its revolutionary inventions – the internal combustion engine, electro-magnetic power and chemistry, just to name a few – still defines our civilization today, namely the notion that that we can no longer live and flourish without rapid technological advancement. It has become part of our nature to expect to perpetually grow our economies, invent, and replace our innovations with new ones at the fastest possible pace.

A large part of humanity, however, is still trying catch-up. Elderly, poor or technologically unskilled people are at an increasing disadvantage compared to their younger, richer and tech-savvy counterparts. On the global scale, a similar divide exists between countries, geographical regions and entire business or social sectors: the gap between pioneers and laggards. The first will thrive and dominate the world, while the second will likely end up in misery.

Representing a series of new technological breakthroughs, the fourth industrial revolution is transforming whole sectors of life for billions of people. By the end of this century there may be a succeeding fifth or even a sixth one. Artificial intelligence is well on its way to surpass humans in almost every skill imaginable. It has already beaten human champions in high-intelligence games such as chess and Go. It is driving cars, running shops, and curing diseases. And it is starting to create other artificial intelligence sources. According to some predictions, machines may become self-aware and thus could deliberately marginalise or eliminate humans in the future. To counter this, some on-going programmes, military and civil, aim to equip human brains with AI-enhanced abilities to enable humanity to defend itself or effectively compete with the machines. A characteristic example is Neuralink Corporation, the neurotechnology company founded by Elon Musk, which is working on implantable "brain-machine interfaces."[253]

Life science is advancing too. Synthetic biology, gene technologies, and biomedical engineering will prolong and profoundly change our lives. At some point we likely will be able to see, hear, touch and do things in a way currently possible only for machines or animals. The genetic codes of people will be designed before they are born. Today's terminal or incurable diseases will become routine cases or things of the past. Our lives will be significantly extended. It is possible we may also reach some kind of immortality thanks to cell rejuvenation, the replacement of organs, or the preservation of intellect and personality in certain forms. Reproduction will also be revolutionised through cloning or related techniques. The impact of life science will seep into all life's domains, as well as our food: our diet will soon include laboratory-grown proteins.

Together, these developments will throw into question the very definition of human beings. How to harness all the technologies and maximise their potential in the service of humanity and not its enslavement? This should be one of Europe's major strategic objectives.

In 2015 the European Parliament published a report on 10 technologies that could overhaul our lives: autonomous vehicles, graphene, 3D printing, massive open online courses, virtual currencies, wearable technologies, drones, aquaponic systems, smart home technologies and electricity storage (hydrogen).[254] There is much more to come – for instance, blockchain was not mentioned in that report but has greatly advanced since then. Many still lie far beyond imagination, but one of the existential challenges Europe faces is its ability to cope with technological change, life science and artificial intelligence. If it fails to seize the initiative in these areas, it risks becoming the "third world" or "fourth world" of the future.

As the 2020s unfold, Europe is clearly outclassed by America or Asia in the development and application of advanced technologies. Further, it has entered a long process of de-industrialisation strongly accelerated by the financial and economic crisis of 2008. Manufacturing in Europe faces serious difficulties, illustrated by the constant reduction of the sector's share in many areas of the economy.[255] While European manufacturing has benefited from the EU's internal market, it has also been widely challenged by globalisation. European workers face the prospect of unemployment because many of them cannot yet catch up with the skills required by the competitive new technologies and professions that have emerged. Moreover, the COVID-19 pandemic has generated nascent work patterns which, at this point, raise more questions than answers about how productivity and economic competition will be organised in future.

Against that background, several strategic objectives can be identified: (1) support for new-tech business; (2) a code of technological ethics governing the use of advanced technologies to boost social cohesion; (3) support for small and medium-sized enterprises (SMEs); (4) a new strategic direction to support and modernise European industry; (5) improvement of the quality of research and development of new employment skills; (6) a high level of protection for employment rights and adaptation of employment to new modes of work.

9.2. Strategic objectives

9.2.1. Support of new-tech business

Since 2011 the EU has been developing its strategy, "Key Enabling Technologies (KETs)", for six technology groups: micro and nano-electronics, nanotechnology, industrial biotechnology, advanced materials, photonics, and advanced manufacturing technologies. As the Commission noted, these technologies have applications across many sectors and can help tackle societal challenges. However, it has also identified a serious problem, namely that *"one of the major weaknesses of Europe with regards to KETs lies in the difficulty of translating its knowledge base into marketable goods and services. This innovation gap has been identified as the European 'Valley of Death'. KETs-related manufacturing is decreasing in the EU and patents are increasingly being exploited outside the EU".*[256]

The EF would inevitably have to deal with more than those six technology areas, while also addressing other pressing policy challenges. We reference the Commission strategy, however, as a useful starting point since it identifies the broader problems that touch so many other areas of our region's economic and technological future.

A major European obstacle to new technologies and their commercial application lies in the internal market's fragmentation, the regulatory differences between EU member states, and discriminatory enforcement by national authorities. All these would categorically be eliminated by the very nature of the EF: its fully integrated market would have to guarantee the same rules for everybody, the same legal certainty and thus same fair competition for all stakeholders.

On the other hand, the EF would have to find answers to issues of financing. Inventing advanced technology products is very capital intensive and requires long periods of research and development. The necessary "venture" or "risk" capital can be hard to find in Europe. SME start-ups often are forced to quit at mid-stream, their innovations never entering the market because they run out of money or lack realistic commercial prospects.

Europe's inability to attract foreign venture capital is one of its major weaknesses. For example, a 2017 report by the European Commission's Joint Research Center (JRC) observed that, although the total amount of venture capital invested in Europe was second only to the US, it receives only 15 % of total international venture capital investments. Moreover, the behaviour of venture capital investors in Europe has changed over the last two decades for the worse. They are now investing less in younger or smaller companies and more in older or larger ones. Contrary to popular perception, Europe's venture capitalists do not support young or high-risk enterprises[257] or, when they do, they impose very tight conditions that restrict the recipient's margin to take risks. It is "risk-averse capital."

As a result, more European companies, especially the innovative ones, seek alternative sources beyond Europe or by techniques such as crowdfunding (finding money for a project or venture by raising small amounts of money from a large number of people) via the Internet. So far, the European crowdfunding regulatory landscape resembles a mosaic of different regimes at national level.

The EF would use resources provided by the European Bank on Advanced Technologies and Tertiary Industries mentioned in Chapter 4. Its specialised units would help innovative enterprises to create fruitful business and research partnerships. The bank would also urge private banks to specialise in this kind of financing as well by defining strategies to support innovative start-ups. The EF's public funding would focus on the early and more risky stages of start-ups. By financing risky, early-stage projects, the public sector would complement private funding that usually goes to more mature business projects and research. This is important to encourage more daring research and enterprises to pursue advanced technologies.

It is interesting to mention here the example of SoftBank, a Japan-based multinational company that owns stakes in many technology companies and also runs the Vision Fund, the world's largest technology-focused venture capital fund, with over $100 billion in capita. This is the most important fund developed outside the U.S. and Silicon Valley environment, and has attracted financial support from many different financial sources, from Europe to Saudi Arabia and East Asia. One or more similar 'vehicles' could be set up in the EF to function as the European locomotive of high-tech development.

The EF would further simplify the environment of crowdfunding for start-ups. It would remove any hurdles that block access for small investors and businesses to this form of finance. This would also require more transparent rules on information disclosures for project owners, risk management, and the supervision of crowdfunding platforms.

It should be also stressed that the EF's unified economic space would offer a huge structural advantage for knowledge-intensive industries and the economy as a whole, enabling large homogeneous pools of data. This is currently enjoyed only by China and the USA. This advantage would help European tech firms improve their machine learning, which involves the feeding of data to algorithms so they learn to interpret other data such as images of faces or patterns of commercial transactions. The EF would ensure that AI firms have the easiest possible access to that ocean of information. Supercomputers, consisting of thousands of processors delivering more than ten million the computational power of common laptops, would be crucial to support business and government. They are projected to soon reach the ability to execute one billion billion (10^{18}) operations per second. Supercomputers will be the ultimate tool for performing computational or data-intensive tasks across all branches of government, academia and industry, and especially for climate change predictions, medicine, cybersecurity, and manufacturing. Unfortunately, the EU's situation in 2020 was not satisfactory enough. As the Commission reported, only one of the world's 10 leading supercomputers was located in the EU, and said it intended to increase the number of such computers across Europe. Demand in Europe was at eight times bigger than available supply, forcing many users to process their digital applications and data outside the EU; that alone raises immediate issues of data privacy and the protection of commercial trade secrets. Indeed, while Europe consumed 30 % of supercomputing resources worldwide, it only supplied about 5 % in 2020.[258] This situation would not be tolerated under EF policy which would strive to make Europe *the* global hub for supercomputing. As a strategic imperative for the future of Europe's digital economy, the EF would spend whatever required to make sure that the supercomputing needs of its companies were fully served within its territory, and it would be net exporter of those services to governments and companies across the globe.

At the same time, the EF would ensure respect for private data. One cannot overlook the fact that European citizens are extremely sensitive about matters of privacy, far more than the Chinese for instance. Europe could become a global leader in governance of artificial intelligence and set international standards in this respect. It is worth mentioning that the EU's General Data Protection Regulation, adopted in 2018, has introduced principles already accepted by many other countries around the world.

To support these initiatives, the establishment of an independent European Council of Advanced Technologies (ECAT) is needed. It would be mandated to: co-ordinate financing and research on advanced technologies and artificial intelligence together with the European Bank on Advanced Technologies and Tertiary Industries; advise on ethical matters; and co-ordinate access to the benefits and use of advanced technologies for society's marginalized population. The ECAT would consist of representatives from the EF government, parliament, the judicial sector, academia, business associations, and civil society. As a fully-fledged body with its own secretariat and experts, it would be granted executive and regulatory competences to implement essential policies.

9.2.2. New-tech ethics and social cohesion

The ethics of new technologies would become integral to all EF policy. Certain ethical limits would be set by law, taking into account contemporary societal values. In our view, artificial intelligence should by no means be allowed to replace people in positions that require respect and care, such as therapists, judges or police officers. Certain modes of human genetic engineering should be banned, as should the mechanisation of the human body and brain, at least beyond a certain point. There would be rules establishing the basic rights of humanoid machines and entities with artificial consciousness, such as the right to property, non-discriminatory taxation or access to justice. Such rights are enjoyed by commercial companies and other legal persons today, so why not by machines tomorrow, if they become individual economic entities? On the other hand, certain basic rights should be reserved only for human beings. In any event, the distinction between acceptable or not acceptable rights for artificial intelligence is going to be difficult and always debatable.

A very cautious approach should be taken in areas where humanity's survival and well-being could be at stake. This implies that it should be ensured that machines do not overpower humans when conscious and strategic decision-making are needed. ECAT would need to develop protocols to limit the delegation of tasks to machines or to control the expansion of their power in certain sectors.

ECAT would screen all EF regulations relevant to advanced technologies and be consulted on related ethical matters. It would issue guidelines and carry out its own surveys. It could possess veto powers to block attempts by the EF government or parliament to pass laws that seriously undermine human dignity or safety. ECAT would co-operate with equivalent bodies from other continents to address the ethical challenges of advanced technologies that demand international solutions. It would serve as the ultimate guardian of European tech-ethics, and a leading one globally.

The new industrial revolution, however, does not only raise ethical challenges. It also offers opportunities to close societal gaps and help people, especially young ones, to climb the social ladder faster. While the benefits of technology will reach society's marginal and poorer segments with enough time, the EF would accelerate the diffusion across all corners of its territory.

Cheap and smart energy and transport could make a big difference in marginalised areas.

Poor people connected through smartphones to their homes and appliances could enjoy considerable energy savings, for example, not to mention other technological benefits for their health and overall well-being. Massive on-line courses can provide millions of students, entrepreneurs, professionals and other citizens in less privileged areas with knowledge and information they otherwise would not be able to access. Similarly, 3D printing offers many opportunities to young business people for innovative creation, while countless new applications in the health sector, including e-health, will revolutionise health care in rural and remote areas (see Chapter 6).

EF authorities would develop an extensive network of local training programmes and seminars to familiarise local business and households in poor or remote regions with the latest opportunities offered by advanced technologies. ECAT would support and co-ordinate all such policies via financial resources from the European Bank on Advanced Technologies and Tertiary Industries. An annual amount of €20 billion would be allocated from the EF budget for that specific task.

Finally, the EF would develop a network of "digital social infrastructure" to bring European people closer, expand their economic and creative potential, and connect all to the information they need for a better quality of life. This would be part of the broader social infrastructure network of energy, transport, and water that we lay out in the next chapter. The digital infrastructure would inevitably include the 'Internet of things' (IoT), which will make daily life easier and more efficient. The IoT is the network of physical objects embedded with sensors and software to connect and exchange data with other devices across the internet. By connecting devices to smart information networks such as the IoT, huge economic savings can be generated and billions of tonnes of waste and pollution can be avoided. But the EF would first need to make very substantial public investments to enable that to happen.

The experiences during the COVID-19 pandemic have clearly indicated that the infrastructure does not exist yet for fast, clear and uninterrupted professional communications to large numbers of people at the same time. Despite big improvements in 2020-21, systems are still overloaded and sometimes perform poorly. The EF would invest substantial amounts to make sure that tele-meetings become more reliable and useful. The expansion of tele-conferences would spare people and the environment the burden of frequent transport, its related pollution and time wasted on getting to physical meetings. Investment in 5G (5th generation) and later generations of telecommunication technologies would be instrumental to boosting European business and society in this respect. It would permit much higher data transmission rates for end-users, reduce end-to-end latency, and create far better connectivity, reliability, and support for very high mobility of data. They would tremendously increase the potential of the business and services, as these moved online and would need the best infrastructure possible for this kind of work.

9.2.3. Small and medium enterprises: Support for their special nature and needs

SMEs lie at the heart of our vision for a free and creative society, as they embody the spirit of people who take risks for the joy of creation, innovation, and wealth production. This is in line with the liberal position, the "entrepreneurship-first" principle, and the vision for a dynamic and ambitious European society that underscores our analysis.

SMEs are an important source of employment, innovation, and tax revenues. As a group, in 2020 they represented 90 % of all business in the EU and provided about 100 million jobs.[259] They are traditionally called 'the backbone' or 'engine' of Europe's economy.

SMEs have a particular profile. Their work methods are less formal than those of large enterprises. Their labour relations, safety rules and internal procedures are – whether in practice or by law – simpler and less demanding. SMEs often have few or no internal departments, and rarely employ in-house accountants, lawyers, managers, or consultants. As a result, their compliance with safety, labour and environmental regulations is more costly and time consuming. And, as the COVID-19 pandemic has shown, they are more vulnerable to external shocks because of small size and lower levels of capital to lean on in hard times. According to the OECD's report in July 2020, the pandemic would force half of all SMEs to go out of business within three months without financial support.[260]

The EF would support SMEs as part of its growth agenda by encouraging innovation and quality, and by nurturing hi-tech innovation and green entrepreneurship. It is clear that a society's growth and wealth can only be generated through vibrant business. Following measures for Europe's SMEs are proposed:

(1) *Reduction of red tape*: under the EF framework, SMEs would enjoy lower inspection or license fees, fast-track procedures for their initial creation, minimal paperwork, more proportionate safety standards, and more flexible rules for hiring, employing and firing employees (see proposals in the next sections on employment).

(2) *Facilitation of access to credit and capital*: SMEs would enjoy access to relatively favourable credit terms by the European Bank on Entrepreneurial Development ("EBED", as mentioned in Chapter 4). Their credit rates would be slightly lower than the ordinary market rates and proportionate to the amount of the loan and the size of the company. The EBED would prioritise the support of partnerships and business plans, which would offer added social value and respect for environmental and health standards. The credits would be granted carefully, under strict conditions for sound business management: Europe cannot afford a further accumulation of non-performing corporate loans. This would build on the existing EU "Investment Plan for Europe", which supports thousands of SMEs and provides guarantees that allow banks to finance start-ups and innovative projects, with the advantage that young companies with a short business history can take part. It offers EU guarantees to mobilise private investment and provides technical assistance for investment opportunities. It also improves the business environment by removing regulatory barriers to investment, both nationally and at EU level.[261]

(3) *Connection to European and international markets*: The EF would create a favourable environment for export-oriented business.

European SMEs would be encouraged to seek growing opportunities in other constituent states of the EF and in emerging
foreign markets. A good start has been the EU's extant web-por-
tals, which support the internationalisation of SMEs and inform
them about potential clients, markets, and partners around the
world. (see, for example, the page 'SMEs Internationalisation
support'[262]). The EF would continue this support, politically and
practically. The EF Ministry of Economy and other specialised
services would develop guidance for European SMEs regarding
access to international markets. It would actively promote alert-
lists to inform them about emerging opportunities around the
world such as the following examples: "Growing demand for bio-
juices in China!" or "Rising demand for leather shoes in Nigeria!"

(4) *Digitalisation*: Small enterprises can be frequently seen as more
traditional than bigger business and slower to adapt to digital
and technological advances. The EF would encourage them to
change. Digitally savvy entrepreneurs save time and cost by using
efficient tools. The Internet has already made it easier for SMEs of
all sizes to overcome some of the barriers to internationalization,
while the COVID-19 pandemic has caused many EU companies
to increase their use of e-commerce. The EF would facilitate the
latter's growth through wider acceptance of electronic signatures,
the issuance of electronic licenses, and the promotion of blockchain, cloud computing and partnerships. It would also support
the dissemination of 3D printing, whose customized production
could offer substantial solutions to business. An extended network of digital infrastructure, described above, would immensely
help achieve this objective.

(5) *Name and fame*: The EF would create a favourable attitude towards
entrepreneurs by promoting them as models, celebrating their
successes. Annual awards would be handed out by sector (e.g.
for innovative production, efficiency gains, social responsibility,
etc.), granted to the respective "enterprise of the year" at local
or European levels. The awards would offer substantial financial
support and the invaluable benefit of an embellished reputation.
Public campaigns to promote entrepreneurship would help shift
things in that direction. In a word: people should fully embrace
the idea of creating businesses and working for them.

(6) *Enhancement of educational and training support*: EF authorities
would offer to SMEs relevant educational and fit-for-purpose

training to respond to the diversity of their needs. Many local upstarts have difficulties growing as planned due to skill shortages in their sector. For example, special training for energy saving or new forms of accounting could prove very useful, even vital, for those SMEs who know little about these techniques.

(7) *Tax regime*: The EF would not favour specific tax incentives for SMEs since we propose low tax rates as a general policy line for all companies and individuals (see Chapter 4 on fiscal policy). However, tax reporting and collection rules for SMEs could be simplified.

9.2.4. Industrial manufacturing: A new strategic direction

Big manufacturing is important in its own right. The 551 biggest EU-based companies employed more than 19.4 million people in 2019.[263] Manufacturing is the key to exploiting the new knowledge economy, as more than 80 % of the EU's private sector expenditure on research and development goes to that sector.[264] It generates the products responsible for three-quarters of the EU's annual exports. It also creates economic growth and jobs, generates demand for primary production and business services and, finally, supplies key inputs to services industries. However, from a long-term perspective, Europe's industry seems to be in retreat, considering its share of EU employment falling from 20.7 % in 1996 to 15.3 % in 2016.[265]

Two opposing strategic options can be considered: one favours the exclusive specialisation of European manufacturing in targeted sectors; the second argues for raising the skills and competences, and thus the opportunities, of the entire European manufacturing sector to cover all products. The latter option is preferred as a matter of principle, as well as necessity.

First, there is the issue of principle: Europe has been the cradle of modern industrial innovation and production. There is no reason to back away from that heritage. Where opportunities and demand exist, European business people should be encouraged to produce everything possible, at all levels whether for internal consumption or export: cheap and high-end shoes, staple foods and luxury ones, and so on. Why should the production basis be narrowed down by focusing only on niche manufacturing?

Second, there is the matter of necessity: Europe needs to be as self-sufficient as possible. It cannot afford to be dependent on other countries for entire sectors of its economy. In case of global crises, it might lack vital supplies. Europe can certainly afford to competitively produce and consume screws and screwdrivers, furniture, computers, smartphones, elevators, tires, bricks, tiles, toothpastes, and whatever else.

This is certainly not an easy task. Our analysis argues in favour of open markets and against protectionism. However, it also acknowledges that it would be difficult for Europe to compete with the world's emerging markets in certain sectors. On the other hand, we need to try. As emerging economies grow and mature (e.g. China, India, Brazil, Mexico, South Africa) they will also become less competitive while demanding high-end European products. It is notable that, in 2018, China had its first current-account deficit after many years of economic expansion. Though that turned to a surplus in the following quarters, the signs are there for a possible reversal of China's seemingly permanent trade surpluses with the rest of the world.[266] The business regime proposed in Chapter 4 and, in particular, the policies suggested of low taxation, foreign investment incentives, the abolition of social security contributions, and reductions of red tape would, together, make European industry attractive for investment and far more powerful in the arena of global competition.

Another dilemma concerns the strategic decision on whether Europe should create fewer but bigger firms ('champions') across its manufacturing sectors or simply foster more competition among more numerous but smaller ones. There are good arguments for both strategies. The proposed EF opts for the "big champion" choice because it is the most realistic way to compete with the big conglomerates of other continents, which often benefit from (direct or indirect) state aid and strong political support by their governments. In doing so, of course, the principles of the internal market should be safeguarded. Soft tools should be used, such as financing to facilitate the merger of European companies in the strategic sectors of telecommunications, energy, networks infrastructure, defence, and biotechnology. The creation of industrial champions would have to be linked, as much as possible, to a healthy business environment that enables smaller suppliers and sub-contractors to collaborate with their big partners.

Moreover, the EF regulatory activity would evolve in a more innovation-friendly direction. Each EF regulation would first examine a product's benefits instead of disproportionately focusing on its potential risks. A new technique or product would be authorised or regulated on the basis of a cost-benefit analysis, with a view to encourage innovation and the progress of Europe and humanity. It would also be possible to introduce certain tax exemptions or other incentives for novel products and services to ease their introduction and acceptance in the marketplace.

Finally, the EF government's overall role would consist of creating a favourable legislative framework and institutions for European industry, research and development. EF authorities would focus primarily on correcting 'systemic failures' to ensure that rules and bureaucracies do not block firms' growth and industrial development. We should always bear in mind that sometimes the best regulatory approach is not to regulate at all, thus leaving enterprises free to develop their potential according to the needs and trends of their era.

Two strategic priorities are proposed in areas where European industry currently lags: higher quality of research and investment in labour skills.

9.2.5. Improving the quality of research and investing in new labour skills

Business research and development (R&D) across our continent competes with other developed regions of the world, accounting for approximately 2 % of the EU's GDP in 2019. By contrast, the US, Japan, and South Korea achieved rates in 2019 of 2.76 %, 3.28 % and 4.22 %, respectively.[267] In one ranking of the world's 2500 largest private R&D investors, the US comes first, with 769 companies (€313 billion), followed by 551 EU-based ones (€208 billion) and 507 Chinese companies (€96 billion).[268]

Private venture capital – crucial for start-up companies to ensure investment in innovation – was five times higher in the US than in Europe in the late 2010s. Despite the rise of new technologies with the potential to boost productivity, such as the Internet-of-things or artificial intelligence, productivity growth in the EU has been sluggish due to the slow diffusion of innovations across its economy.[269]

As noted in the opening chapters, the fourth industrial revolution is both capital- and knowledge-intensive. Intellectual property protection

(e.g. patent registration) has become a key instrument for modern industrial policy. Worldwide patent applications per year have increased from
roughly one million in 1990 to more than three million in 2018.[270] In
2019, for the first time, China was the top filer of international patents,
surpassing the US.[271] Of course, not all patents have the same added
value; some are of little or no use and do not reflect any societal needs.
But in the big picture, Europe is definitely being challenged by the other
big powers. In the chemical sector, for instance, and since the start of the
century, China has increased its global share of scientific publications
from 7 % to 28 %, while its share of world trade involving research-
intensive goods has jumped from 3 % to nearly 10 %.[272]

In the area of research on advanced technology, the EF would strive
to make this substantial indeed. It would arrange for a minimum of
3 % of its GDP –approximately €400 billion – toward that goal, a
rate exceeded today only by Israel, Japan and South Korea. Its public
budget would contribute €200 billion for matching with another €200
billion from industry and private funds. Joint public-private partnerships in R&D production would be actively pursued. EF authorities
would take a leading role in co-ordinating business and research on
advanced technologies. The EU has already made a good start with
its framework of 'Advanced Communities', or networks of scientific
communities whose research infrastructures rest on a high degree of
co-ordination.[273]

European industries would receive funding from the Bank of Secondary Industries, private equity and international sources. They would
be supported and guided by EF authorities and banks into international
research partnerships. A main task of the EF public services would be
to bring innovation back to the core of European industrial production, encouraging partnerships and strategic teaming within their own
departments as well as classic public-private partnerships with industry.
They would second top-level experts within the governmental departments and agencies to coach, rather than referee, innovation within the
business community. And they would be innovators themselves in their
areas of responsibility, such as public infrastructure and managers of
public utilities.

It would be crucial to ensure the results of research projects are dif-
fused across Europe's industrial sectors. Each project's output would be
shared from its early stages with chambers of commerce and industry
associations, with innovative solutions discussed with the companies

most directly concerned. EF authorities would vigorously urge industry to take advantage of applied research, while creating ad-hoc "innovation groups" where business, researchers, banks, and public authorities would sit together to review the best innovative methods for industrial manufacturing. They would also examine the investment and cost issues linked to adopting innovations as early as possible, the training implications of innovations, and so on.

Given that too much innovation takes place elsewhere, the EF would seek to join the other continents' most important programmes. EF embassies would have special innovation and research units to engage with foreign projects of most interest to European industry. Europe's enterprises should participate and contribute in innovation hubs across the world. This would imply that industries should invest money and resources in these projects. This could apply, for instance, to innovative projects on Chinese solar panels, American electric vehicles, African food production, or computer and telecom manufacturing.

This strategic approach would be further linked and complementary to the second one, namely to develop new labour skills that would match demand and offer of the new jobs.

Millions of "blue collar" (unskilled or low skilled) jobs in the manufacturing sector will be lost in the next decades as robots take over to perform the tasks better, quicker, and cheaper. Studies vary in their estimates of how many jobs will disappear in the long-term due to automation and artificial intelligence, but all agree the impact will be significant. One study, for example, predicts the loss of 800 million jobs worldwide by 2030.[274]

A major consequence is that self-employment will increase in several sectors. The same upward trend will happen to remote work: millions of people will no longer need to work in an office or store as long as they are digitally connected to their employer or client. The COVID-19 pandemic has already given its first taste of what lies ahead.

According to the most pessimistic scenario, human work will become obsolete, with all its negative consequences. Many unemployed persons will be drawn to margins of a society dominated by large corporations and machines. However, in spite of this doom thinking, human skills and knowledge will always be needed in emerging sectors. For many jobs, human emotions and discretion will be requisite, even in the most automated areas such as manufacturing.

EF policy would proactively match the supply and demand of employment by establishing the 'European Employment Portal'. This would be a public database that registers all vacancies per sector/region/skill-set, etc. across the EF's territory. Its mission would be to connect prospective employers with employees from all corners of the EF. It would be equipped with special algorithms and big data processing tools to make the best use of each applicant's profile and offer them the best possible chances for jobs in the nearest location. In this way, each prospective employer and employee in Europe would be only three or four mouse clicks away from each other.

EF authorities would foster a supportive social and business environment that guides citizens towards those jobs that are expected to survive the new technological developments. The USA Bureau of Labor Statistics, for example, releases every two years its projections for job growth for the next 10 years and the types of work that will remain in high demand despite automation. In 2020, it highlighted the following work profiles: wind turbine technicians, solar photovoltaic installers, occupational therapy assistants, statisticians, information security analysts, and physician assistants.[275] The BLS report offers a picture of a future economy based on high-value services, sectors where the vast majority of new jobs will be created. EF authorities would carry out the same analysis on a regular basis to inform its business, public administration, academia and other citizens about employment trends.

We should also highlight the potential benefits of emerging technologies for the circular economy and renewable energy. A low carbon economy will require particular skills, especially in construction, engineering, and research. The EF would exploit this by offering vocational training to develop "green-collar" skills across its labour force. The EU's renewables industry has increased its work force by 20 % since 2000, for example. By 2017, this accounted for 4.2 million jobs,[276] being only the beginning of a predicted long-term boom. As early as 2011, the European Commission emphasised *"the positive employment benefits if revenues from the auctioning of ETS (Emissions Trade Scheme) allowances and CO2 taxation are used to reduce labour costs, with the potential to increase total employment by up to 1.5 million jobs by 2020."*[277]

The EF would invest €20 billion per year in training to create these needed skills. It would also support, in a targeted manner, the creation of new employment posts in sectors of high social value, such as the circular economy and carbon-free energy. To increase "green collar" occupations, the EF would promote across Europe the model of vocational training, as described in Chapter 6 on education. It would also develop labour capital through the European Institute for Industrial and Entrepreneurial Skills, following the good example set by Austria.

– Best practices from Austria

Producers in emerging economies are upgrading the skills of their workers in export industries, a factor that undermines the EU's competitive edge on world markets. European industry should rapidly adapt its labour skills to advanced technologies and new production methods. There are several ideas on how to achieve this objective. In the following, relevant current upgrading practices in Austria are shown as examples. Such approaches should be emulated in other EU member states today, and in the EF tomorrow.

Austria's Institute for Economic Promotion (Wirtschaftsförderungsinstitut, or "WIFI"), within the country's Federal Economic Centre, promotes the strong performance and competitiveness of Austrian companies, across all branches of the economy. Its main mission is to translate economic, social and technical developments into innovative and attractive training courses.

It is interesting to see how WIFI works. Leading business representatives submit their views via advisory boards about the content of the training courses that WIFI should offer. Company experts in human resources and education help develop "qualification concepts" for various sectors such as machinery, vehicles, plastics, construction or eco-buildings. In this way, entrepreneurs and experts from all sectors of the economy can influence WIFI's training and education programmes, which help Austrian authorities develop insights into the economy's future employment needs.

WIFI trainers come directly from companies, and most of them teach part-time. This ensures that what they teach is up-to-date and directly applicable to everyday business. WIFI participates in Austria's "Standing Committee on New Skills" to support its companies and employees, as well as those seeking work. Conclusions that emerge from the committee meetings directly influence the content of training courses for companies and their employees.[278]

The EF would establish its own WIFI – it could be named the "European Institute for Industrial and Entrepreneurial Skills". It would focus on nurturing the most appropriate labour skills as required by the market and technological developments. It could include top experts from other continents too and co-operate with the respective institutes of those countries. Branches of the Institute would be established within major business and technological clusters across Europe, as hubs of excellence.

9.2.6. Employment policy: Protection of labour rights and mutual boost of business and employment

Employment policy is traditionally seen as part of the "class struggle" opposing employers to employees. However, it should be better conceived as the synthesis of "class co-operation".

Employment is a vital part of personal fulfilment, social harmony, business performance and overall prosperity. It counts among the basic indicators of a society's success and is rapidly evolving: one has only to ponder the kind of jobs from the 1920s, 1950s or 1980s that no longer exist. More important, as the 21st century progresses, are the jobs that will emerge or disappear due to automation, artificial intelligence, or new societal needs.

EU law contains a rich arsenal of legal acts for protecting workers' rights – too many to list here. We nevertheless highlight a few to illustrate the depth and versatility of European employment policy. These include: the Community Charter of the Fundamental Social Rights of Workers (1989); Minimum Workplace Safety Directive (1989); Health and Safety of Atypical Workers Directive (1991); Part-time Workers Directive (1997); Fixed-term Work Directive (1999); Employee Involvement Directive (2001); European Works Council Directive (2009).

The level of employee protection in the EU is very high and must remain so under the EF. Here below we focus on the most important aspects of workers' rights, which we deem essential for productive employment and the accomplishment of our broader social objectives.

First comes the right to rest and paid leave. This is the foundation of productive employment and a balanced life. Under EF law, all workers would be entitled to annual leave of 25 work days. There would be a maximum 40-hour work week, extendable only with the employee's express consent. There would be six public holidays for the entire EF

(25–26 December, 1 January, Easter Monday, 1 May and a "European" day) plus another six public holidays determined by each constituent state to honour religious, national or regional anniversaries (for instance in Greece: 25 March, 15 August and 28 October).

Commodity shops would be closed every Sunday, with no exceptions. Making or spending money is not everything in life: societies should take a collective break from consumerism once per week to focus on other important activities and values. We should also bear in mind that the gradual advance of e-commerce and flexible working schedule is going to make shopping on Sundays less necessary.

The EF would preserve existing EU legislation that secures important rights such as collective bargaining, representation in corporate governance or the right to strike. Some simplification would be needed, however, to incorporate those EU directives into a single, shorter, and more transparent EF labour code. This would be an important step towards legal certainty and for attracting domestic and foreign investment.

– A new landscape after the COVID-19 pandemic

However, the COVID-19 pandemic is shaping an entirely different employment landscape, as technologies do have a serious impact on it. Uncertainty prevails. Both employees and employers are still sending contradictory signs about the benefits and disadvantages of these technologies. While Jack Dorsey, Twitter's head, has declared that Twitter's staff can work forever from home, Reed Hastings, the founder of Netflix, described tele-work as a "pure negative".[279] In September 2020 *The Economist* presented a very interesting report on the future of the workplace,[280] noting that only 3 % of Americans regularly worked from home prior to the pandemic, while huge numbers were doing it afterwards. After the end of Germany's pandemic lock down of spring of 2020, 74 % of its workers returned to their place of employment, but only half of them did so for a full five days a week. The teleworking platforms of Microsoft Teams, Zoom, Google Meet and Cisco Webex already reached over 300 million users in the midst of the pandemic. Civil courts, notaries and other services were quick to abandon bureaucratic hurdles and offer their services online, something unimaginable before the coronavirus hit the world.

Many people favoured that shift, given that, in the USA, the average American spends four hours a week commuting to work. Brussels is another example, where many people spend as much as 10 hours per week to travel from the Belgian countryside to the heavily congested city every day for professional reasons.

This raises questions about the future of work relations in labour intensive service economies such as those of Europe. Offices will become more like hubs for occasional meetings rather than 'second homes', as they used to be for many people prior to the pandemic. Staff interactions will change: due to distance, they will become more restricted and formal, and this will also affect procedures such as employee performance evaluation, promotions, dismissals or access to professional development. There will be new legal issues such as assigning liability if an employee suffers an injury or sickness while working at home. Another risk, perhaps the most serious, is that many people could simply burn out from spending their life closed off from the world, at home where their work environment and private sphere will become inseparable.

In this new environment the EU today, and the EF tomorrow, should design a strategy that is mutually satisfactory for business and employees. Physical presence of employees in offices and other working places should be favoured as much as possible. While this is costly in terms of space and commuting, it is also beneficial for personal interactions, creativity and productivity. Many cases of personal burn-out would likely be avoided. At the same time, teleworking will inevitably become the pattern for millions of companies and people, meaning that some performance and working protocols should be set for this form of work. Working time would be less fixed and more flexible, according to the needs of both the employers and the employees. The EF would bring business, academia and employees together to draw up the new protocols and turn them into a set of new labour rules.

Some of the labour rules would also have to cover limited-service contracts since, unfortunately, predictions are that more and more people will be employed as part-timers and freelancers. According to one study, full-time salaried work peaked around the year 2000, with Europe's number of independent workers growing since then. Indeed, at 11-million strong, freelancers are the fastest-growing segment of the EU labour market in the early 2020s, and rising.[281]

Therefore, special consideration would be given to the rights and obligations of both sides, to make sure that employees are not subject to abusive treatment by much stronger companies. Freelancing would be recognised as a stand-alone work category, with its particular training and mentorship needs, guidance and employment rights.

Moreover, new policies would be needed to mutually boost business and the interests of the employees.

The "entrepreneurship first" principle is based on the need to liberate European business from social security costs and administrative burden. It is in the interest of society – and of the unemployed and underemployed who seek steady and better jobs – to have vibrant and profitable enterprises. Therefore two basic labour policy steps should be supported as necessary conditions to boost business and investment: (i) freedom from social security contributions and (ii) freedom to hire and fire in the best interest of the enterprise.

– Freedom for social security contributions

As explained in Chapter 6 on social protection, employers and employees would be relieved from any obligatory social security contributions, thanks to a universal pension paid directly from the EF state budget for anyone older than 65. This would give a big boost to all types of enterprises by sparing them from serious financial costs, while saving human resources and administrative time otherwise spent to manage an organisation's social protection obligations. It would imply that no more money, time and personnel are wasted in dealing with this issue. Enterprises could instead focus on what they do best: creating wealth for themselves, their employees, and society. Consequently, we could expect enterprises to generate larger profit margins, and hire more people. At the same time, a minimum EF salary would be set to prevent abuses and ensure dignified employment conditions.

It is worth mentioning that at the end of 2010s Europe's employers paid for approximately 34 % of total social security contributions.[282] In the EU28 that amounted to hundreds of billions of euros. One could easily imagine the stimulus to Europe's economy if employers could direct that money toward higher salaries, new jobs, investments, training, and research instead of social security outlays.

– freedom to hire and fire in the best interest of the enterprise

In respect of the regulatory area, employment legislation is notoriously complex. It contains thousands of pages of rules, and often contains more exceptions than the rules themselves. The result is a heavily regulated labour market where employers think twice before hiring an employee. In many parts of the EU, the labour market has become too tight. As a result, many people, especially young ones, are excluded from productive employment.

This situation should be reversed. Today, when a company's financial situation becomes difficult, legally compelling it to retain workers, maintain high salaries or other requirements at the expense of its balance sheet can lead to disaster. Companies shut down and all -instead of only a few- employees can lose their jobs. Enterprises in the EF, however, would be free to do their planning as circumstances require and, if necessary, reduce or alter their workforce. In that regard, the reforms proposed in 2017 in France by the Macron government to introduce more flexible and open labour laws, are going in the right direction.[283]

Firing someone is always unpleasant; in some cases it destroys lives and families. Certain safeguards should therefore be introduced. Employees would only be fired following a reasonable warning period and compensation. In the EF they would have priority access to vocational training and other programmes of rehabilitation. At any rate, with the EF's social protection system analysed in Chapter 6, there would always be the universal basic support's safety net of 300 euros per month for every member of the household of the employee. A fired parent of a family of four, for example, would have guaranteed monthly support of 1200 euros.

Business should also have more liberty to hire people on a part-time basis and on more flexible terms, as circumstances require. This would increase overall real employment. At a minimum, it would offer the opportunity for millions of young people to enter the labour market as a first step towards work experience and a career. Internships for training purposes would be decently paid. The current widespread practice in Europe, whereby companies exploit interns by paying them nothing, while offering little training in return, would stop.

Overall, and as mentioned earlier, balancing the interests of companies and their employees is a delicate equation. The interest, as a society, is to make sure that both sides develop their potential within a prosperous economic environment.

9.3. Concluding summary and budgetary issues

The EF would promote the integration of advanced technologies into all productive sectors of society. Advanced technologies will constitute our best means to bridge societal gaps, bring new wealth to the poor and help Europe better compete with the rest of the world, thus contributing to humanity's overall progress.

The EF would pursue the strategic objectives of supporting new tech companies, integrating the fourth industrial revolution into our production models, developing a code of technological ethics, and bridging Europe's societal gaps. It would establish the European Council of Advanced Technologies (ECAT) with enhanced co-ordination and regulatory competences pertaining to the use of technologies and their ethical dimensions.

The EF would establish a favourable framework for SMEs tailored to their particular needs and nature. It would strive to reduce red-tape and facilitate SME access to capital markets and new skills. It would also promote a revival of European big industry in as many sectors as possible, with a view to making them more competitive on the global stage. That framework would focus on new labour skills and qualitative research and innovation.

Employment is a fundamental social right and one of the cornerstones of personal fulfilment. At the same time the traditional concepts and opportunities for employment are rapidly evolving. The EF would have to confront the challenges of automation. It would support business-friendly policies, balanced with the need to provide dignified and meaningful employment for all citizens. The EF's strategic objectives would aim for a labour policy that boosts business and adapts society to the forthcoming world of artificial intelligence and automation. It would also focus on the challenges of a post-COVID-19 employment landscape characterised by remote working and wide-spread freelancing.

The EF would earmark some €200 billion per year, co-funded by equal private funding, for research into advanced technologies to match the investment rates of the world's leading R&D nations (Japan and South Korea). It would further allocate €20 billion for innovative start-up businesses and to help enterprises and households in marginal areas adapt to advanced technologies.

The EF would allocate another €20 billion to support the working skills, especially, "green collar" skills and jobs that are needed for a future circular economy. This would complement our vision for a carbon-free economy and social cohesion, as outlined elsewhere in this text.

Finally, the EF would allocate €30 billion each year to the European Bank on Secondary Industries and the European Bank on Entrepreneurial Development to subsidise interest rates for SMEs; promote their digitization; help them gain access to energy and transport infrastructure; develop new labour skills and industrially innovative projects; and finance public-private investment schemes for "smart industrial economy" projects.

Chapter 10

Climate policy, infrastructure networks and circular economy

10.1. Introduction: Basis for optimism and pessimism

Great optimism is expressed about humanity's ability to reach a stage of low or no carbon energy production. Whether accompanied or not by specific policies from government, many important environmental concerns today will be resolved in the not-too-distant future by technology and science. Road transport, which consumes almost half of global oil production in the EU,[284] will become fully electric in a few decades, thus rendering oil largely obsolete. Solar and wind energy production will constantly increase their share in the total energy mix. Nuclear power production will become safer and more effective, thanks to thorium, fusion or other technologies. Other forms of energy such as tidal or geothermal are also destined to expand. There is therefore good reason to believe that the production and consumption of fossil fuels will soon be relegated to history. This is good news for humanity, nature and especially for Europe, as it is relatively poor in fossil fuels. Its dependency on other continents for gas and oil supplies weakens its geopolitical and economic position – a situation that needs to be reversed.

However, there is more cause for pessimism about the climate situation. As explained in detail in Chapter 1, global average temperatures are relentlessly increasing. They are projected to rise by two or more degrees Celsius before the end of the century.[285] Although it is impossible to project with precision the effects of global warming on Europe and elsewhere, some trends are certain: melting glaciers and an increase of droughts, causing water and food scarcity in some regions; rising sea levels and the devastation of certain coastal areas; new kinds of diseases; and more frequent extreme-weather events.

Europe should prepare to adapt to global warming while trying to mitigate it to the greatest extent possible. Even a reduction in the rise of global temperatures by 0.5 or 1 degrees Celsius would save many lives, properties and irreplaceable aspects of nature.

EF authorities would map out strategies for a more viable way of life, building on the European Green Deal, currently being designed by the EU. The EF would establish extended networks of clean energy and transport, it would promote solar, wind, hydrogen, and a safer use of nuclear power. Moreover, it would turn its economy into a sustainable circular one to make best use of planet's resources. These policies are explained in more detail in the next sections of this chapter.

10.2. The European Green Deal

The EU28's energy mix has been positively transformed since the beginning of the century. In 2018, renewable energy represented 18.9 % of energy consumed in the EU –more than double the share in 2004.[286] During 2008–2018 the EU's production of natural gas fell by 46 % and that for oil and petroleum products by 35 %.

Those trends are good news. Europe is gradually using cleaner and more efficient energy. It is on the right track and we are confident it will remain a leader in this global effort. However, there are reasons for alarm: in 2021, Europe is still consuming large quantities of fossil fuel, still dependent on other continents and Russia for its energy needs and faces the major threat of global warming. The EU today, and the EF in future, must urgently devote substantial means for creating the necessary infrastructure to switch to its own cheaper and more effective renewable energy.

Fortunately, the EU has recognised the urgency of change, with the unveiling in December 2019 of its European Green Deal. As the European Commission noted at the time, the Green Deal is a new growth strategy aiming to *"transform the EU into a fair and prosperous society, with a modern, resource-efficient and competitive economy where there are no net emissions of greenhouse gases in 2050 and where economic growth is decoupled from resource use"*. However, climate policy is not the programme's only objective: it also addresses the risk of biodiversity loss, overproduction of waste, water and air pollution, and the need to protect quality of life in general.

The EU will offer financial and technical support to those most affected through the Green Deal's 'Just Transition Mechanism', which will mobilise at least €100 billion between 2020 and 2027. EU countries with high employment in greenhouse-emission sectors, such as oil and coal industries, will be the main beneficiaries of the mechanism.

The Commission has also proposed a 'European climate law', a programme of legal acts to make the Green Deal's objectives more specific and legally binding. The programme focuses on environmentally-friendly technologies, decarbonisation of the energy sector, cleaner forms of transport, energy efficiency for buildings, and new ways of overall production and consumption.[287] The European Green Deal also includes the 'Farm to Fork' strategy, as described in Chapter 8, to integrate agriculture as part of Europe's climate policy. The European Green Deal is thus not simply an environmental project: it is a new concept for life. It rests on the fact that all growth aspects can be coupled with low carbon economy. This can be done: from 1990 to 2018, for example, the EU reduced its greenhouse gas emissions by 23 %, while its economy grew by 61 %.[288]

The EF would embrace and expand these policies. Its more integrated structure and robust financial mechanisms would enable it to introduce more ambitious targets while providing strong support to economic sectors that need to adapt. Contrary to the current situation in many EU member states, the EF would abolish all subsidies for fossil fuels. Thanks to its geopolitical weight, it would endeavour to turn the European Green Deal into a global one, rallying all other countries in the effort. As a complement to its vision of a global federation of rules, peace and democracy, the EF would strive for a global community of ecological values. A further elaboration, based on the principles of the ecological development, follows in the next sections.

10.3. Integrated networks of clean energy (wind, solar power, hydrogen and nuclear energy)

Serious investment would be needed to achieve a high level of 'social infrastructure' networks to ensure the access of all EF citizens to clean and cheap energy, transport, water supply, and the digital networks mentioned in the previous chapter. Together, these networks would create the basic conditions for social justice and a new, smart, and sustainable economy. They would be the most important factor for achieving the European Green Deal's strategic goals.

The EF would assign priority to the networks' construction to produce more solar, wind, geothermal, and tidal power, and distribute that power more widely and efficiently across Europe. The objective would be to ensure that, by 2050, more than half of all households produce – and not merely consume – their energy through renewable sources. A move to "energy democracy" would be necessary in sectors where renewable production and consumption have been decentralised. Citizens would have the opportunity to generate their own energy and provide any surplus to others via solar panels, for instance. The EF would follow best practices as applied in Italy, where the government applies an "eco-bonus" system to renovation projects involving photovoltaic installations and storage systems.[289] The practice of several countries which tax the energy used by households for their own consumption, would not be applied by the EF.

The EF would partially subsidise the initial installation of such technology in households, while investing in research to make the materials and systems more affordable. The subsidies could take the form of low-interest loans, based on reimbursement by contributing energy to the grid. The EF would also ensure that grids are "smarter" by using digital technologies to create interactive communication along power lines between users and utilities. The mix of computers, automation and power equipment would quickly match supply and demand. Their intelligence makes them more efficient.

The networks would require private investment and function within a framework of fair competition between operators. Such an approach, if managed with transparent rules, would ensure lower costs for consumers and much higher levels of energy efficiency for society as a whole. EF authorities would retain a significant part of the networks' ownership, however, due to the networks' strategic importance. Those networks would make best use of the available renewable sources of clean energy, such as hydroelectric or geothermal, however we would focus in particular on wind, solar power, hydrogen and nuclear power, which are the most common and easiest to use.

10.3.1. Wind power

A major investment goal would be to develop offshore electricity grids to exploit the huge potential of the Atlantic and other European seas to produce wind energy. Progress so far in these areas is impressive. The EU currently has the largest floating wind energy capacity in the world – about 70 % of the total. In 2020, its total installed wind energy capacity was more than 210 GW, supplying 14 % of electricity demand. Its future target are even more ambitious: 350 GW of power for 24 % of total electricity demand by 2030.[290]

The EF would continue that trend, increasing the production of wind power, both in absolute terms and as a percentage of its overall energy mix. Energy produced offshore is based on stable and abundant resources, whose use is cheap and publicly acceptable, thus it would be worth investing more in it. Production is currently concentrated in the North Sea, whose waters are relatively shallow. But for reasons of diversification, wind farms should be expanded to the deeper waters of the Atlantic and Mediterranean, investing more in floating systems. Such installations could also be placed in the Black Sea to support energy distribution in the Balkans and central Europe.

The EF would treat wind power as one of the pillars of its industrial development. According to "Wind Europe", the sector's trade association, three of the five largest turbine manufacturers in the world are European, which has a 40 % share of all wind turbines sold globally. In 2020, the wind industry accounted for 300,000 jobs in Europe.[291] It is estimated that, in the next year, the EU wind energy sector generated €37bn to EU GDP, operated 248 factories across the EU, and each new wind turbine installed in Europe would contribute €10m of economic activity.[292]

The EF would allocate the necessary funds to expand its wind power network, with a clear preference for European manufacturers of turbines and other infrastructure. Thanks to its more integrated structure, the EF could be expected to achieve a more rational use of grids across today's national borders, efficiently using power where it is most needed. Energy would be traded from where it is cheapest, while reducing the electricity system's overall environmental footprint. "Wind Europe" has urged European institutions to support offshore hybrid wind projects that combine the transmission and generation of power.[293] The EF authorities would review this and other approaches, in close consultation with business actors.

10.3.2. Solar power

Like wind power, solar energy production has become one of the cheapest technologies in the world. According to the Commission, the cost of electricity production in Europe from solar power decreased by 75 % between 2008 and 2019.[294] In the EU, its growth has been spectacular, from 7.4 TWh in 2008 to 115.0 TWh in 2018.[295]

The major form of solar energy production is photovoltaics, based on solar cells assembled into panels, which can be installed in diverse ways, but usually on rooftops or on the ground. It lends itself to small scale, decentralised energy production carried out by any individual who can afford it. In an ideal world, each household would be energy-sufficient thanks to this kind of infrastructure, and the EF would set ambitious targets to enable the majority of households to profit from the technology. That is the basic step to achieve the "energy democracy", as noted above. It would be a win-win strategy for all: for citizens, as both producers and consumers of clean energy, for the state that would benefit from a reduction of energy imports, for nature (spared the intensive and dirty extractions emissions of fossil fuels), and of course, for the European photovoltaic industry. In 2018 alone, the solar panel industry accounted for 117,000 full-time jobs, which should grow to as much as 300,00 by the end of this decade.[296] A Europe-wide scheme supporting the household use of solar panels based on subsidies and other incentives would offer a huge boost to the industry and its employment opportunities.

In addition, proximity to Sahara, the world's sunniest area, should be an advantage. The EF would substantially invest in connectivity, via joint partnerships, with North Africa's solar power production for its dissemination to Europe. Tens of billions of dollars have already been invested in renewable energy projects in Egypt, Algeria, Tunisia, and Morocco. For example, the 580-megawatt Noor Ouarzazate complex in Morocco, the world's largest solar plant, was built with the help of Spanish companies and technology. Europe offered to that project $2.5 billion in financing, a huge investment.[297] Elsewhere, Egypt's 150 MW Kuraymat solar power field supplies nearly 2 million people with electricity.[298] Once operational, Tunisia's TuNur solar project will forge a new intercontinental energy corridor between North Africa and Europe by delivering power to homes in Italy and France.

The EF would prioritise the development of those energy links. It would also develop solar power parks across the European continent, especially in its southern regions where they would be most effective. Additional investment would focus on energy storage via more efficient battery systems to achieve all-weather energy production. In sum, the

EF would increase the overall share of solar power in Europe's total energy mix, with the idea of making it our top energy source, along with wind power.

10.3.3. Hydrogen: A special opportunity for our future

Hydrogen generated power is perhaps one of the future's greatest opportunities for clean and efficient energy production. Hydrogen fuels emit no greenhouse gases, cause negligible air pollution and can be used for a number of applications, such as internal combustion engines or fuel cells. It can provide power to heavy industry, cars, trains, boats, airplanes, rockets, and cell applications that can power any electric motor. Its use in cars, however, remains a technical challenge because it is difficult to store it in a tank.

With the new decade, the majority of hydrogen will still be produced from fossil fuels ("blue hydrogen"). This is a dirty production mode as it causes the release of up to 100 million tonnes of CO_2 annually in the EU, according the Commission's hydrogen strategy.[299] However, there is a gradual shift to cleaner hydrogen production from hydro electrolysis ("green hydrogen"). According to the strategy, the share of hydrogen in Europe's total energy mix is projected to rise from less than 2 % today to 13–14 % by 2050. Industry seems to be on board. In May 2020, an alliance of major European electricity groups – including Enel, Iberdrola, Ørsted, and EDP – sent a joint letter to the Commission, urging it to prioritise renewable hydrogen produced via electrolysis in its pandemic recovery plan.[300]

The EF would follow programmes to increase the use of hydrogen as power source. It would gradually move to the production of 100 % green hydrogen, where renewable sources (e.g. wind or solar) are used to extract hydrogen from electrolysis instead of fossil fuels. It would invest in the installation of renewable hydrogen electrolyser plants across its territory to produce many gigawatts of power. Green hydrogen would become part of its intrinsic energy system, alongside expanded solar and wind energy networks. To that end, segments of today's gas distribution grid would be used for the long-distance transport of green hydrogen. The EF would cluster hydrogen stations across Europe's islands and less populated areas to ensure decentralised production, and Europe's roads would be dotted with hydrogen refuelling stations to serve vehicles.

The hydrogen sector would need to be financially viable, meaning the EF would do its utmost to boost demand by end-users. Heavy industry would be given incentives to abandon fossil fuels (and blue hydrogen produced from them) and use green hydrogen instead. The same could be done for heavy duty road vehicles which would be encouraged to use hydrogen at the initial stage, perhaps at subsidised prices. Public campaigns advertising its benefits and opportunities could be launched as well.

10.3.4. Nuclear energy

Nuclear plants generated around 28 % of the electricity produced in the EU-27 in 2018. However, the total percentage of electricity generation from nuclear plants in the EU-27 decreased by 16.7 % between 2006 and 2018, partly as a result of the Fukushima accident in Japan, in 2011. At the end of 2010s, 14 EU member states had operational nuclear reactors: Belgium, Bulgaria, Czechia, Germany, Spain, France, Hungary, the Netherlands, Romania, Slovenia, Slovakia, Finland, Sweden and the UK.[301] More than half of nuclear energy power in the EU is generated in France.

The use of nuclear power for energy production remains a controversial issue in Europe. It is considered as an unacceptable risk by a significant part of the European population, and for good reasons. There are many nuclear plants concentrated in a small and densely populated continent, thus any new Chernobyl-style accident would have a devastating impact on millions of people's lives, health and properties. In the aftermath of the Fukushima nuclear disaster of 2011, stress tests were developed within the EU with the goal of making all 132 operating European reactors[302] follow the same safety standards and to have the same safety level for a list of possible catastrophic events (e.g. earthquake, flooding or plane crash). Moreover, the disposal of nuclear waste carries high safety concerns too.

However, nuclear power offers indisputable advantages for the society as a whole: it is cheaper, more reliable, does not depend on weather conditions, emits no greenhouse gases and causes no air pollution. Historically, it has proven much less lethal than the use of fossil fuels. According to one study, it has caused 330 times fewer deaths than coal, 250 times fewer than oil and 38 times fewer than gas.[303]

EF energy policy would pursue all the options for a safer and more efficient use of nuclear power. We are in favour of fusion energy and in particular ITER, the project in southern France where 35 nations are collaborating to build the world's largest "tokamak", namely a device which uses a powerful magnetic field to confine plasma in the shape of a torus. ITER will test and prove the feasibility of fusion as a large-scale, carbon-free source of energy. Fusion is the energy source of the sun and stars whose heat and gravity at their core cause hydrogen nuclei to collide and fuse into heavier helium atoms, releasing tremendous amounts of energy in the process. If successful, ITER will be the first fusion device to produce net energy and the first to sustain it for long periods of time. It is expected to be fully operational by the 2030s.[304] The EF would systematically invest in fusion energy and the exploitation of ITER's results.

Additional research should be funded on the production of nuclear power based on thorium instead of uranium. This type of production offers several potential advantages, including superior physical and nuclear fuel properties, reduced nuclear waste production and the fact that thorium is much more abundant than uranium. It is seen as perhaps the safest mode of nuclear power production.[305] However, development of thorium power is not yet commercially viable due to its high initial development costs. The EF would seek the best ways to reduce the number of uranium-based nuclear plants across Europe and replace them with thorium-based plants, if such an option is proven feasible.

Overall, the amount of nuclear power would fill part of the gap created by the abolition of fossil fuels. It should be stressed that, in October 2021, ten EU member states, led by France and Poland, openly supported nuclear power as part of the solution to the climate crisis and the rise in energy prices of that time.

10.4. Integrated networks of clean transport and water supply

The green transition of Europe will further require the development and modernization of continental networks of clean transport and water supply. This can best be achieved at European federal level due to the scale and importance of the process.

10.4.1. Transport networks

In the 2010s transport represented almost a quarter of Europe's greenhouse gas emissions and was the main cause of air pollution in cities. The transport sector has not seen the same gradual decline in emissions as other sectors: these only started to decrease in 2007 but, in 2020, still remained higher than in 1990. Road transport was by far the biggest emitter, accounting for more than 70 % of all greenhouse gas emissions by the transport sector.[306]

The EF would switch to low carbon transport as a matter of urgency. Electric cars and trucks must enter the markets and streets on a massive scale. The EF would ensure that such vehicles become cheaper by sponsoring related research. It would heavily invest in battery technology, electric vehicles, and fuel cells. Our research and marketing strategies would focus on areas such as vehicle efficiency via new engines, materials, and design; cleaner energy use through new propulsion systems; and safer operations through information and communication systems.

Key would be the development of a European battery industry. In 2017, the European Commission launched the "European battery alliance" – bringing together chemical groups, engineering companies, and car firms – to compete with American and Asian manufacturers. Encouraging signs appeared in 2020 with the emergence of potential industry champions. One of them is Swedish manufacturer Northvolt which obtained a €350 million loan from the European Investment Bank to build Europe's first battery giga-factory. At the same time, Volkswagen and other players started backing a similar project in Germany. In September 2021, Opel was scheduled to receive a €437 million grant by the German government for its battery cell factory in Kaiserslautern, as part of a wider European initiative[307]. The UK is also developing its own giga-plant in Wales. Although trailing China, Europe is now increasingly investing in this kind of production.[308] The EF would designate batteries for electric cars as a key industrial sector and ensure supplies of the necessary raw materials such as lithium, cobalt, and nickel by, for example, gaining preferential access to them in other regions, and especially in Africa.

The EF's railway network would be expanded to become one of the major transport means for a significant part of the population. Trains should replace airplanes and cars as much as possible. This would imply the acceptance of today's expensive costs of railways, though mitigated by actual investments in the sector's infrastructure and research. It should be stressed that today there is still no pervasive European high-speed rail network, as its development depends on fragmented national investments and plans. This is neither efficient nor logical in a densely populated continent with so many cities and small countries next to one other. The EF would thus offer an ideal political and administrative framework for such a programme.

Cities should dig deeper and wider to expand their metro systems. The example of Brussels today is characteristic: although at the heart of European politics, it has a sparse metro system and its traffic jams are among the worst in Europe. Regional and local governments across the EF would be required to draw up and enforce plans to ensure that people living in the cities and suburbs have good access to public transport, such as a maximum of 10 minutes' walking distance from the nearest tram, bus or metro station. They would be legally obliged to launch programmes for expanded use of bicycle lanes and walking routes, car-sharing/pooling schemes, and other measures to reduce congestion in their jurisdictions. They would receive financial assistance from the EF federal, national and regional budgets. But they would be strictly supervised to implement their plans as swiftly as possible, with clear and measurable targets tailored to their particular landscapes, population, and other local factors.

Big transport axes would be developed across the continent. The EU has made a good start with its transport-oriented "Trans-European Networks" (T-TEN corridors) and the development of nine transport routes that connect Europe, north to south and east to west. They bring together public and private resources to remove bottlenecks, fill in missing cross-border connections, and promote modal integration. These cover some very long routes such as the Scandinavia-Mediterranean or Baltic-Adriatic corridors. They comprise roads, tunnels and shipping routes that link major urban centres or ports with industrialised area.[309] The EF's transport policy would build on, and enhance, those networks to reduce Europeans' time and mileage spent on travel. Doing so would obviously reduce transport costs and pollution, while also creating wealth and boosting the general population's well-being.

10.4.2. Water supply networks

In parallel, the EF would modernize as a priority its water supply network. This would be vital for its ecological development and climate policy at a more integrated federal level.

The quality across Europe's water supply networks is uneven. People in certain cities dare not drink their tap water unfiltered. Parts of the EU's 7 million-kilometre long system of pipes have been in operation for over 100 years, with investment in water infrastructure failing to keep pace with Europe's growing population, urbanisation or global warming. According to one estimate, the EU would need to invest €135 billion to modernise its infrastructure. This is important to protect public health, the environment and, where possible, reduce the costs of water supply.[310]

Water supply in the EU is the responsibility of each member state, meaning the task is handled inconsistently from one state or region to the next. Fortunately, due to its many mountains and high rates of rainfall, renewable water remains abundant in Europe. Water resources are nonetheless limited and under rising pressure from urbanisation and climate change. The European Environmental Agency (EEA) finds that one European out of ten already suffers a degree of water scarcity. For example, the 1960–2010 years saw a 24 % decrease in renewable water resources per capita across Europe, particularly in its southern regions. There are pressing water stress conditions in the densely populated river basins of Europe, which correspond to 11 % of its total area, with 86 million inhabitants there. In many parts of Europe, groundwater resources and rivers continue to be overexploited. The situation is most worrisome in the Mediterranean region, where 40 % of its inhabitants live under water stress conditions.[311]

As a result of its inadequate infrastructure, Europeans over-consume bottled water, which produces mountains of plastic waste and hikes our continent's demand for imported oil to produce the bottles in the first place. Moreover, as mentioned in Chapter 8 on agriculture, large quantities of water are wasted due to inefficiencies and leakages from irrigation systems.

Access to clean, drinkable water and to water supplies for critical functions, such as farming and food production, would be one of EF's policy priorities. It would focus on new networks for capturing the water supplies of the richest areas, especially mountainous ones. The oldest networks, some of which are literally rotting, would be gradually replaced. The most egregious leakage points would be repaired and consumption meters installed consistently across pipeline systems. There would be regular auditing, inspections, and standardisation of networks, and a solid data trail updated with modern analytical technologies. In addition, investment in advanced wastewater treatment methods would raise levels of water reuse and efficiency. For example, the removal of potential nutrients such as algae for re-purposed use elsewhere would be explored as one option for cleaning water and producing energy.

The management of water utilities is a socially sensitive issue where the EF would need to find realistic solutions. Within the EU today, four models apply to the sector: direct public management; delegated public management (where the public sector retains ownership of the network but delegates certain tasks to management entities), delegated private management (the public sector retains ownership but authorises a private company to manage the system for a limited period in the form of lease or concession contract), and direct private management where the ownership of water utilities lies with the private sector.[312] Due to the strategic significance of water supply, a solution between the second and third option should be favoured by the EF authorities. This would imply that the public sector retains ownership but delegates, partly or fully, the management of a water network to other contractors or allows them to lease and exploit it for a fixed period under strict conditions.

At any event the EF would allocate, as a joint public and private investment, around €135 billion to modernise Europe's aged water supply network within a period of 10 years (€13,5 billion annually). In addition, it would set aside each year €20 billion for investment in new technologies and infrastructure to improve the capture, use, re-use and protection of all water resources.

10.5. Switching to a circular economy: Reducing material and energy losses

A move from the current model of a linear economy (produce-consume-dispose) to a circular one is imperative. A circular economy is a regenerative system where resource input, emissions, energy leakage and waste are minimised by maintaining, repairing, reusing, refurbishing, and recycling the material and energy we use.

According to a report of the Dutch think-tank 'Circle Economy', only 9 % of the world's exploited natural resources are re-used, with more than two-thirds of all greenhouse gases emitted by the exploitation of natural resources. A fully circular economy would cut those emissions by 72 %, argues the report.[313] The Dutch policy group suggests seven strategies to bridge the circularity gaps: prioritising renewable resources, preserving existing resources and goods, re-using and recycling waste, favouring a "functional" economy, optimising and incorporating the use of digital technology, eco-design and, finally, promoting collaboration to create joint value.

We fully subscribe to this analysis. Resources are finite and nature is under heavy pressure, risking being swamped by our own garbage. The figures are alarming: on average 476 kg of garbage per person (municipal waste) is produced every year. This waste translates into more than 240 million tonnes for the EU27 and the UK. Only 40 % of municipal waste is re-used or recycled and, in some countries, more than 80 % goes straight to landfills.[314] A great deal of industrial and other types of waste also ends up literally 'wasted' and not re-used.

Switching to a model of circular economy can, and should, be coupled with economic growth. A recent study of Cambridge Econometrics, Trinomics, and IF International suggests that applying circular economy principles in the EU could increase its GDP by 0.5 % by 2030, creating around 700 000 new jobs.[315] As part of its European Green Deal, the European Commission announced in 2020 its action plan on circular economy,[316] based on win-win strategies where business and consumers would both benefit financially from more efficient use of our resources. The action plan advocates new types of activities such as collaborative and sharing economy, digitisation, blockchain and artificial intelligence that would dematerialise the economy and make us less dependent on primary materials.

The EF would place the circular principle at the heart of its economic policies. It would elaborate a broad set of measures to reach that goal, per the principles of ecological development. It would adopt more ambitious recycling targets. The existing EU target of recycling 55 % of plastic by 2030 is inadequate, and would be increased to at least 70 %.[317] Recyclable goods would not be allowed to end-up to landfills – still abundant in countries like Greece or Bulgaria – that would be eventually abolished. Certification schemes would be expanded to cover a wide range of waste streams to ensure high quality recycling. Municipal waste would be taxed above a certain threshold (e.g. in excess of 1.5 kg per person per day) and monitored through the installation of digital garbage collection systems. Smart meters for electricity, gas and other forms of energy would be subsidised and actively promoted for daily consumption. Large companies would be subjected to energy audits on a regular basis.

Moreover, the EF would introduce a new legal framework for the design of products to improve their durability and re-usability. Such goods initially might be expensive to build, make, refurbish or buy, but the extra costs would be soon recovered through substantial energy savings.

Eco-design would become the mainstream manufacturing mode for hundreds of products such as boilers, electric devices, and any type of machinery. All would be subject to energy efficiency standards and labelling. The single use of products would be subject to tighter restrictions and penalties. Recycling of material would be increased. Resource-intensive goods such as electronics, steel or textiles would have to meet sustainability criteria, with financial incentives for compliance such as fiscal advantages. Plastic bags and plastic produced from non-recycled material would be taxed and progressively banned.

The application of digital technologies for tracking and traces of resources during production processes would become the norm. An EF certification scheme would apply across the board to verify compliance with upgraded standards for circular economy business practices. Devices such as mobile phones, tablets, laptops, desk computers or chargers would be designed and manufactured to be repairable, reusable, and recyclable. A consistent EF-scheme would be set up in all regions, especially the least developed ones, to ensure the return or buy back of old devices. Batteries would be subject to specific rates of recycled content to ensure the materials' recovery. Non-rechargeable batteries would be banned. Overpackaging and packaging waste would be drastically reduced and fined, especially regarding the complexity and use of polymers. Microplastics would be heavily restricted in all products. Textile products would be designed to fit into circularity and reuse, with collections of textile waste carried out at industrial and consumer levels. Separate and more narrowly defined collection steams would be laid down for different types of paper, textile, aluminium, plastic, batteries, electronic devices and so on.

All new buildings in the EF would have to be designed as intelligent, low-energy consumption structures. Efficiency has to be increased along all stages of the energy chain, from energy generation to final consumption. Heating and cooling in buildings and industry accounts for currently half of the EU's energy consumption. Moreover, 84 % of that energy is generated from fossil fuels, while only 16 % comes from renewable energy sources. To fulfil the EU's climate and energy goals, Europe's heating and cooling sectors must sharply reduce their energy consumption and the use of fossil fuels.[318] This would imply, of course, substantial public and private investment.

The EF would explore all means to finance the above measures. Several EU member states, for example, have already implemented financing schemes such as preferential interest rates to encourage private sector investment in the most efficient solutions for buildings. These and other private financing models would be promoted under the EF.

Finally, the EF would seek to introduce circularity as a principle in its international relations too. It would inject obligations into its free trade agreements and other partnerships for the others to shift to circular economy and apply equivalent European policies for each of their production lines. Particular attention would be paid to poorer partners where the need is most urgent to modernise how they produce and manufacture goods. The European Commission's "Global Circular Economy Alliance" has identified the knowledge gaps and supports international partnerships to help close them. The EF would make best use of that initiative, using its financial and diplomatic resources to ensure success. The European Green Deal must become a Global Green Deal, with a "circular Europe" contributing to a "circular world".

10.6. The EU post COVID-19 stimulus package for green and digital transition

Special reference must go to the very important stimulus package the EU has put together, designed to overcome the pandemic's economic blow to Europe and to help its societies adapt to and mitigate the effect of climate change. It focuses heavily on two big issues examined in the last part of our analysis: the transitions toward a digital and green future. This touches many aspects laid out by our vision for an EF in the 21st century, based on paths already forged by the EU today. The stimulus package is the largest ever financed by the EU, worth a total of € 1.8 trillion. It consists of €1.07 trillion for the EU's multiannual budget for 2021–2027 and €750 billion as a special post-COVID-19 recovery programme, entitled 'NextGenerationEU'.[319] Together, the package's two components aim to create more flexible financing mechanisms for the EU to deal with an unpredictable future. It is a budget focused on resilience, designed to handle tomorrow's uncertainties.

Specifically, more than 50 % of the amount dedicated to 'NextGen-erationEU' will support three policy goals: research and innovation via Horizon Europe; climate and digital transition via the Just Transition Fund and Digital Europe Programme; and, finally, preparedness, recovery and resilience via the package's Recovery and Resilience Facility, rescEU, and a new health programme ("EU4Health"). In addition, the package pays special attention to reforming some of the EU's longstanding instruments such as its Cohesion fund and Common Agricultural Policy. Big part of that programme will focus on climate policies and gender equality.

The Recovery and Resilience Facility is the centrepiece of NextGen-erationEU. Some €672.5 billion will be set aside for loans and grants to support the wider aim of mitigating the pandemic's economic and social impact. Each member state has had to define its own recovery and resilience plans in order to gain access to the Facility. Greece, for instance, submitted a plan that, among other things, calls for connecting its islands to the country's mainland power network and to phase out Greece's energy production from lignite coal.

One of the most interesting aspects of the Recovery Plan is its implied shift to a more federal dimension for Europe. One example is the common borrowing by all EU member states for a common purpose, a crucial step towards fiscal federalism. Another is health policy, an area that has historically hewed to national competence. Now it is part of broader EU planning. To wit: it was, and remains, the European Commission that negotiated and ordered the EU's Covid vaccines on behalf of all its national capitals. Moreover, the member states readily exchanged resources to deal with the pandemic, leading to patients hospitalised across national borders in a number of cases. In its broadest sense, the Recovery Plan recognises the importance of the social dimension to EU policies as a building block for the future of Europe. And, due to the pandemic, it has introduced 'resilience' as a central concept for common EU policies.

10.7. Concluding summary and budgetary issues

The EF would pursue a policy of carbon neutrality, decentralised "energy democracy", and a circular economy. It would build on, and develop further, the European Green Deal that was launched by the EU in 2019 to achieve a carbon neutral economy by 2050. The EF would expand a network of social infrastructure for sustainable energy, transport, and water for all. It would adopt a model of circular economy affecting all aspects of European production and consumption. It would take measures to make recycling and the reuse of resources affordable activities of our everyday life.

Those policies would require major, sustained investments. According to estimates by the European Commission, an increase in public and private investment of around €270 billion per year will be needed in the coming 40 years to switch Europe's economy to a low carbon one.[320] The EF would aim for a total of €400 billion per year. It would annually allocate €250 billion from its public budget toward this goal by financing activities such as: development of smart energy grids for renewable energy, with emphasis on wind and solar power; research and development for fusion and thorium-based nuclear power; digital connections; development of the Internet of Things, with a focus on more marginalised areas; electrification of auto-mobility; expansion of key transport corridors, with a focus on low carbon transport and the inter-connection of less developed areas; renovation of Europe's water supply infrastructure; energy efficiency of buildings; dissemination of smart meters for energy consumption; the creation of digitally automated garbage collection to reduce municipal waste.

This budgetary outlay would be complemented to a significant extent (€150 billion) by industry and other segments of the private sector with a view to reaching a combined private-public investment target of €400 billion per year.

Epilogue

This forward-looking and visionary analysis has been written in the 21st year of the 21st century. It dares to introduce a far-reaching proposal for policies for all of Europe for the remainder of the century. With the benefit of hindsight, we would like to play a mental game: what would a similar political proposal and analysis have looked like in the 21st year of past centuries?

In 321 A.D. this analysis could have been written by a Roman citizen. He or she would argue for the re-organisation of the Roman Empire in a century of emerging dynamic groups (the Germanic tribes) and an emerging dynamic religion (Christianity). A new vision would be required for the incorporation of those groups and religion into a new and more inclusive empire.

In the year 1521, such an analysis could have been written by an English citizen. He or she would call for the urgent establishment of a strong English navy, because that would be the century of exploration and global commerce. They would argue that a nation's progress could only be accomplished through robust power projection, new resources and expansion of trade.

In 1821, such a text could have been written by a German citizen who would argue for a united German kingdom, replacing more than 30 different German statelets. The author would also call for expertise in engineering and the development of an industrialised economy to accommodate the century's advancing industrial revolution.

In 1921, after World War I, such a text could have been written by any European citizen who would make the case, as we do today, for a united Europe. The text would elaborate a new model for peace, and argue against the unnecessary suffering of war. It would lobby for European integration and co-operation in order to compete or collaborate with the emerging powers of the time (the USA and Bolshevik Russia).

All these imaginary visionary elaborations would have several things in common: a call for unity, inclusiveness, and adaptation to the circumstances of their time. There seems to be a historic pattern in the demand for integration and the re-organisation of nations during critical periods. Such a message is pertinent for Europe in the 21st century too.

Europe yesterday, today and tomorrow

The European project was conceived originally in the early 1950s as a peace project to avoid the repetition of two devastating world wars. It started as the European Economic Communities and then evolved into the European Union as we know it today. It was a remarkable step forward for humankind, significantly contributing to people's freedom and well-being. Its prime objective was to deliver economic growth and prosperity. It moved further ahead with the principles of sustainable development, social cohesion, human rights, rule of law, international co-operation, and solidarity. Despite some serious ups and downs, it only took less than 70 years to accomplish all of that – a relatively short period of history. We should appreciate that achievement and continue building on it.

But the European project has now reached a new crossroads. It faces the novel landscape of globalisation and cross-border issues: climate change, trade competition, immigration, and the fourth industrial revolution. A globalised world offers tremendous possibilities, but it also poses new threats to stability and prosperity. Combining pragmatic proposals with an ambitious re-envisioning of the European governance, our analysis and proposal represent an understanding of how to best achieve a competitive, sustainable, and inclusive Europe.

"Europe cannot survive unchanged", according to a 2017 article written both by Manfred Weber, then chairman of the European Parliament's EPP political group, and Guy Verhofstadt, then head of the ALDE political group.[321] We agree with that view. National policies have fallen short of tackling the 21st century's existential challenges. Each individual member state of the EU is too weak to stand alone in a globalised world. Together, they could become the most powerful entity on the planet – the world champions of economic growth, technological progress, social justice, environmental protection, and humanistic values. This is why we believe that the political unification of Europe is neither a luxury, nor a utopic vision, but an absolute necessity.

To paraphrase what Stefan Auer and Nicole Scicluna wrote in their book, "Whose Liberty is it anyway? Europe at the Crossroads":

For writers and artists, Europe's greatness was its culture...

For economists and more practically minded people, its tremendous wealth...

For liberals, its commitment to liberty and the rule of law...

For socialists, its devotion to equality and fairness...

For visionaries, its transformation into a *European Federation!*

Appendix

Annual expenses of the proposed EF budget

The policy items in the left column are based on Eurostat's classification of government expenses by function[322] and the specific policy proposals laid down in the various chapters of this book. The number of the chapter, where each respective policy has been analysed, is also indicated in that column.

The proposed annual figures for each policy item are indicated in the right column. Most of them have been analysed in the respective chapters. They are based on the objective of restricting public spending to less than 50% of the EF's annual GDP (namely less than €8 trillion of the approximately €16 trillion for the EU28 in 2019).[323]

In order to offer a sense of comparison, the annual EU budget for 2019 was a mere €148 billion compared to approximately €7.5 trillion of the total sum of the national public spending of each EU member state.

All figures represent rough estimations and are indicated in 2021 prices. They are by no means the results of a full impact assessment. However, they aim to show that a common European federal budget could replace the respective national ones in an effective manner. They also imply that the objectives presented in this text for a federal Europe are feasible.

Policy item	Annual expenses in €billion
1. Social protection (including universal basic support, universal basic pension, universal health coverage and special health coverage for disabilities serious cases (Chapter 6))	3,480 *1,440 for universal basic support* *840 for universal basic pensions* *900 for health infrastructure and universal health coverage* *200 for special health coverage* *100 for disability allowances*
2. Education (pre- and primary education, secondary education, post-secondary and non-tertiary education, tertiary education, development of common curricula, programs for reduction of educational poverty, school buildings, subsidised school meals, salaries and training programmes for teachers (Chapter 6))	750 (incl. 100 for universities)
3. Salaries of 15 million civil servants (Chapter 3), including increased salaries of 150,000 judges and prosecutors (Chapter 5)	720
4. Anti-corruption authority (Chapter 3)	10
5. Annual debt servicing (Chapter 4, worst case scenario)	500
6. Support of the sovereign wealth fund ('rainy day fund') (Chapter 4)	200
7. Clean-up of red banking loans (Chapter 4)	50
8. Defence (Chapter 5)	300
9. Public order and security (Chapter 5)	320

Policy item	Annual expenses in €billion
10. International development aid (Chapter 5)	100
11. Social cohesion, housing and community amenities, including housing development, community development, water supply, street lighting, research, other costs (Chapter 6)	200 *75 for social cohesion projects* *75 for housing projects* *30 for other housing amenities* *20 for penitentiary system*
12. Agricultural and food policy (Chapter 8)	140
13. Networks of social infrastructure, including energy, transport, water and digital (Chapters 9 and 10)	250
14. Circular economy, climate policy and environmental protection, including waste management, waste water management, pollution abatement, protection of biodiversity and landscape, research, other costs, transition measures to circular economy (Chapter 10)	250
15. Research and development on advanced technologies and measures to adapt to them (Chapter 9)	200
16. Support of innovative start-up businesses (Chapter 9)	20
17. Support of working skills needed for a circular economy (Chapter 9)	20

Policy item	Annual expenses in €billion
18. €30 billion allocated to development banks for support of SMEs (Chapter 9)	30
19. Demographic policy (Chapter 7)	120
20. Immigration policy (Chapter 7)	60
21. Recreation and culture, including cultural diplomacy, recreational and sporting services, cultural services, broadcasting services and €10 billion allocated for the programmes of cultural diplomacy (Chapter 5)	30
Total	7,750

Notes

Prologue

1 Officially entitled, *For a Free and United Europe. A Draft Manifesto* (*Per un'Europa libera e unita. Progetto d'un manifesto*), 1941.

Part I Conceptual framework for a European Federation

2 Price Waterhouse Cooper, "The World in 2050", https://www.pwc.com/gx/en/issues/economy/the-world-in-2050.html

3 World Population Review 2020, http://worldpopulationreview.com/

4 International Monetary Fund, World Economic Outlook Database 2021, https://www.imf.org/en/Publications/WEO/weo-database/2021/April/weo-report?a=1&c=998,&s=NGDPD,PPPGDP,NGDPRPPPPC,PPPPC,&sy=2018&ey=2026&ssm=0&scsm=1&scc=0&ssd=1&ssc=0&sic=0&sort=country&ds=.&br=1

5 European Commission, DG TRADE, "EU position in world trade", https://ec.europa.eu/trade/policy/eu-position-in-world-trade/

6 European Commission, "Recipients and results of EU aid", https://ec.europa.eu/info/aid-development-cooperation-fundamental-rights/recipients-and-results-eu-aid_en

7 United Nations Development Programme, Human Development Reports, http://hdr.undp.org/en/content/2019-human-development-index-ranking

8 CEIC, "European Union real GDP growth 1996–2019", https://www.ceicdata.com/en/indicator/european-union/real-gdp-growth

9 Statista, "National debt in EU countries in the 1st quarter 2019 in relation to gross domestic product (GDP)", https://www.statista.com/statistics/269684/national-debt-in-eu-countries-in-relation-to-gross-domestic-product-gdp/

10 Trading Economics, "Country List Government Debt to GDP", https://tradingeconomics.com/country-list/government-debt-to-gdp

11 See IMF Data mapper, http://www.imf.org/external/datamapper/PPPSH@
    WEO/OEMDC/ADVEC/WEOWORLD

12 Mikkel Barslund, Daniel Gros, "Europe's Place in the Global Economy –
    What Does the Last Half Century Suggest for the Future?", *Intereconomics,*
    2016.   https://www.intereconomics.eu/contents/year/2016/number/1/arti-
    cle/europes-place-in-the-global-economy-what-does-the-last-half-century-
    suggest-for-the-future.html

13 United Nations Conference on Trade and Development, UNCTAD, *Key
    Statistics and Trends in International Trade 2018*, p. 10, https://unctad.org/
    en/PublicationsLibrary/ditctab2019d2_en.pdf

14 Barslund, Gros, *Op. cit.*

15 Darrell M. West, Christian Lansang, "Global manufacturing score-
    board: How the US compares to other nations", *Brookings,* 2018, Table 1.
    https://www.brookings.edu/research/global-manufacturing-scorecard-
    how-the-us-compares-to-18-other-nations/

16 Eurostat, "The EU in the world – Population", http://ec.europa.eu/eurostat/
    statistics-explained/index.php/The_EU_in_the_world_-_population

17 World Population Review, "Countries by Median Age 2018", https://world-
    populationreview.com/country-rankings/median-age

18 Eurostat, "Fertility rates", https://ec.europa.eu/eurostat/statistics-explained/
    index.php/Fertility_statistics#The_birth_rate_in_the_EU_decreased_at_
    a_slower_pace_between_2000_and_2017_than_before

19 Eurostat, "The EU in the world – Population", http://ec.europa.eu/eurostat/
    statistics-explained/index.php/The_EU_in_the_world_-_population

20 European Parliament, *Demographic Outlook for the European Union in
    2019*,   http://www.europarl.europa.eu/RegData/etudes/IDAN/2019/
    637955/EPRS_IDA(2019)637955_EN.pdf

21 European Parliament, *op. cit.*, http://www.europarl.europa.eu/RegData/
    etudes/IDAN/2019/637955/EPRS_IDA(2019)637955_EN.pdf

22 Eurostat, "Extra-EU trade in agricultural products", https://ec.europa.eu/
    eurostat/statistics-explained/index.php/Extra-EU_trade_in_agricultural_
    goods#EU_trade_in_agricultural_products:_slight_deficit

23 National Oceanic and Atmospheric Administration, "2020 was Earth's
    second warmest year, just behind 2016" https://www.noaa.gov/news/2020-
    was-earth-s-2nd-hottest-year-just-behind-2016

24 Copernicus Climate Service and Europenews, "Climate Now: 2019 was
    warmest year on record in Europe", https://www.euronews.com/2020/01/
    13/climate-now-2019-was-warmest-year-on-record-in-europe

25 Copernicus Climate Service as reported by Climate Home News, https://www.climatechangenews.com/2020/01/08/2019-second-warmest-year-record-ends-hottest-decade-yet-says-eu-observatory/

26 European Environmental Agency, "Glaciers", https://www.eea.europa.eu/data-and-maps/indicators/glaciers-2/assessment

27 Ana Garcia Valdivia, "Desertification: A Serious Threat To Southern Europe", *Forbes*, 2019, https://www.forbes.com/sites/anagarciavaldivia/2019/07/30/desertification-a-serious-threat-to-southern-europe-lands/#439898b13021

28 European Court of Auditors, "Combating Desertification in the EU: a growing threat in need of more action", 2018, p. 7, https://www.eca.europa.eu/Lists/ECADocuments/SR18_33/SR_DESERTIFICATION_EN.pdf

29 Joint Research Centre, European Commission, "Climate Impacts in Europe, The JRC PESETA II Project", 2014, https://bit.ly/3grgoFi

30 Joint Research Centre, "Global food security", https://ec.europa.eu/jrc/en/research-topic/global-food-security

31 Newsletter for the European Union, "Which Strategy for European Energy Security?", http://www.newslettereuropean.eu/strategy-european-energy-security/. For the sake of this analysis, we are not using data from the years 2020 and 2021 due to the pandemic-related irregular fall of overall consumption and import of energy.

32 European Commission, "From where do we import energy and how dependent are we?", https://ec.europa.eu/eurostat/cache/infographs/energy/bloc-2c.html

33 World Economic Forum, "Fourth Industrial Revolution", https://www.weforum.org/focus/fourth-industrial-revolution

34 Regarding: internet companies, World Atlas, https://www.worldatlas.com/articles/the-25-largest-internet-companies-in-the-world.html ; semiconductor companies, EPSNews, https://epsnews.com/2019/11/18/intel-to-reclaim-no-1-semiconductor-supplier-ranking-in-2019/; IT companies, mbasKOOL.com, https://www.mbaskool.com/fun-corner/top-brand-lists/17611-top-10-it-companies-in-world.html

35 Barslund, Gros, *op. cit.*

36 European Commission, "Shaping the Conference on the Future of Europe", https://ec.europa.eu/commission/presscorner/detail/en/ip_21_1065. The launch was initially scheduled for 9 May 2020, but it was finally launched on 10 March 2021 due to the COVID-19 pandemic.

37 Conference on the Future of Europe, Rules of Procedure of the Conference on the Future of Europe, https://futureu.europa.eu/uploads/decidim/attachment/file/4522/Consolidated_text_Rules_of_Procedure.pdf

38 "Initiative for Europe", Speech by M. Emmanuel Macron, President of the French Republic, 26 September 2017, http://international.blogs.ouest-france.fr/archive/2017/09/29/macron-sorbonne-verbatim-europe-18583. html

Chapter 2 The ideological framework of the European Federation

39 "Liberalism", *Encyclopaedia Britannica*, https://www.britannica.com/topic/liberalism/Rights

40 *Idem.*

41 World Bank, "Decline of Global Extreme Poverty Continues but Has Slowed", 2018, https://www.worldbank.org/en/news/press-release/2018/09/19/decline-of-global-extreme-poverty-continues-but-has-slowed-world-bank

42 It is the definition first developed by the United Nations World Commission on Environment and Development, "Our Common Future", 1987.

43 Suggestions for further reading on the principles of social ecology: Murray Bookchin, *The Ecology of Freedom,* Stirling: AK Press, 2005; and Andrew Light, *Social Ecology After Bookchin,* New York: Guilford Press, 1998. See also website of Institute for Social Ecology, www.social-ecology.org

44 Suggestions for further reading on political ecology see: Michael Watts, "Political Ecology", in *A Companion to Economic Geography*, E. Sheppard and T. Barnes (eds.), Blackwell, 2002; Susan Paulson, Lisa L. Geson, and Michael Watts, "Locating the Political in Political Ecology: An Introduction", *Human Organization* Vol. 62, issue 3 (2000), pp. 205–217; and R. Bryant (ed.), *International Handbook of Political Ecology*, Edward Elgar, 2015.

45 For an overview of EU legislation on environment and climate change see: European Commission, Eur-Lex, "Environment and Climate Change", https://bit.ly/2H44gg8

46 The European Green Deal, "Communication from the European Commission", 11 December 2019, https://ec.europa.eu/info/sites/info/files/european-green-deal-communication_en.pdf

47 *Humanism – What's in the Word*, London: Rationalist Press Association, 1997; Richard Norman, *On Humanism (Thinking in Action)*, London: Routledge, 2004; Vito Giustiniani, "Homo, Humanus, and the Meanings of Humanism", *Journal of the History of Ideas,* Vol. 46, no. 2 (April-June 1985), pp. 167–95.

48 Robert Grudin, "Humanism", *Encyclopedia Britannica*, https://www.britannica.com/topic/humanism

49 Steinar Stjerno, "The Idea of Solidarity in Europe", *European Journal of Social Law*, No. 3 (September 2011).

50 Sven-Eric Liedman, "Solidarity, A conceptual history", 2002, *Eurozine*, https://www.eurozine.com/solidarity-a-conceptual-history/

51 Classic readings on social contract: Jean-Jacques Rousseau, *Du contrat social*, 1762; John Locke, *Second Treatise of Government*, 1689; Thomas Hobbes, *Leviathan*, 1651. For more contemporary analyses of the theories of social contract: J. W. Gough, *The Social Contract*, Oxford: Clarendon Press, 1936; Otto Friedrich Von Gierke and Ernst Troeltsch, *Natural Law and the Theory of Society 1500 to 1800*, translated by Sir Ernest Barker, with a lecture by Ernst Troeltsch, "The Ideas of Natural Law and Humanity", Cambridge University Press, 1950; Patrick Riley, *Will and Political Legitimacy: A Critical Exposition of Social Contract Theory in Hobbes, Locke, Rousseau, Kant, and Hegel*, Cambridge, MA: Harvard University Press, 1982.

52 Some reading on the Idea of Progress: F. J. Teggart, *The Idea of Progress: A Collection of Readings*, Berkeley: University of California Press, 1949; David Spadafora, *The Idea of Progress in Eighteenth Century Britain*, Yale University Press, 1990; and Arthur M. Melzer, et al. eds, *History and the Idea of Progress*, 1995, where scholars discuss Machiavelli, Kant, Nietzsche, Spengler and others.

53 "Progress", *Stanford Encyclopedia of Philosophy*, 2011.

54 Encyclopedism was a movement of the 18th century that promoted the advancement of science and secular thought in support of tolerance, rationality, and the Enlightenment's open-mindedness.

55 The website of the organization: http://www.international-paneuropean-union.eu/#

56 L. Bekemans, D. Mahncke and R. Picht, *The College of Europe, Fifty Years of Service to Europe*, Europacollege: Brugge, 1999.

57 The European Movement, History, https://europeanmovement.eu/who-we-are/history/

58 Union of European Federalists, "The Spinelli Group", https://www.federalists.eu/spinelli-group

59 Volt Europe, https://www.volteuropa.org/about

60 A more descriptive analysis of the principle can be found in Protocol 2 to the European Treaties, https://europa.eu/european-union/sites/europaeu/files/docs/body/treaty_on_european_union_en.pdf

61 For a full list of the agencies, see: European Commission, Agencies and other EU bodies, https://europa.eu/european-union/about-eu/agencies_en

62 European Commission, "European Neighbourhood Policy And Enlargement Negotiations", https://ec.europa.eu/neighbourhood-enlargement/policy/glossary/terms/accession-criteria_en

63 European Commission, http://ec.europa.eu/citizens-initiative

64 European Commission, "Public administration characteristics and performance in EU 28", Introduction, page 3, file:///C:/Users/PCEUROPA/AppData/Local/Temp/0%20-%20KE-01-18-782-EN-N_Introduction.pdf

65 The model of Estonia's electronic governance is outlined in "E-stonia", https://e-estonia.com/

66 Special Eurobarometer 397, "Corruption", February 2014, http://ec.europa.eu/commfrontoffice/publicopinion/archives/ebs/ebs_397_en.pdf

67 Special Eurobarometer 397, "Corruption", February 2014, http://ec.europa.eu/commfrontoffice/publicopinion/archives/ebs/ebs_397_en.pdf

68 European Commission, Corruption, https://ec.europa.eu/home-affairs/what-we-do/policies/organized-crime-and-human-trafficking/corruption_en

69 Transparency International, Corruption Perception Index, 2020, https://www.transparency.org/en/cpi/2020/index/nzl

70 "Artificial Intelligence – a promising anti-corruption tool in development settings?", Per Aarvik, Series editor: Arne Strand U4 Anti-Corruption Resource Centre, Chr. Michelsen Institute (U4 Report 2019:1), https://www.u4.no/publications/artificial-intelligence-a-promising-anti-corruption-tool-in-development-settings

71 World Bank blogs, "Can artificial intelligence stop corruption in its tracks?", https://blogs.worldbank.org/governance/can-artificial-intelligence-stop-corruption-its-tracks

72 "The Role of Education" A Forthcoming Education Policy Task Force Position Paper from the *Communitarian Network*, September 1998, http://civiced.org/papers/articles_role.html

73 EU Code of Practice on Disinformation, October 2018, file:///C:/Users/PCEUROPA/AppData/Local/Temp/1CodeofPracticeonDisinformation.pdf

74 European Parliament, Briefing, EU policies – Delivering for citizens, 2019, https://www.europarl.europa.eu/RegData/etudes/BRIE/2018/628293/EPRS_BRI(2018)628293_EN.pdf

75 European Institute for Gender Equality, "Gender Equality Index 2019: Gender Equality Index 2020: Still far from the finish line", https://eige.europa.eu/gender-equality-index/2020

76 Eurostat, news release, 7 March 2019, "8 March 2019: International Women's Day: Only 1 manager out of 3 in the EU is a woman…even less in senior management positions", https://ec.europa.eu/eurostat/documents/2995521/9643473/3-07032019-BP-EN.pdf/e7f12d4b-facb-4d3b-984f-bfea6b39bb72

77 For full statistics about the length and content of court cases, see European Commission, The 2017 EU Justice Scoreboard: https://ec.europa.eu/info/sites/info/files/justice_scoreboard_2017_en.pdf

78 The 2019 EU Justice Scoreboard, Figure 5, https://ec.europa.eu/info/sites/info/files/justice_scoreboard_2019_en.pdf

79 *Idem*, figure 16.

80 JRC Technical Reports, The judicial system and economic development across EU Member States, 2017, Vincenzo Bove and Elia Leandro, Unit I.1 – Competence Centre on Microeconomic Evaluation (CC-ME), http://publications.jrc.ec.europa.eu/repository/bitstream/JRC104594/jrc104594_ _2017_the_judicial_system_and_economic_development_across_eu_ member_states.pdf

81 European Commission, "Study on the functioning of judicial systems in the EU Member States", 05/04/2018, https://ec.europa.eu/info/sites/info/files/20180405_-_eu_scoreboard_-_indicators.pdf

Chapter 4 Economic governance through an economic, fiscal, monetary and banking union

82 EU digital single marker, *Business Europe*, https://www.businesseurope.eu/policies/digital-economy/eu-digital-single-market

83 Communication of the European Commission, "The European Green Deal", 11.12.2019, https://ec.europa.eu/info/sites/info/files/european-green-deal-communication_en.pdf

84 European Commission, DG Internal Market, Industry, Entrepreneurship and SMEs, "Clusters as drivers of the European economy: results from the 2020 European Panorama Report, March 2020", https://ec.europa.eu/growth/content/clusters-drivers-european-economy-results-2020-european-panorama-report_en

85 "European Union Government Spending to GDP", *Trading Economics*, https://tradingeconomics.com/european-union/government-spending-to-gdp

86 Statista, 'Gross domestic product of the European Union from 2009-2020, https://www.statista.com/statistics/279447/gross-domestic-product-gdp-in-the-european-union-eu/

87 European Court of Auditors, "Public Private Partnerships in the EU: Widespread Shortcomings and limited benefits", 2018, https://www.eca.europa.eu/Lists/ECADocuments/SR18_09/SR_PPP_EN.pdf

88 Communication of the European Commission, 10 March 2020, "Identifying and addressing barriers to the Single Market", https://ec.europa.eu/info/sites/info/files/communication-eu-single-market-barriers-march-2020_en.pdf

89 Corona virus and the cost of non Europe, European Parliamentary Research Service, May 2020, https://www.europarl.europa.eu/RegData/etudes/IDAN/2020/642837/EPRS_IDA(2020)642837_EN.pdf

90 Communication of the European Commission, 10 March 2020, "Identifying and addressing barriers to the Single Market", https://ec.europa.eu/info/sites/info/files/communication-eu-single-market-barriers-march-2020_en.pdf

91 Euractiv, "Nine member states ask for eurobonds to combat coronavirus", 25 March 2020 https://www.euractiv.com/section/economy-jobs/news/nine-member-states-ask-for-eurobonds-to-face-coronavirus-crisis/

92 Eurostat, Euro area government deficit at 0.6 % and EU at 0.5 % of GDP, https://ec.europa.eu/eurostat/documents/portlet_file_entry/2995521/2-22102020-AP-EN.pdf/7a9993de-a07d-4223-d8bb-83d1df836055#:~:text=In%202019%2C%20the%20government%20deficit,from%200.4%25%20to%200.5%25.

93 European Commission, "Convergence criteria for joining", https://ec.europa.eu/info/business-economy-euro/euro-area/enlargement-euro-area/convergence-criteria-joining_en

94 Eurostat, News release, 22 October 2019, https://ec.europa.eu/eurostat/documents/2995521/10064364/2-22102019-AP-EN/e0daab94-5418-21d7-a621-17730c7772b0

95 Eurostat, News release 21 January 2021, "Third quarter of 2020, Government debt up to 97.3 % of GDP in euro area", https://ec.europa.eu/eurostat/documents/portlet_file_entry/2995521/2-21012021-AP-EN.pdf/a3748b22-e96e-7f62-ba05-11c7192e32f3

96 "China's debt tops 300 % of GDP, now 15 % of global total: IIF", *Reuters*, 18 July 2019, https://www.reuters.com/article/us-china-economy-debt/chinas-debt-tops-300-of-gdp-now-15-of-global-total-iif-idUSKCN1UD0KD

97 "China's debt surpasses 300 percent of GDP, IIF says, raising doubts over Yellen's crisis remarks", *CNBC*, 28 June 2017, https://www.cnbc.com/2017/06/28/chinas-debt-surpasses-300-percent-of-gdp-iif-says-raising-doubts-over-yellens-crisis-remarks.html

98   European Commission, VAT rates applied in the Member States of the European Union, 1 January 2018, https://ec.europa.eu/taxation_customs/sites/taxation/files/resources/documents/taxation/vat/how_vat_works/rates/vat_rates_en.pdf

99   European Commission, VAT rates applied in the Member States of the European Union, 1 July 2019, https://ec.europa.eu/taxation_customs/sites/taxation/files/resources/documents/taxation/vat/how_vat_works/rates/vat_rates_en.pdf

100 Trading Economics, List of Countries per Income tax rates, https://tradingeconomics.com/country-list/personal-income-tax-rate?continent=europe

101 European Commission, European Semester Tax Sheet, https://ec.europa.eu/info/sites/info/files/file_import/european-semester_thematic-factsheet_taxation_en_1.pdf

102 The National Asset Register, HM Government, January 2007, https://assets.publishing.service.gov.uk/government/uploads/system/uploads/attachment_data/file/228846/7022.pdf

103 In 2021 the following EU member states are still using their national currencies: Bulgaria, Croatia, Czech Republic, Denmark, Hungary, Poland, Romania and Sweden.

104 Bank for International Settlements, "Triennial Central Bank Survey, Foreign Exchange Turnover in April 2019", https://www.bis.org/statistics/rpfx19_fx.pdf

105 European Commission, "The international role of the euro", https://ec.europa.eu/info/business-economy-euro/euro-area/international-role-euro_en

106 European Commission, "The benefits of the euro", https://ec.europa.eu/info/about-european-commission/euro/benefits-euro_en

107 European Central Bank, "The definition of price stability", https://www.ecb.europa.eu/mopo/strategy/pricestab/html/index.en.html

108 EurActiv, "Eurozone economy's growth 'best in nearly seven years'", 5 January 2018, https://www.euractiv.com/section/economy-jobs/news/eurozone-economys-growth-best-in-nearly-seven-years/

109 European Central Bank, "Pandemic Emergency Purchase Programme (PEPP)", https://www.ecb.europa.eu/mopo/implement/pepp/html/index.en.html

110 For further reading on this topic: "Helicopter money: A cure for what ails the euro area?", European Parliamentary Research Service, April 2016;

Willem Buiter, *Helicopter Money: Why it works – Always*, 2014; "Helicopter Money reloaded", *Bruegel*, 2016, https://www.bruegel.org/2016/03/hel icopter-drops-reloaded; Frank van Lerven, *Recovery in the Eurozone: using money creation to Stimulate the economy*, 2015; Simon Wren-Lewis, "What do people mean by helicopter money?", *mainly macro*, 2012, https://main lymacro.blogspot.com/2012/10/what-do-people-mean-by-helicopter-money.html.

111 CNBC, "Fourth stimulus checks are unlikely. Here's what federal aid could be coming next, 31 March 2021", https://www.cnbc.com/2021/03/31/fourth-stimulus-checks-are-unlikely-what-aid-could-be-coming-next.html

112 Euronews, 14/04/2021, 'Cryptocurrencies combined are now worth more than Apple, the world's most valuable company', https://www.euronews.com/2021/04/14/cryptocurrencies-combined-are-now-worth-more-than-apple-the-world-s-most-valuable-company

113 Josef Ackermann, "Europe suffers from the sorry state of its banks", *Financial Times*, 3 January 2019, https://www.ft.com/content/497d4d9e-0f3a-11e9-b2f2-f4c566a4fc5f

114 Deloitte, "Deleveraging Europe", October 2019, https://www2.deloitte.com/content/dam/Deloitte/uk/Documents/corporate-finance/deloitte-uk-deleveraging-europe-2019.pdf

115 European Commission, "Questions and Answers: Tackling non-performing loans to enable banks to support EU households and businesses", https://ec.europa.eu/commission/presscorner/detail/en/qanda_20_2376

116 European Central Bank, "ECB 2018 stress test analysis shows improved capital basis of significant euro area banks", 1 February 2019, https://www.bankingsupervision.europa.eu/press/pr/date/2019/html/ssm.pr190201~6114ab7593.en.html

117 "Deutsche Bank derivative dumbness", *Financial Times*, 8 July 2019, https://ftalphaville.ft.com/2019/07/08/1562575972000/Deutsche-Bank-derivative-dumbness/

118 Full title of the Liikainen report: "High-level Expert Group on reforming the structure of the EU banking sector", See summary of the European Commission: https://ec.europa.eu/commission/presscorner/detail/en/IP_12_1048

119 See European Commission, "Deposit Guarantee Schemes", https://ec.europa.eu/info/business-economy-euro/banking-and-finance/financial-supervision-and-risk-management/managing-risks-banks-and-financial-institutions/deposit-guarantee-schemes_en

120 OECD, "Regulatory of OTC Derivatives and its Implications for Sovereign Debt Management Practices", https://www.oecd-ilibrary.org/docserver/5k9gz2n0sgq2-en.pdf?expires=1590156263&id=id&accname=guest&checksum=D59D81137F283B7EEAA139EC40725D55

121 Eurostat, "Number of banks decreasing", https://ec.europa.eu/eurostat/cache/digpub/european_economy/bloc-3d.html?lang=en

Chapter 5 Security governance: Common foreign, defence and security policy

122 SIPRI (Stockholm International Peace Research Institute), "Military expenditure per country in constant (2019)", Fact Sheet, https://sipri.org/sites/default/files/Data%20for%20all%20countries%20from%20 1988%E2%80%932020%20in%20constant%20%282019%29%20 USD%20%28pdf%29.pdf

123 In 2020, Russia's population was 145 million compared to 508 million in the EU-28, and in 2019 its GDP was $1.63 trillion compared to EU-28's $18.75 trillion. Source: International Monetary Fund, http://www.imf.org/external/datamapper/LP@WEO/OEMDC/ADVEC/WEOWORLD

124 "United Nations might run out of money in a few weeks", *CBS News*, 8 October 2019, https://www.cbsnews.com/news/united-nations-could-run-out-of-money-in-october-secretary-general-antonio-guterres-says-today-2019-10-08/

125 SIPRI, "Military expenditure per country in constant (2019)", *op. cit.*

126 U.S. Congretional Research Service, Government Expenditures on Defense Research and Development by the United States and Other OECD Countries: Fact Sheet, 28 January 2020, https://fas.org/sgp/crs/natsec/R45441.pdf

127 David A. Slapak and Michael W. Johnson, "Outnumbered, outranged and outgunned: How Russia defeats NATO", *War on the Rocks*, 2016, https://warontherocks.com/2016/04/outnumbered-outranged-and-outgunned-how-russia-defeats-nato/

128 "Europe Wants Its Own Anti-Nuclear Ballistic Missile Defence System", *The National Interest*, 18 March 2020, https://nationalinterest.org/blog/buzz/europe-wants-its-own-anti-nuclear-ballistic-missile-defense-system-134317

129 See "Missile defense advances to better protect Europe", *POLITICO*, 7/8/2016, By Wes Kremer, president, Raytheon Integrated Defense Systems,

https://www.politico.eu/sponsored-content/missile-defense-advances-to-better-protect-europe/

130 "Top 10 navies in the world", *Military today*, http://www.military-today.com/navy/top_10_navies.htm

131 Samantha Bradshaw and Phillip N. Howard, "The Global Disinformation Order", University of Oxford, 2019, Figure 3, https://comprop.oii.ox.ac.uk/wp-content/uploads/sites/93/2019/09/CyberTroop-Report19.pdf

132 One military space agency's plan for 1,000 new satellites by 2026, https://www.c4isrnet.com/battlefield-tech/space/2020/01/21/one-military-space-agencys-plan-for-1000-new-satellites-by-2026/

133 "NATO, Summit Season", *The Economist,* Edition June 12th – 18th 2021, page 19

134 RUSI, "Artificial Intelligence and UK National Security: Policy considerations", https://rusi.org/publication/occasional-papers/artificial-intelligence-and-uk-national-security-policy-considerations; BBC, "UK spies will need artificial intelligence – RUSI report", 27 April 2020, https://rusi.org/publication/occasional-papers/artificial-intelligence-and-uk-national-security-policy-considerations

135 NATO press release, "Defence expenditure of NATO countries (2012 – 2019)", https://www.nato.int/nato_static_fl2014/assets/pdf/pdf_2019_06/20190625_PR2019-069-EN.pdf

136 "NATO just turned 70 – and it's showing its age", Carnegie Europe, Judy Dempsey, 4 April 2019, https://carnegieeurope.eu/2019/04/04/nato-just-turned-70-and-it-s-showing-its-age-pub-78795

137 Source: European Commission, DG TRADE, "EU position in world trade", http://ec.europa.eu/trade/policy/eu-position-in-world-trade/

138 European Commission, DG TRADE, "Trade for All - New EU Trade and Investment Strategy", https://ec.europa.eu/trade/policy/in-focus/new-trade-strategy/

139 World Bank, "The global costs of protectionism, 2017", http://documents.worldbank.org/curated/en/962781513281198572/The-global-costs-of-protectionism

140 European Environmental Bureau, "Race to the Bottom: How the trade deals are undermining standards that protect us", 2019, https://meta.eeb.org/2019/04/09/race-to-the-bottom-how-trade-deals-are-undermining-standards-that-protect-us/

141 See inflation calculator: https://www.in2013dollars.com/us/inflation/1948?amount=12000000000

142 "The Marshall Plan", *Encyclopaedia Britannica*, https://www.britannica.com/event/Marshall-Plan

143 European Commission, "European Development Policy", https://ec.europa.eu/europeaid/policies/european-development-policy_en

144 European Commission, "The European Union remains world's leading donor of Official Development Assistance with €75.2 billion in 2019", https://ec.europa.eu/international-partnerships/news/european-union-remains-worlds-leading-donor-official-development-assistance_en

145 Kimberly Ann Elliot, "Evidence on the Costs and Benefits of Economic Sanctions", Peterson Institute of International Economics, 1997, https://www.piie.com/commentary/testimonies/evidence-costs-and-benefits-economic-sanctions

146 European Union External Action, "European Neighbourhood Policy", https://eeas.europa.eu/headquarters/headquarters-homepage/330/european-neighbourhood-policy-enp_en

147 *Cultural Times*, report by CISAC and UNESCO, 2015, pages 15 and 16 https://en.unesco.org/creativity/sites/creativity/files/cultural_times._the_first_global_map_of_cultural_and_creative_industries.pdf

148 Joint Communication to the European Parliament and the Council, "Towards an EU strategy for international cultural relations", JOIN (2016) 29 final, https://eur-lex.europa.eu/legal-content/EN/TXT/?uri=JOIN%3A2016%3A29%3AFIN

149 Press release of the European Commission, 8 June 2016: http://europa.eu/rapid/press-release_IP-16-2074_en.htm

150 See EU – Russia trade figures in European Commission, DG Trade: https://ec.europa.eu/trade/policy/countries-and-regions/countries/russia/

151 Carnegie Endowment for International Peace, "The EU and Ukraine, Taking a Breath", 27 February 2018: https://carnegieendowment.org/2018/02/27/eu-and-ukraine-taking-breath-pub-75648

152 European Commission, DG TRADE, Country profiles, Ukraine: https://ec.europa.eu/trade/policy/countries-and-regions/countries/ukraine/

153 European Commission, DG TRADE, Countries and regions, Turkey: https://ec.europa.eu/trade/policy/countries-and-regions/countries/turkey/

154 The Energy Charter is a multilateral agreement covering investment promotion and protection, trade, transit, energy efficiency and dispute resolution. Its members include, among others, European and post-Soviet states. See website of Energy Charter: https://energycharter.org/

155 Eurostat, Government expenditure on public order and safety, February 2020: https://ec.europa.eu/eurostat/statistics-explained/index.php/Government_expenditure_on_public_order_and_safety

Chapter 6 Socio-cultural governance

156 European Commission, DG Education and Training, Linguistic Diversity: https://ec.europa.eu/education/policies/multilingualism/linguistic-diversity_en

157 Eurostat, Social protection statistics – social benefits: https://ec.europa.eu/eurostat/statistics-explained/index.php?title=Social_protection_statistics_-_social_benefits#Expenditure_on_social_protection_benefits_by_function

158 Eurostat, "Population structure and ageing", https://ec.europa.eu/eurostat/statistics-explained/index.php/Population_structure_and_ageing#The_share_of_elderly_people_continues_to_increase

159 Eurostat, "Government expenditure on social protection", https://ec.europa.eu/eurostat/statistics-explained/index.php?title=Social_protection_statistics_-_social_benefits

160 "Finnish basic income pilot improved wellbeing, study finds" *The Guardian*, 7 May 2020: https://www.theguardian.com/society/2020/may/07/finnish-basic-income-pilot-improved-wellbeing-study-finds-coronavirus

161 For a more general reading on education and Europe, read Bekemans, Léonce, "Education for European Citizenship-building", in Bekemans, L., *Globalisation vs Europeanisation. A Human-centric Interaction,* Peter Lang: Brussels, 2013, pp. 263–287; and Bekemans, Léonce, "The Future of Education in a (drastically) changing Europe", *Foreign Policy Review*, Institute for Foreign Affairs and Trade, Dec. 2018, pp. 22–51.

162 European Commission, "Education and Training Monitor 2019", https://ec.europa.eu/education/sites/education/files/document-library-docs/volume-1-2019-education-and-training-monitor.pdf

163 Publications Office of the EU, "Education and Training Monitor 2017", https://op.europa.eu/en/publication-detail/-/publication/38e7f778-bac1-11e7-a7f8-01aa75ed71a1

164 European Commission, "Education and Training, Early school leaving", https://ec.europa.eu/education/policies/school/early-school-leaving_en

165 "A shadow epidemic of school dropouts risks worsening Italy's north-south divide", *POLITICO*, 8 June 2021, https://politi.co/35dGKqN

166 European Commission, "Education and Training Monitor 2019", pp. 18–19, https://ec.europa.eu/education/sites/education/files/document-library-docs/volume-1-2019-education-and-training-monitor.pdf

167 European Commission, "Education and Training Monitor 2019", p. 30, https://ec.europa.eu/education/sites/education/files/document-library-docs/volume-1-2019-education-and-training-monitor.pdf

168 "Vocational training in Germany – how does it work?", Discover Germany, https://www.make-it-in-germany.com/en/for-qualified-professionals/training-learning/training/vocational-training-in-germany-how-does-it-work. See also: "The German Vocational Training System", Federal Ministry of Education and Research, https://www.bmbf.de/en/the-german-vocational-training-system-2129.html

169 uniRank, Universities in Europe, https://www.4icu.org/Europe/

170 Academic Ranking of World Universities, 2020, https://www.shanghairanking.com/rankings/arwu/2020

171 Eurostat, "Majority of health jobs held by women", https://ec.europa.eu/eurostat/web/products-eurostat-news/-/DDN-20200409-2

172 World Health Organisation, "What is health financing for universal coverage?", http://www.who.int/health_financing/universal_coverage_definition/en/

173 World Economic Forum, Harvard School of Public Health (2011), "The Global Economic Burden of Non-Communicable Diseases".

174 OECD, "Health At a Glance, Europe 2016", https://ec.europa.eu/health/sites/health/files/state/docs/health_glance_2016_rep_en.pdf

175 EU anti-tobacco campaigns, European Commission, https://ec.europa.eu/health/tobacco/ex_smokers_are_unstoppable_en

176 Study of Public Health France, BBC report of 28.05.2018, "One million French smokers quit in a year amid anti-smoking measures", http://www.bbc.com/news/world-europe-44282138

177 Eurostat, "Overweight and Obesity BMI Statistics", https://ec.europa.eu/eurostat/statistics-explained/index.php/Overweight_and_obesity_-_BMI_statistics

178 *Idem.*

179 Alcohol consumption, European Commission, DG Mobility and Transport, https://ec.europa.eu/transport/road_safety/specialist/knowledge/alcohol/prevalence_amp_rate_of_alcohol_consumption/alcohol_consumption_en

180 See World Health Organisation, "Alcohol use", Data and Statistics, https://www.euro.who.int/en/health-topics/disease-prevention/alcohol-use/data-and-statistics

181 World Health Organisation, "Road traffic injuries", http://www.who.int/news-room/fact-sheets/detail/road-traffic-injuries

182 Harvard Health Publishing, Harvard Medical School, "Can exercise extend your life?", Marwa A. Ahmed https://www.health.harvard.edu/blog/can-exercise-extend-your-life-2019031316207

183 Health Literacy Europe, "Making health literacy priority a priority in EU policy", https://www.eu-patient.eu/globalassets/policy/healthliteracy/health-literacy-consensus-paper_2016.pdf

184 "Premature deaths attributable to air pollution", European Environment Agency, https://www.eea.europa.eu/media/newsreleases/many-europeans-still-exposed-to-air-pollution-2015/premature-deaths-attributable-to-air-pollution

185 "Swiss medical tourism continues to grow", *International Medical Travel Journal*, 2014, https://www.imtj.com/news/swiss-medical-tourism-continues-grow/

186 Eurostat, "Government expenditure on health", March 2018, http://ec.europa.eu/eurostat/statistics-explained/index.php/Government_expenditure_on_health

187 Eurostat, "Government expenditure on health", https://ec.europa.eu/eurostat/statistics-explained/index.php/Government_expenditure_on_health

188 Mario Glowik, Slawomir Smyczek, *Healthcare. Market Dynamics, Policies and Strategies in Europe*, De Gruyter, 2015, p. 7, https://cutt.ly/whEAEc6

189 See for instance the Oxfam report, "Richest 1 percent bagged 82 percent of wealth created last year – poorest half of humanity got nothing", January 2018, https://www.oxfam.org/en/press-releases/richest-1-percent-bagged-82-percent-wealth-created-last-year-poorest-half-humanity

190 Camilo Maldonado, "Credit Suisse: Top 1 % Own Nearly 50 % Of Global Wealth And China's Wealthy Now Outnumber America's", *Forbes*, 2019, https://www.forbes.com/sites/camilomaldonado/2019/10/23/credit-suisse-top-1-own-nearly-50-of-global-wealth-and-chinas-wealthy-now-outnumber-americas/#7256cbc92ede

191 Eurostat, "Living conditions in Europe – poverty and social exclusion", https://ec.europa.eu/eurostat/statistics-explained/index.php/Living_conditions_in_Europe_-_poverty_and_social_exclusion

192 Bertelmanns Stiftung, 2013, "Social Cohesion Radar Measuring Common Ground", https://www.bertelsmann-stiftung.de/fileadmin/files/Projekte/Gesellschaftlicher_Zusammenhalt/englische_site/further-downloads/information/Findings_USA_Social_Cohesion.pdf

193 Eurostat Social Indicators, http://ec.europa.eu/social/main.jsp?catId= 756; see also: OECD Social Indicators, http://www.oecd.org/social/soci ety-at-a-glance-19991290.htm; see also: UN Human Development Index, http://hdr.undp.org/en/content/human-development-index-hdi

194 European Cohesion Policy in Sweden, https://ec.europa.eu/regional_pol icy/sources/docgener/informat/country2009/sv_en.pdf

195 European Commission, "New community centre helps build social cohesion in Širkovce, Slovakia", https://ec.europa.eu/regional_policy/en/projects/Slovakia/new-community-centre-helps-build-social-cohesion-in-sirkovce-slovakia

196 European Commission, "Cohesion Policy and Spain", https://ec.europa. eu/regional_policy/sources/information/cohesion-policy-achievement-and-future-investment/factsheet/spain_en.pdf

197 European Commission, "Available budget 2014–2020, EU regional and urban development", https://ec.europa.eu/regional_policy/en/funding/available-budget/

198 Eurostat, "Housing statistics", http://ec.europa.eu/eurostat/statistics-explained/index.php/Housing_statistics

199 Statista, "Number of Airbnb listings in selected European cities as of 2019", https://www.statista.com/statistics/815145/airbnb-listings-in-europe-by-city/

200 European Social and Economic Committee, 4 December 2019, "We need an EU strategy in social and affordable housing, says EESC", https://www.eesc.europa.eu/en/news-media/press-releases/we-need-eu-strategy-social-and-affordable-housing-says-eesc

201 €75 billion would correspond to something barely higher than 0.1 % of the annual EF budget.

202 Report of the European Parliament, October 2017, http://www.europarl. europa.eu/sides/getDoc.do?type=TA&language=EN&reference=P8-TA-2017-0385

203 European Prison Observatory (EPO), "Prison in Europe: overview and trends, 2013"; EPO, "From national practices to European guidelines", 2013, http://www.prisonobservatory.org/upload/EPOinterestinginitia tives.pdf

204 Report of the European Parliament, "Prison conditions in the Member States: selected European standards and best practices", 2014, http://www.europarl.europa.eu/RegData/etudes/BRIE/2017/583113/IPOL_BRI(2017)583113_EN.pdf

205 Council of Europe, SPACE – Council of Europe Annual Penal Statistics, 20 March 2018, https://www.coe.int/en/web/prison/space

206 Report of United Nations Office on Drugs and Crime (UNODC), "Introductory Handbook on the Prevention of Recidivism and the Social Reintegration of Offenders", 2012, http://www.unodc.org/documents/justice-and-prison-reform/crimeprevention/Introductory_Handbook_on_the_Prevention_of_Recidivism_and_the_Social_Reintegration_of_Offenders.pdf

207 Joseph A. Califano Jr., "What Was Really Great About The Great Society", *The Washington Monthly*, October 1999, https://web.archive.org/web/20140326175845/http://www.washingtonmonthly.com/features/1999/9910.califano.html

208 Eurostat, "Government expenditure on health", February 2020, https://ec.europa.eu/eurostat/statistics-explained/index.php/Government_expenditure_on_health

209 Eurostat, "Government expenditure on education", February 2020, https://ec.europa.eu/eurostat/statistics-explained/index.php/Government_expenditure_on_education

Part III Major policy sectors of the new European Federation

210 IMF Blog, "The Macroeconomic Effects of Global Migration," *by Philipp Engler, Keiko Honjo, Margaux MacDonald, Roberto Piazza (team leader) and Galen Sher, under the guidance of Florence Jaumotte, 19 June 2020,*

211 Eurostat, "Immigration and immigration population statistics", https://ec.europa.eu/eurostat/statistics-explained/index.php/Migration_and_migrant_population_statistics

212 Eurostat, "Statistics on enforcement of immigration legislation", http://ec.europa.eu/eurostat/statistics-explained/index.php/Statistics_on_enforcement_of_immigration_legislation

213 Gov.UK, Policy paper, "The UK's points-based immigration system: policy statement", 19 February 2020, https://www.gov.uk/government/publications/the-uks-points-based-immigration-system-policy-statement/the-uks-points-based-immigration-system-policy-statement

214 "Attracting and retaining international students in the EU", 2017, EMN (European Migration Network) study, https://ec.europa.eu/home-affairs/sites/homeaffairs/files/00_eu_international_students_2018_synthesis_report.pdf

215 Eurostat, "Residence permits", https://cutt.ly/phEA6a3

216 , "Germany's immigrants better integrated than 10 years ago, study says", *Deutsche Welle*, 21.11.2018, https://www.dw.com/en/germanys-immigrants-better-integrated-than-10-years-ago-study-says/a-46388938

217 "Von der Leyen seeks to bridge chasm on migration", *POLITICO*, 23 September 2020, https://www.politico.eu/article/european-commission-ursula-von-der-leyen-proposal-common-eu-migration-policy/

218 European Commission, "European Neighbourhood Policy and Enlargement Negotiations", 'EU delivers support and border management in Libya', 16.07.2020, https://cutt.ly/qhESthb

219 See Eurostat: http://ec.europa.eu/eurostat/statistics-explained/index.php/Fertility_statistics.

220 "Fertility rate in Germany rises to 33-year high", *The Guardian*, https://www.theguardian.com/world/2016/oct/17/fertility-rate-germany-rises-33-year-high-births-children-population

221 Directive 92/85/EEC.

222 European Parliament, "At a Glance", Infographic December 2014, "Maternity and paternity leave in the EU", http://www.europarl.europa.eu/RegData/etudes/ATAG/2014/545695/EPRS_ATA(2014)545695_REV1_EN.pdf

223 The University of Sidney, "Paid parental leave increases fertility intentions", 25 March 2016, https://www.sydney.edu.au/news-opinion/news/2016/03/25/paid-parental-leave-increases-fertility-intentions.html

224 European Parliament, "Adoption of children in the European Union", June 2016, https://www.europarl.europa.eu/RegData/etudes/BRIE/2016/583860/EPRS_BRI(2016)583860_EN.pdf

225 Hague Convention of 29 May 1993 on Protection of Children and Co-operation in Respect of Intercountry Adoption, https://www.hcch.net/en/instruments/conventions/full-text/?cid=69

226 European Parliament, "Adoption of children in the European Union", June 2016, https://www.europarl.europa.eu/RegData/etudes/BRIE/2016/583860/EPRS_BRI(2016)583860_EN.pdf

227 Eurostat, "Migration and migration population statistics", https://ec.europa.eu/eurostat/statistics-explained/index.php/Migration_and_migrant_population_statistics

Chapter 8 Agriculture and food policy

228 Eurostat, "Agriculture, forestry and fisheries statistics", 2018 edition, p. 12, https://ec.europa.eu/eurostat/documents/3217494/9455154/KS-FK-18-001-EN-N.pdf/a9ddd7db-c40c-48c9-8ed5-a8a90f4faa3f

229 European Commission, DG Agriculture and Rural Development, "CAP at a glance", https://ec.europa.eu/agriculture/cap-overview_en

230 "Extra-EU trade in agricultural goods", Eurostat Statistics Explained, http://ec.europa.eu/eurostat/statistics-explained/index.php/Extra-EU_trade_in_agricultural_goods

231 See Communication of the European Commission, 8.3.2011, COM(2011) 112 final, "A Roadmap for moving to a competitive low carbon economy in 2050", http://eur-lex.europa.eu/legal-content/EN/TXT/PDF/?uri=CELEX:52011DC0112&from=en

232 European Commission, "Farm to Fork Strategy: for a fair, healthy and environmentally friendly food system", https://ec.europa.eu/food/farm-2fork_en

233 European Commission, "From Farm to Fork", https://ec.europa.eu/info/strategy/priorities-2019-2024/european-green-deal/actions-being-taken-eu/farm-fork_en

234 "All You Wanted to Know About the Green Revolution", *Thought.Co* , https://www.thoughtco.com/green-revolution-overview-1434948

235 "15 Emerging Agriculture Technologies that Will Change the World", *Business Insider*, 5 May 2014, http://www.businessinsider.com/15-emerging-agriculture-technologies-2014-4?IR=T

236 See: European Commission, Directorate General Agriculture, "Water and Agriculture", https://ec.europa.eu/agriculture/envir/water_en

237 See: "Four ways to reduce water use in agriculture", *One Billion Hungry: Can we feed the world?*, https://canwefeedtheworld.wordpress.com/2013/03/22/four-ways-to-reduce-water-use-in-agriculture/

238 See European Environment Agency, "From production to waste", August 2016, https://www.eea.europa.eu/signals/signals-2014/articles/from-production-to-waste-food-system

239 See IME (Institution of Mechanical Engineers) food waste report – data, https://docs.google.com/spreadsheets/d/1nzLDn1LbiwVe2TL4y4kie-juUQKpIx4Z3R5GHOguwvmo/edit#gid=0

240 VegNews, "Price of Lab-Grown Meat to Plummet from $280,000 to $10 Per Patty By 2021", https://vegnews.com/2019/7/price-of-lab-grown-meat-to-plummet-from-280000-to-10-per-patty-by-2021

241 Fusions, "Estimates of European food waste levels", http://www.eu-fusions.org/phocadownload/Publications/Estimates%20of%20European%20food%20waste%20levels.pdf

242 See Eurostat, "Overweight and obesity – BMI statistics", Statistics explained, http://ec.europa.eu/eurostat/statistics-explained/index.php/Overweight_and_obesity_-_BMI_statistics

243 Food Waste Alliance, http://www.foodwastealliance.org/about-our-work/policy/

244 European Commission, Directorate-General Agriculture, "What is Organic Farming?", https://ec.europa.eu/agriculture/organic/organic-farming/what-is-organic-farming_en

245 Eurostat, "Organic farming statistics", January 2020, https://ec.europa.eu/eurostat/statistics-explained/index.php/Organic_farming_statistics#-Fully_organic_farms

246 Eurostat, "European Commission, Organic farming statistics", https://ec.europa.eu/eurostat/statistics-explained/index.php/Organic_farming_statistics, and "Facts and Figures on organic agriculture in EU", http://ec.europa.eu/agriculture/rica/pdf/Organic_2016_web_new.pdf

247 Food and Agricultural Organisation, FAOSTAT, http://www.fao.org/faostat/en/#data/countries_by_commodity/visualize

248 "The food rush: Rising demand in China and west sparks African land grab", *The Guardian*, 3 July 2009, https://www.theguardian.com/environment/2009/jul/03/africa-land-grab

249 European Commission, "Common Agricultural Policy: Key Graphs and Figures", https://ec.europa.eu/info/sites/info/files/food-farming-fisheries/farming/documents/cap-expenditure-graph1_en.pdf

Chapter 9 Enterprises, industry and employment during the fourth industrial revolution

250 Statista, "Number of employees of JP Morgan Chase from 2008 to 2019", https://www.statista.com/statistics/270610/employees-of-jp-morgan-since-2008/

251 "An AI Completed 360,000 Hours of Finance Work in Just Seconds", *Futurism.com*, 8 March 2017, https://futurism.com/an-ai-completed-360000-hours-of-finance-work-in-just-seconds/

252 UNCTAD report, "Robots and Industrialisation in developing countries", October 2016, http://unctad.org/en/PublicationsLibrary/presspb2016d6_en.pdf

253 Financial Times, "Musk-backed Neuralink unveils upgraded brain implant technology", 29 August 2020, https://www.ft.com/content/fa214593-c7ba-4fb0-93a5-cd35c78abd7a

254 European Parliament report, "Ten technologies which could change our lives", January 2015, http://www.europarl.europa.eu/EPRS/EPRS_IDAN_527417_ten_trends_to_change_your_life.pdf

255 For more details on the state of play of European manufacture: Claire Dhéret and Martina Morosi with Andrea Frontini, Annika Hedberg and Romain Pardo, "Towards a New Industrial Policy for Europe", European Policy Centre, November, 2014 page 3, http://www.epc.eu/documents/uploads/pub_4995_towards_a_new_industrial_policy_for_europe.pdf

256 European Commission, "High level expert group on Key Enabling Technologies", Final report, June 2011, file:///C:/Users/karamis/AppData/Local/Packages/Microsoft.MicrosoftEdge_8wekyb3d8bbwe/TempState/Downloads/hlg_report_final_en%20(1).pdf

257 JRC Science for Policy Report, 2017, "7 ways to boost digital innovation and entrepreneurship in Europe", https://publications.jrc.ec.europa.eu/repository/bitstream/JRC104899/jrc104899_formatted_final_20170426.pdf

258 European Commission, "A digital economy and society powered by High-Performance Computing", https://ec.europa.eu/digital-single-market/en/digital-economy-and-society-powered-high-performance-computing

259 European Commission, "Entrepreneurship and Small and Medium Enterprises", https://ec.europa.eu/growth/smes_en

260 OECD Policy response to Coronavirus (COVID-19), SME policy responses, section on "transmission channels", 15 July 2020, http://www.oecd.org/coronavirus/policy-responses/coronavirus-covid-19-sme-policy-responses-04440101/

261 European Commission, "Investment Plan for Europe", https://ec.europa.eu/commission/strategy/priorities-2019-2024/jobs-growth-and-investment/investment-plan-europe_en

262 European Commission, "Support for SME Internationalisation beyond the EU", https://ec.europa.eu/growth/smes/sme-strategy/access-to-markets/internationalisation/support-tools_en

263 European Commission, "2019 Industrial Research and Development Scoreboard: EU companies increase investment amidst stiff global competition", https://ec.europa.eu/info/news/2019-industrial-research-and-development-scoreboard-eu-companies-increase-investment-amidst-stiff-global-competition-2019-dec-18_en

264 Communication from the Commission – Implementing the Community Lisbon Programme: A policy framework to strengthen EU manufacturing – towards a more integrated approach for industrial policy, "THE IMPORTANCE OF EU MANUFACTURING"

265 Eurostat, "Which sector is the main employer in the EU", https://ec.europa.eu/eurostat/web/products-eurostat-news/-/DDN-20171024-1

266 Trading Economics, "China current account 1998–2020", https://tradingeconomics.com/china/current-account

267 Eurostat, "R&D expenditure in the EU increased slightly to 2.07 % of GDP in 2017", 10 January 2019, https://ec.europa.eu/eurostat/documents/2995521/9483597/9-10012019-AP-EN.pdf/856ce1d3-b8a8-4fa6-bf00-a8ded6dd1cc1

268 European Commission, "2019 Industrial Research and Development Scoreboard: EU companies increase investment amidst stiff global competition", https://ec.europa.eu/info/news/2019-industrial-research-and-development-scoreboard-eu-companies-increase-investment-amidst-stiff-global-competition-2019-dec-18_en

269 McKinsey & Company, "What the future of work will mean for jobs, skills and wages", 2017, by James Manyika, Susan Lund, Michael Chui, Jacques Bughin, Jonathan Woetzel, Parul Batra, Ryan Ko, and Saurabh Sanghvi, https://www.mckinsey.com/featured-insights/future-of-work/jobs-lost-jobs-gained-what-the-future-of-work-will-mean-for-jobs-skills-and-wages#

270 Statista, "Number of patent applications worldwide from 1990 to 2018", https://www.statista.com/statistics/257610/number-of-patent-applications-worldwide/

271 Francis Gurry, "China Becomes Top Filer of International Patents in 2019 Amid Robust Growth for WIPO's IP", WIPO (World Intellectual Property Organisation),7 April 2020, https://www.wipo.int/pressroom/en/articles/2020/article_0005.html

272 Marijn Dekkers, "Why Europe lags on innovation, The problem is not regulation. It's Europe's obsession with risk", *POLITICO*, 4/21/16, https://www.politico.eu/article/why-europe-lags-global-innovation-modern-science-enlightenment/

273 European Commission, CORDIS, 2018, "Integrating Activities for Advanced Communities", https://cordis.europa.eu/programme/id/H2020_INFRAIA-01-2018-2019

274 McKinsey & Company, "What the future of work will mean for jobs, skills and wages", 2017, by James Manyika, Susan Lund, Michael Chui,

Jacques Bughin, Jonathan Woetzel, Parul Batra, Ryan Ko, and Saurabh Sanghvi, goo.gl/7pxYaG.

275 US Bureau of Labor Statistics, Employment Projections, 2019–2029, 1 September 2020, https://www.bls.gov/emp/

276 European Commission, "Jobs for a Green Future", 13/07/2017, https://ec.europa.eu/environment/efe/themes/economics-strategy-and-information/jobs-green-future_en

277 Communication from the European Commission 8.3.2011, COM(2011) 112 final, "A Roadmap for moving to a competitive low carbon economy in 2050", http://www.europarl.europa.eu/meetdocs/2009_2014/documents/com/com_com(2011)0112_/com_com(2011)0112_en.pdf

278 WIFI, https://www.wko.at/service/WIFI_(Wirtschaftsfoerderungsinstitut)_-_Institute_for_Econ.html

279 Joe Flint, "Netflix's Reed Hastings Deems Remote Work 'a Pure Negative'", *The Wall Street Journal*, 7 September 2020, https://www.wsj.com/articles/netflixs-reed-hastings-deems-remote-work-a-pure-negative-11599487219

280 *The Economist*, September 12–18, 2020, "Office politics", page 11.

281 EFIP, "Freelancing in Europe", https://news.malt.com/wp-content/uploads/2019/02/FREELANCING-IN-EUROPE-2-1.pdf

282 Eurostat, "Social protection receipts, EU-28, 2014", https://ec.europa.eu/eurostat/statistics-explained/index.php?title=File:Social_protection_receipts,_EU-28,_2014_(%25_of_total_receipts)_YB17.png&oldid=345666

283 "What are French President Emmanuel Macron's labor reforms", *Deutsche Welle*, 31.08.2017, https://www.dw.com/en/what-are-french-president-emmanuel-macrons-labor-reforms/a-40310100

Chapter 10 Climate policy, infrastructure networks and circular economy

284 Eurostat, "Statistics explained, Oil and petroleum products, a statistical overview", 2020, https://ec.europa.eu/eurostat/statistics-explained/pdfs-cache/43212.pdf

285 United Nation, Climate Change, Paris Agreement. The Paris Agreement central aim is to strengthen the global response to the threat of climate change by keeping a global temperature rise this century well below 2 degrees Celsius above pre-industrial levels and to pursue efforts to limit

the temperature increase even further to 1.5 degrees Celsius, https://unf-ccc.int/process-and-meetings/the-paris-agreement/the-paris-agreement

286 Eurostat, "Renewable energy statistics", https://ec.europa.eu/eurostat/statistics-explained/index.php/Renewable_energy_statistics

287 European Commission, 11.12.2019, COM (2019) 640 final.

288 *Idem.*

289 Emiliano Bellini, "Italian homeowners can now install PV systems for free", *PV Magazine*, 22 May 2020, https://www.pv-magazine.com/2020/05/22/italian-homeowners-can-now-install-pv-systems-for-free/

290 European Commission, "Wind energy", https://ec.europa.eu/info/research-and-innovation/research-area/energy-research-and-innovation/wind-energy_en

291 Wind Europe, https://windeurope.org/about-us/new-identity/

292 Elina Morhunova, "Why is offshore wind the 'Cinderella' of EU climate policy?", *EU Observer,* 23 July 2021, https://euobserver.com/opinion/152503

293 Wind Europe response to targeted consultation on TEN-E Regulation revision, https://windeurope.org/policy/position-papers/

294 European Commission, "Solar power", https://ec.europa.eu/energy/top-ics/renewable-energy/solar-power_en

295 Eurostat, "Renewable energy statistics", https://ec.europa.eu/eurostat/statistics-explained/index.php/Renewable_energy_statistics#Share_of_renewable_energy_almost_doubled_between_2004_and_2018

296 European Commission, "DG Energy, Solar energy", https://ec.europa.eu/energy/topics/renewable-energy/solar-power_en

297 HELI-SCSP, "Why carbon-free Europe will still need North African energy", https://www.politico.eu/article/why-carbon-free-europe-will-still-need-north-african-energy/

298 Quartz Africa, "Sub-Saharan Africa is still in the dark but North Africa will soon be selling power to Europe", 28 September 2017, https://qz.com/1084847/sub-saharan-africa-is-still-in-the-dark-but-north-africa-will-soon-be-selling-power-to-europe/

299 European Commission, COM(2020)301 final, "A hydrogen strategy for a climate-neutral Europe", https://ec.europa.eu/energy/sites/ener/files/hydrogen_strategy.pdf

300 Open letter to Vice-President Franz Timmermans, "Choose Renewable Hydrogen", 22 May 2020, https://www.euractiv.com/wp-content/uploads/sites/2/2020/05/Open-letter-on-renewable-hydrogen_.pdf

301 Eurostat, "Nuclear energy statistics", February 2020, https://ec.europa.eu/
      eurostat/statistics-explained/index.php/Nuclear_energy_statistics

302 European Commission, "EU Nuclear Stress Tests: Legally binding reviews
      every six years", https://ec.europa.eu/commission/presscorner/detail/en/
      IP_13_532

303 Our World in Data, "What are the safest sources of energy?", 10 Febru-
      ary 2020, https://ourworldindata.org/safest-sources-of-energy

304 ITER, https://www.iter.org/

305 International Atomic Energy Agency. "Thorium fuel cycle – Potential
      benefits and challenges" (PDF). Retrieved 27 October 2014, https://www-
      pub.iaea.org/MTCD/Publications/PDF/TE_1450_web.pdf

306 European Commission, "Transport emissions", "A European strategy for
      low-emission mobility", https://ec.europa.eu/clima/policies/transport_en

307 Euractiv, "Opel battery cell plant to get $500m German grant", 3 September
      2021, https://www.euractiv.com/section/batteries/news/opel-battery-cell-
      plant-to-get-500m-german-grant/?fbclid=IwAR09fPv1BvEsSeZ2vky-
      FHM7go5iFwdVLoJp9Z_WgqoeN8HXYru5_c6bQUWg

308 Frédéric Simon, " 'Europe is closing the gap in battery manufactur-
      ing', Northvolt says", *Euractiv*, 28 August 2020, https://www.euractiv.
      com/section/energy-environment/news/europe-is-closing-the-gap-on-
      battery-manufacturing-northvolt-says/?fbclid=IwAR2mHxkbx
      LFv2TwkNX8yGKO5-HLGKAiA4q4u8n_W_WfYz7tfcnPHUv8KN7A

309 See European Commission, "Mobility and Transport, Infrastructure –
      TEN-T – Connecting Europe", Corridors, https://ec.europa.eu/transport/
      node/2443

310 See report of Klara Ramm, chair of the EurEau Committee on Economics
      and Legal Affairs and an expert at IGWP, the Polish Waterworks Cham-
      ber of Commerce, EURACTIV.COM, 2 May 2018, "Time to invest in
      Europe's water infrastructure", https://www.euractiv.com/section/energy-
      environment/opinion/time-to-invest-in-europes-water-infrastructure/

311 EEA, "Water use and environmental pressures", https://www.eea.europa.
      eu/themes/water/european-waters/water-use-and-environmental-pres-
      sures/water-use-and-environmental-pressures

312 EurEau, "The governance of water services in Europe", http://www.
      eureau.org/resources/publications/150-report-on-the-governance-of-
      water-services-in-europe/file

313 The "Circularity Gap Report", January 2018, https://www.circle-econ-
      omy.com/the-circularity-gap-report-our-world-is-only-9-circular/
      #.WmsxBa6nGUl

314 European Commission, DG Environment, Waste, http://ec.europa.eu/ environment/waste/ and Environmental Data Centre on Waste, Eurostat.

315 Cambridge Econometrics, Trinomics, and ICF (2018), "Impacts of circular economy policies on the labour market".

316 European Commission, COM(2020)98 final, 11 March 2020, "A new circular economy action plan. For a cleaner and more competitive Europe", https://eur-lex.europa.eu/resource.html?uri=cellar:9903b325-6388-11ea-b735-01aa75ed71a1.0017.02/DOC_1&format=PDF

317 European Council, 23.02.2018, Press release, "EU ambassadors approve new rules on waste management and recycling", http://www.consilium. europa.eu/en/press/press-releases/2018/02/23/eu-ambassadors-approve-new-rules-on-waste-management-and-recycling/

318 European Commission, DG Energy, "Energy Efficiency", https://ec.europa.eu/energy/topics/energy-efficiency_en

319 European Commission, "Recovery Plan for Europe", https://ec.europa.eu/ info/strategy/recovery-plan-europe_en

320 See "Communication from the commission to the European Parliament, the Council, the European Economic and Social Committee and the Committee of the Regions. A Roadmap for moving to a competitive low carbon economy in 2050", COM/2011/0112 final/2, https://eur-lex.europa.eu/ legal-content/EN/TXT/PDF/?uri=CELEX:52011DC0112&from=EN

Epilogue

321 "Why the EU cannot survive unchanged", *Politico*, 25 March 2017, https://www.politico.eu/article/why-the-eu-cannot-survive-unchanged/

Appendix

322 Eurostat, "General government expenditure by function – COFOG", https://ec.europa.eu/eurostat/statistics-explained/index.php/Government_expenditure_by_function_%E2%80%93_COFOG

323 According to World Bank figures, in 2019 EU-27 GDP stood at $15.592 trillion and UK stood at $2.827 tillion, namely a total of $18,419 trillion. This translates to an amount of approximately €16.5 trillion, if we calculate on the basis of a euro / dollar exchange rate of 1,12 at the end of 2019. For the purpose of this text, we will calculate on a more conservative basis of €16 trillion for EU-28. https://data.worldbank.org/indicator/NY.GDP.MKTP.CD?locations=EU and https://data.worldbank.org/ indicator/NY.GDP.MKTP.CD?locations=GB

Europe of Cultures

Dialogues

"Europe of Cultures" is a series of studies, monographs, stories, research projects, reports on conferences and debates devoted to the complexities and changing realities in European societies. It bridges the past with the future at the cross road of challenges and opportunities of the transformation of European societies. The management of changes in societies refers to the interconnection of various dimensions and levels of policy-making impacting on economic, social, political, democratic, communication, philosophical, artistic, religious as well as ethical traditions and behaviour. As an editorial project the series is structured along two interconnected and complementary sub-series: i.e. the "(Europe of) Dialogues" series and the "(Europe of) Living Stories".

The sub-series "(Europe of) Dialogues" mainly deals with (cultural) diversities, identity and citizenship building in Europe as well as with the relevant multi-level governance and communication structures in the transformation of European societies. Europe is a laboratory for understanding this multi- and intercultural reality. The purpose is to contribute to a better understanding and communication of the changes taking place by looking at the European societies in general, and the specificities of different national, regional and local cultures and communities in a framework of dialogues. The series presents interdisciplinary and critical views of value-driven and policy-oriented reflections. Moreover, it offers new insights into understanding how to manage, value and communicate cultural diversity, identity and citizenship. It also wants to contribute to the development of new ways of "living together", in which cultures and communities are perceived as binding forces in creative society building.

The sub-series "(Europe of) Living Stories" (formerly "Mémoire de l'Europe en devenir", Director Gabriel Fragnière †) is devoted to inspiring narratives for a broad public with a view to contribute to a better understanding, communication and contextualisation of the newly emerging

Europe. It mainly focusses on stories, memories and testimonies of persons, events, institutions and issues that have transformed mentalities, fostered European awareness and finally shaped Europe's future. These stories serve as important references and communication tools for future developments of Europe in the world. This collection wants to be open and diverse, original and dynamic in its content, method and pedagogy faithful to Europe's role and reference in the globalising world.

Series Editor : Léonce Bekemans,
Jean Monnet Professor ad personam, Bruges, Belgium

Editorial Board

Series titles

www.peterlang.com

www.ingramcontent.com/pod-product-compliance
Lightning Source LLC
Chambersburg PA
CBHW020526270326
41927CB00006B/457